UNAMERICAN

UnAmerican

*The Resident's Story
and
Our Country's Last Chapter*

by James Rogers

Copyright © 2016 by James Rogers

All rights reserved. No part of this publication may be reproduced or transmitted in any form or by any means electronic or mechanical, including photocopy, recording, or any information storage and retrieval system now known or to be invented, without permission in writing from the author, except by a reviewer who wishes to quote brief passages in connection with a review written for inclusion in a magazine, newspaper, website, or broadcast.

Ordering Information:

U.S. trade bookstores and wholesalers: Please contact the author through our email address: lastchapter.book@hotmail.com.

Library of Congress Control Number: 2016906085

A CIP catalog record for this book is available from the Library of Congress.

ISBN   978-0-9974409-2-8
ISBN   978-0-9974409-1-1   (pbk)
ISBN   978-0-9974409-0-4   (eBook)
ISBN   978-0-9974409-3-5   (EPUB)

Dedication

To Jack,

for I do not look forward to telling you during my sunset years what it was once like in the United States where men were free.

Contents

Preface ix

Definitions xix

Introduction 1

I NEEDED A RACE

Dunham 17

Seeds 25

Blackness 33

THE PROPHET

Direction 45

Community Organizer 57

Politics 67

THE SAVIOR

Stealing Senate 73

Serendipity 83

Myth-Building 91

Residency 113

Barack Obama Comes Out 123

Preparations 129

The Real Campaign 137

Failure Again 159

OCTAVIAN

Purpose 167

No More Distractions 173

Legacy 179

The Campaign Continues 191

AUGUSTUS

Matriculation 207

Corrective Actions.. 227

Conclusion.. 237

Acknowledgements 241

APPENDIX

The Constitution of the United States of America 245

Amendments to the Constitution of the United States of America 259

NOTES 271

Index.. 291

Preface

> *Government is not reason; it is not eloquence; it is force! Like fire, it is a dangerous servant and a fearful master.*
> *- President George Washington*

Looking back almost 25 years, it seems like it was almost a different country. It was during Desert Shield and Desert Storm when I first began to realize the truly awesome gift it is to be born in the United States of America. It was easy to take for granted the family, culture, and values which surrounded the American at that point.

The year was 1991, and it would be the year of Earth-shaking events. It was the last year of the Cold War. The immoveable object to our unstoppable force, the Soviet Union would collapse suddenly, leaving the United States, whose military had just completed the most devastating and overwhelming 100 hour defeat of a respectable belligerent, as the lone super power on the globe. It would also be the year of the Japanese asset price bubble, where their economy began a decade long decline, called the Lost Decade, caused by inflated real estate and stock market prices. We would not heed the warning, and would earn a similar fate less than two decades later. Our country, that is, because the thieves, who became very wealthy, in money and power, would not feel its effects.

It was also a more innocent era when a letter was still the standard long-distance communication method, before the electronic devices we consider little more than a utility today, and a long-distance telephone call was a financial consideration. The internet had just 'gone public'; the cell phone was still only a rich person's accessory in very limited areas; and although MTV had existed for almost a decade already, their core programming content was still music videos. The MTV logo paid homage to the greatness of America with the Astronaut on the Moon; it was not that long before when men in space was science fiction.

"I did NOT do anything wrong. The hatch just BLEW. It was a GLITCH. It was a...a technical malfunction. Why in hell won't anyone believe

me?" Astronaut Gus Grissom, a national hero can provide no better example of what it means to be an American, will be forever remembered for those words through the pages of Tom Wolfe's *The Right Stuff*[1].

Enlisting during World War II after he graduated from high school, it was already 1944, and he would never make it to either theater. But he would go to college on the GI Bill, graduate from Purdue University majoring in Mechanical Engineering, and return to the Air Force to serve as a fighter pilot during the Korean War, flying around 100 missions, awarded the Air Medal and Distinguished Flying Cross. But his goal was to be a test pilot. After three years serving as a flight instructor, he was accepted for graduate study in Aeronautical Engineering at the Air Force Institute of Technology, and then the United States Test Pilot School, which prepared him for the rigors of flight test.

But the Space Race had just begun, and Gus heard the call. Selected as one of what was to become called the Mercury Seven, he would be one of the first Americans to risk space travel. It would be his first mission, and he was to become only the second American to launch into space. But another Astronaut, Gordon Cooper, would warn him just prior to launch, "Just make sure you don't screw the pooch, Gus." The launch would go well, and his flight would be a short 15 minutes and 37 seconds. But it's what happened after his return which would forever change his trajectory.

Liberty Bell 7 was Grissom's Mercury capsule which splashed into the Pacific on July 21, 1961. The hatch, sealed throughout the flight, would prematurely open as the explosive bolts restraining it blew without warning, allowing the ocean water to enter. By the time the recovery team could attempt to retrieve the capsule, too much water had entered. It was too heavy; the capsule couldn't be retrieved and eventually would sink to the bottom of the Pacific.

Such are the events surrounding risky operations like space launches, and flight testing. Six years later, the country would lose this great American to the tragic Apollo I capsule fire. A truly great American, Gus Grissom will forever be remembered a hero who sacrificed for his country.

Preface

The country was still riding on the patriotic high resurrected by the last President, Ronald Reagan, hoping his successor, the very respectable, but establishment George H.W. Bush wouldn't "Screw the Pooch" as the country had fully recovered from the "malaise" resulting from the lackluster performance of the last Democratic President, Jimmy Carter. But Bush '41 would not govern conservatively, and would lose the country's support. So frustrated was the country, that in 1992 they decided to give the Democratic Party candidate a try. It was this election where I first became aware of how the establishment and the media would create the product necessary to win over the gullible public. It was not that the Republican candidate was proving himself a worthy successor to Reagan, but the complete obfuscation of the Democratic candidate's unscrupulous past while in office, not to mention the blisteringly long list of alleged criminal activity in his background, which was astounding.

The media carefully pushed aside case after case of sexual assault claims, and would aid in the campaign's attempts to not implicate the candidate with his own wife's past questionable dealings. This would also be a time before the parties appeared to collude and cooperate over the control levers of power inside the beltway. There was still competition, but the Republicans couldn't quite figure out how to overcome the media-supported Democrats.

It turned out that administration would not focus on the diminishment of the country as the Carter administration had. It could be because this administration was focusing on a different prize, a future of wealth transfer built off of arrangements brokered for their own benefit, or possibly the civil and criminal legal issues surrounding the Presidency during those eight years distracted them sufficiently so that they just could find time for destruction. Two years into his administration, the country would also be blessed to have an actual leader as Speaker of the House of Representatives who demonstrated how a disciplined and tough American can challenge the State and win. The result was the first (and last) years of a budget surplus since President Nixon was in the White House. The media complex continues to execute their revisionist desires and place the glory at the foot of the philanderer, but it's the American who knows that Newt Gingrich deserves the praise. God works in mysterious ways.

Although this effort was planned to be an exploration of the person who now sits in the White House, it expanded in an attempt to provide relevant historical insights and events which have provided support and prelude for the deluge of tyrannical behavior the State has graduated to. In addition, I must be honest, the subject was found to be fairly boring. Not the examination of the events and implications for our future, but the person himself. He's just not that interesting! This might explain how the several books written about his life prior to and during the first term whispered propaganda. But that shouldn't come as a surprise as he had a fairly weak resume when he applied for his current position. Periodic excursions are taken to collect historical connections in an attempt to provide some context for the current situations we are facing. They are provided in shaded regions in order to distinguish them from the main subject of the book.

There is no attempt to deal thoroughly with any particular subject, as the effort would cover centuries of the country's activities. If the reader should find interest sparked by the introduction of various events, it's hoped the reader will search out more information about the subjects and learn for themselves the history of this great country. The challenge is to uncover the truth, molded by the actual surrounding events and traditions of the time, in order to understand what had occurred. The more the citizens educate themselves and question the propaganda being projected by the public relations front masquerading as the main stream media (MSM), the quicker the citizen will once again find their inner American. If the reader finds elements counter to their understanding, hopefully a search for the truth will prevail, as much currently thought to be true is mere fantasy.

Like the vast majority of Americans, I would watch the goings-on at Foggy Bottom with almost cynical and disconnected amusement. Sure, the quadrennial circus would allow the voter to select from a couple of people already selected by the establishment, but the Federal Government didn't appear to be a central character in an American's life.

Taxes would be levied, but through a brilliant mechanism where the American would no longer realize the money that was being wasted was their own. The effect was subtle, but effective. However, along the way the government began to change the language; it was now the government's money that the people would use, rather than the people's money that the government was wasting.

It was a time when the impact on the individual's life was small compared to the rewards of a life in this great country. The welfare state was substantial, but appeared manageable. A person's property was their own. The country was about to enter a period of change, where the press or the 'fourth estate'[2], once the critical conscience of a free society, would transition from the pack of insatiable searchers for the truth witnessed during the Watergate scandal of the early 1970's, to the propaganda wing of the Democratic Party during the 1990's, and now to the public relations department of the State. The Gray Lady, *New York Times*, would still maintain effective control of the MSM through the 1990's, unaware of its nearing demise as a result of the explosion of immediate communication on the horizon, and manage the message that the citizenry would be directed to receive. But the ability of the message to immediately reach the populace with the internet has subjugated the Gray Lady to a footnote in the 21st century, and required the State to directly manage the message themselves. The absurdity of controlled access to the administration through the choreographed public pronouncements and press conferences would be entertaining if the system created by the masterminds[3] had not grown to such unwieldy proportions.

Is all lost? Was that light on the hill more like a distant star many light years away, already vanished long before the last ray of light meets the observer's eye?

Like anyone we may cross paths with during our own journey, there are characteristics in others which we see in ourselves. Much like the Resident, I find myself to be much of a 'moviegoer', often a step behind observing the goings-on around me. This book is a collection of those observations spanning not only the life of the present administration, but beyond. Something has happened in the past 25 years, and it's had a devastating effect on what was once our great country. We have lost perspective, our place in history.

Whether you live your life fully integrated in a life based on religion or you consider yourself religious, but unmoored to formal religion, there is at least an understanding and belief that there is a higher power which had made this life possible. Many believe there will be an accounting after this life for the deeds perpetrated. But the author will never understand how a person can look over the wondrous universe, and into a child's eyes, and not accept that the invisible hand of a greater power may have been at work. While many individuals believe religion is no longer a central part of their lives, many of those do not realize they have but substituted another in its place. Regardless, it's fundamentally American to respect the values of those that have a deep belief system. The fact that our neighbor believes differently does not impact an American, for a civil society relies on the mutual respect among its citizens. It would be (and is) fundamentally un-American to impose your own beliefs onto another. For those ideologies that are not willing to integrate into the civil society, they must find another place to exercise the rights they believe are their own. If those beliefs are incompatible with the civil society, or at least supported by only a minority and cannot win in the marketplace of ideas, it is by definition outside of the civil society's norms. The anti-Christian ideology masquerading as a religion currently waging a war on humanity may be a religion for many, but it's fundamentally incompatible with the American civil society.

The compassionate society may tolerate periphery indulgences, but using governmental gimmickry to impose false acceptance and support from society will not change facts: might doesn't make right. As we are watching events unfold, the birth of a police state has never solved social issues, and will not in this case either. This was what made this country unique at its birth. For those who had been educated over the last 25 years, the removal of civic classes, and the diminishment and revisionism of American history has virtually separated the younger generation from the country they were blessed with. They are immersed in presentism, unaware of the fact that the government now represents the State, no longer the people. The State has become the religion of many, looking for a just master to provide the needs for their existence. Ancient history warns us to beware false idols.

In science and engineering, there is a concept of 'frame of reference'. Much of our perspective is based on the reference frame from which we are observing the phenomena. The importance can be perceived based on the simple sound of a train. If you are on the train, the sound is consistent throughout your journey. But if you are on the ground as the train races past, you will hear the pitch of the sound change as it passes you. If the sound never changes while you are on the train, but does when you are not on the train, there must be other factors involved than just the sound. Your frame of reference is critical to accurate assessment.

In the 16th century, Nicolaus Copernicus famously created a mathematical model for Heliocentrism, or the astronomical system with the Sun at its center. Prior to this, the Earth was believed to be the center of not only the solar system, but the known universe. It was here where Ockham's Razor would appear as a philosophical tool for evaluating assumptions, simply observing that among the competing hypotheses, the one with the fewest assumptions should be the one selected. The Geocentric theory of the time required more assumptions, and would lose favor. But Copernicus only shifted the center of the universe from the Earth to the Sun. It would be centuries again before the world would realize that the Sun itself was not even the center of the universe. It was once believed the atom was the smallest particle in existence, only to be proven wrong in the 20th century. But a student of history cannot overlook the fact that no amount of knowledge has ever provided all the answers during that timeframe. The unmerciful march of discovery never ceases to invalidate accepted truths. But one thing has been consistent throughout history, and that would be the unstoppable self-assurance of the individual. It is a human weakness to assume we have all the answers. And if a small group of supporters are found, further entrenchment of superiority results.

Centuries ago it was called Alchemy, which included the ability to change elemental matter from one material to another: turning lead into gold. Based on the mix of science and mysticism, the greatest minds of the time would spend lives experimenting, but any real success claimed was rooted in fraud. The careful manipulation of data and irreproducibility of results were the only consistency found. For the laws of nature are what they are. We can strive to understand them, build models that seem to represent their behavior, and develop theories in an attempt to describe their 'why', but we cannot change them. It's even unclear whether the fraudsters were conscious of their compromises, for with the luxury of time and education we can criticize them only because we have a better frame of reference. Many may have actually believed their results. Recent examples of the same faulty approaches abound. The perennial search for a perpetual motion machine continues, and there was a relatively recent claimant who created a 'cold fusion machine', both of which violate the laws of physics, at least as they are known during our short existence. The modern 'Climate Change' theories are another version of this affliction. But what is consistent across the centuries can be discovered if one would only "follow the money". The consistent thread that dominates these schemes is the researcher's financial support comes from a governmental donor of some type. While a philanthropist may provide some support for whacky schemes now and again, it takes a financial provider, disconnected with the responsibility for positive results, to effectively support these schemes. And that would be the government.

The purpose of this book isn't to go over every issue with today's State-sponsored countrywide bankruptcy, but rather to highlight the crisis the country has placed itself into. By allowing the Federal Government to take over virtually all aspects of life, and placing at its head a person who is clearly detached from the country's traditions and values, has placed us at the precipice of destruction. While the end of the United States of America, as defined in the Constitution, may be nearing inevitability, the American will remain, and will rekindle that light on the hill, even if that hill is the ash heap of the failed police State to which its predecessor had transitioned.

It seems few have actually read the Constitution. It was written by brilliant and visionary men at the dawn of this country. It was written for each of us. It wasn't written for lawyers to decide what the meaning of a word is. It's written in language clear to all grade school graduates. It isn't scripture-laden with randomly placed bits of wisdom which can be pulled from its context in order to build a position. It's a definition of a frame of reference for the Federal Government. No piece of it is independent of the other. It was carefully crafted to constrain those who would not be angels in government, by the states which agreed to it. The Constitution is included in the Appendix so that the reader may actually read it. There are few areas where a new observer may need to read it again to catch the details of what is described, but it is inherently readable, and clearly understandable. And it should be read in its entirety. Once read, the reader should ask themselves whether the government which sits at Foggy Bottom resembles the government of the United States of America. We will delve into several of the many changes made by designing men over the course of the last couple centuries, in order to place into perspective many of the problems created not by the country, but by the presidents, legislators, and judges entrusted during that time.

The life of the Resident is also important to understand why this person, in particular, has found himself in a position to bring finality to this grand experiment we call the United States of America. Presidents of the past may have been corruptible, scandalous, and even incompetent; but we've never had one who clearly despises the country. Not only has this society provided for him a fantastic life, unequaled by any other, but it even elected him to be President, twice! While the final section of this book has yet to occur, I felt duty-bound to find a way to describe what I've seen building over the last 25 years in the hopes it might find the ear of fellow Americans who may be in a position to alter the on-coming chain of events. The foundations of our civil society have been undermined; the battlefield has been prepared; the victory is within the grasp of the State. For those hearing this warning call, and seem unaware of what has been happening, I believe it's not too late. But it soon may be. Evaluate your own frame of reference. Do you think tomorrow will be just like today? Why?

Definitions

American	Person who believes they are born with unalienable rights of life, liberty, and the pursuit of happiness, and respects those rights in others.
Democratic Party	Political party which existed from 1832 until 1990s, the bulwark of America's racist past, but morphed into the champion of modern liberalism, home to all self-determined oppressed groups hoping for government solutions to social and personal problems.
Democratic Wing of the Party	That remainder of the Democratic Party now subsumed into 'The Party' which maintains the illusion of independence through the Democratic National Committee. Controls nomination processes. Struggles to maintain voter base as it relies on a mix of anti- and un-American or Progressive identity-based special interest groups, in addition to those either unaware of the party's transformation or simply the intransigent.
Establishment, The	The uncoordinated, yet coherent motion of the elitist representatives of The Party, reliant on oil of the country's productivity for the machinery of what they decide must be accomplished. The managers of the world's largest money laundering scheme, the Federal Budget.
Executive	The second branch of the government, created to manage the awesome responsibility of protectorate of the country, but now reduced to a damage control command post dedicated to justifying whatever the Resident decides is important for the State, and himself.
Foggy Bottom	The heart of the leviathan, once the seat of the light on the hill, the experiment which was to protect the citizen's liberty. Once the limited expanse of the federal government itself, now but a nerve center for the State.

Judicial	The third branch of the government, created to settle constitutional squabbles, now reduced to a rubber stamp for despotic desires of the State, and justifier for social experimentation activities.
Legislative	The first branch of the government, constitutionally the strongest, but now reduced to the financial wing of the State.
Main Stream Media	See Praetorian Guard.
Mastermind	Politicians, judges, and bureaucrats who are self-appointed as wise and learned beyond the capabilities of the people they rule[1].
Omnibus	Magical authorization document masquerading as fiscally responsible government financial control over almost $4 trillion annually.
Party, The	Borne of circumstances during the 1990s, the go-along-to-get-along establishment realized one plus one equals more (for themselves.) The effect was collusion over competition paving the way for absolute control over electoral choices.
Power of the Purse	Apparently one of Tolkien's 'Rings of Power', forged in the Second Age, but not seen by man for ages.
Praetorian Guard	Media wing providing cover to State activities. Often characterized as the Main Stream Media, as they are able to dominate discussion. Term applied to media by Mark Levin[2].
Republican Party	Political party which existed from 1856 until 1990s and became the champion of modern conservatism during the 1980s, home to all self-determined independent Americans looking to reduce government.

Republican Wing of the Party	That remainder of the Republican Party now subsumed into 'The Party' which maintains the illusion of independence through the Republican National Committee. Controls nomination processes. Struggles to maintain voter base as it relies on a mix of American and un-American special interest groups, in addition to those either unaware of the party's transformation or intransigent.
Resident	A person elected President, but chooses to discard his oath and responsibilities to impose his own un-American doctrine
Several States	The sovereign states once united under an agreement of mutual cooperation, as a nation of states, now reduced to administrative appendages which spend half their time complaining of federal oversight, the other begging for federal support.
State, The	The administrative fourth branch of the government, managed by the establishment, until recently subservient to the three branches of the republican government.
Un-American	The person who believes they have the right to another's life, liberty or pursuit of happiness.

Introduction

> *At what point shall we expect the approach of danger? By which means shall we fortify against it? Shall we expect some transatlantic military giant, to step the ocean, and crush us at a blow? Never! All the armies of Europe, Asia, and Africa combined, with all the treasure of the earth (our own excepted) in their military chest, with a Buonaparte for a commander, could not by force, take a drink from the Ohio, or make a track on the Blue Ridge, in a trial of a thousand years. At what point, then, is the approach of danger to be expected? I answer, if it ever reach us it must spring up amongst us. It cannot come from abroad. If destruction be our lot, we must ourselves be its author and finisher. As a nation of freemen, we must live through all time, or die by suicide.*
> *- Abraham Lincoln[1]*

What is American? American isn't a label one is given because they happened to be within some geographic border. An American doesn't define himself, or herself, based on some central authority that claims to be their caregiver. An American citizen is blessed with certain benefits and responsibilities which come from their allegiance to the Unites States of America. A resident of the United States is often called an American, but that alone doesn't really identify that person as an American. An American is quite the opposite. Observing the citizens of the many countries around this blue planet, American may not even be a quality that is inherent in the human character, but is developed during the early stages of life, reinforced during the struggle toward independence, and actualized when the heart claims liberty.

Merriam-Webster defines 'American' as a person who was born, raised, or living in the U.S. (North or South America). From a simpleton's view, this may be adequate, but this is really equivalent to saying we are human because we live on the Earth. Being American is surely more than just a coincidence of location and time. Surely for the United States citizen, American can be tied to our country's founding, claiming linkage with our Declaration of Independence, governed by the framework defined in the Constitution. But the term American has been used to describe the many inhabitants of this hemisphere since 1568. In fact, the founding documents of the United States of America did not create the

American; it was the American that created those documents and built the greatest country this Earth had ever seen.

An American doesn't have a birthright to position or status. An American doesn't have the right to another's property or labor. An American must find their own position and define their own success. The American is not an individual, however. The American is a member and contributor of a family, a community, or a church. This societal structure provides the opportunity for families, communities, or churches to improve the conditions of their members through mutual support.

As the communities grew, so did the need for a more formal structure of self-management. Governments were created in order to secure the liberties of those within its jurisdiction. The states would be defined by geographical boundaries, but the cultures within them were sometimes very different than their neighbors'. The several states could each trace their roots to the various religious sects of Christianity which fled the oppression of Europe in search of a free society. It's not surprising that that states would find far more in common with their neighbors than differences, as they shared the same language and came from the same culture, based in western civilization. But there would be differences. The social and religious differences were found incompatible by many. But it was these differences, combined with the Constitution, which would become the bedrock for this country.

Each state, having its own collection of values and beliefs, would be in competition with the other. In the free market of ideas, a form of capitalism would result in the success of those cultures most beneficial to the well-being of the population which would claim ultimate victory. It was not an accident that the Federal Government was born of limited powers, allowing the states to survive only as long as they would be of service to the people within. It would be left up to the state and local governments to decide how they would best serve their citizens. The concept of the current welfare state would be as alien to them as an astronaut in space.

While community groups or churches can provide some relief, the real power has been within the American family. A successful parent is able to improve the next generation's initial state and provide much valued guidance which can, over generations, create dynasties. But this is only possible if the latest generation is competent and prepared to assume the increased responsibility that comes with these advantages. Much attention is paid to the families who are able to maintain some hegemony over several generations, but that is actually an anomaly in America. In Europe, the aristocratic families seem entrenched for eternity, defined by blood or name. In American, you are only in that position as long as you justify your position. There are many successful families who move from the elite to join the masses, only to rise again through hard work. It is this lack of predetermined outcomes which the American realizes is what provides the opportunity to create your own success. Knowing that no one else is responsible for your success or failure is not a cross to bear, but rather it's the extent of this privilege which is unavailable to citizens outside of this country. That privilege is what in a nearly prefect alignment of the stars almost 250 years ago motivated the inhabitants of 13 English colonies to claim their God-given unalienable rights.

Most of all, the American understands the United States was not built overnight and may never be a completed project. Formed to ensure that "life, liberty, and the pursuit of happiness" is cherished and protected, the journey over hundreds of years isn't complete and it's their responsibility to leave it to the next generation in an improved state. But there has been relentless progress over the past century to overturn the American Revolution. The Progressive movement has been able to take control of the levers of power in the Federal Government, and is now in position to deal its final blow.

It began with the justification for judicial activism even while many the framers were still alive. A seemingly reasonable assertion on the part of the Supreme Court had laid the foundation for two hundred years of 'legislation from the bench', avoiding the debate and victory or defeat in the public square, which the framers had intended. The next serious blow to republicanism would come at the hands of perhaps our greatest President of the 19th century, as he asserted the Federal Government's authority over the 'several states'. It was a good deed for humanity, but at the cost of our federal system. The relationship between the state and the Federal Government would reverse, and sow the seeds of the country's demise. It was under this new government structure the Progressives would add their own 'fertilizer' of authoritarian rule.

The next major attack on republicanism would be the 17th Amendment, removing the 'several states' from the government decision process, giving birth to the State. No longer having to court the favor of a majority of the state legislatures, the government would be able to rapidly advance agendas unimpeded. For the first one hundred and fifty years, the role of the federal government was primarily to provide collective security for the country, and to regulate commerce between the states in order to maintain a level playing field. But the worldwide crisis of the Great Depression would allow the federal government to justify the New Deal as the right to take over vast areas of the economy as well as state and personal responsibilities. The transfer of authority from the states to the federal government had created the framework for a more devastating attack on republicanism three decades later. The State was growing.

The Great Society would provide the Progressive satisfaction, for it was to be the massive program which would eliminate poverty. As is most progressive thinking, the problems causing the issues were never a concern. There was a lot of money to be made treating the symptoms, and the byproduct was a dependency class which would assure a political base to secure power for the State, which was now becoming self-aware.

The effect of the removal of authority and participation in the federal process, coupled with the creation of federal funding for internal projects and welfare had taken root as entitlements by the 1960's. The growth of the federal government could be measured by the increasing size of the President's cabinet, now having more members representing internal, extra-constitutional responsibilities than those responsible for constitutional authorities. By the 1970's the welfare state was firmly in place, and the 'several states' authority had all but dissipated. The organizational framework was still there, but they had effectively become an administrative appendage of the State by this time, a Governor's main role appearing to be that of corporate manager, and pleader for federal funding in times of crisis. It would be this political class that would become the new aristocracy, which the Revolution fought to save us from.

For approximately the first 200 years of this country's existence, the political parties would participate in this tag team match when it comes to control of the government. A minority party would work its way into majority status through a combination of proclaiming themselves as the better choice through electioneering, and ensuring the other team would lose favor with the help of undermining of their efforts along the way. And the cycle would start again. As one party comes to power, they would replace the key participants with their own team, only to be replaced several years later by the other team. Each time the winning party would gain their offices back, the new team would be made of those from the previous administration who would serve in more senior positions, and the trainees at lower positions. It basically functions as a farm league system for bureaucrats. All was well, until someone got greedy. The golden goose was about to be strangled.

It was the 1990's and the country realized its overwhelming military dominance, as well as the enormous budget which the Department of Defense had. There would be a small effort inserted into the normal, yet inefficient, government acquisition policy during that timeframe. The concept was effectively to transfer all military system development over to contractors, with the justification that they would be more cost conscious and efficient, ultimately improving the return on investment for the ballooning expense of cutting edge, war-winning materiel. The result was the massive 'out-sourcing' movement which has exploded the reach of the State and the authority over which its thousands of rules and regulations would apply. In addition, the contracting policies of the time demanded the government not provide specific requirements for what they are purchasing, but rather provide a description of the capability which was desired, and leave it to the company to develop the best solution to satisfy the need. It would all seem reasonable, at face value. The result has been dismal, but the experiment had become the model for the government in general.

The Federal Government now employs over 4 million people itself[2]. Couple that with the army of support contractors, realizing less than half of our population is actually counted as employed by our own government statistics and roughly 4% of the workers in the United States work for the Federal Government. That's 1 in 25! Add to this the state and local employees, there is a reason why we are bankrupt. But it isn't just the assumption of responsibilities within the various departments that is overwhelming the American; it's the intrusion into all aspects of their lives. The State has become the omnipresent authoritarian for society.

History has seen this movie play out before, and it always has a bad ending. The State, insatiable for power and authority, but incompatible with human independence, will transition to a totalitarian role, impose some form of a police state, struggle for validation at the cost of the lives of its citizens, and collapse of its own weight, and take its place in line behind Venezuela, Cuba, Cambodia, Russia, Spain, Germany, Italy, and more. And that is only the last century.

The other solution is to follow the failed state policies of the current European Union, a policy of cooperative national suicide. The European culture is one where the society dictates what you will be allowed to become. It produces and champions dependency. And with the current tactic of importing their own invasion, it is only a matter of time before the indigenous culture rises up to expel the welcomed invader, or their own culture will be crushed. There are many in key positions of power in the United States who appear enamored by European society. This is another symptom of the Progressive affliction where it seems more acceptable to chase other failed governmental constructs in order to become welcomed into their small inner cocktail circuit, than to proudly represent the greatest country in the history of the planet and the people who for some reason elected them. Leadership is often a lonely burden.

Recent decades have also seen a shift from the competitive nature of the two-party system to a more cooperative collusion for the benefit of both. A glance at Figure 1 illustrates how the variations from congress to congress appear to have significantly diminished since the four decades of Democrat control of the House. And the Senate displays a similar trend since 1979. While each team races to the microphones to claim their support for the electorate's wishes, when all is said and done, the State is strengthened and the people are weakened. The apologies and finger-pointing ensues, but the cattle continue to support this behavior with reelection. It's easy to get caught up in the red versus blue, Yankee versus Red Sox bickering, but once the American realizes that is only a

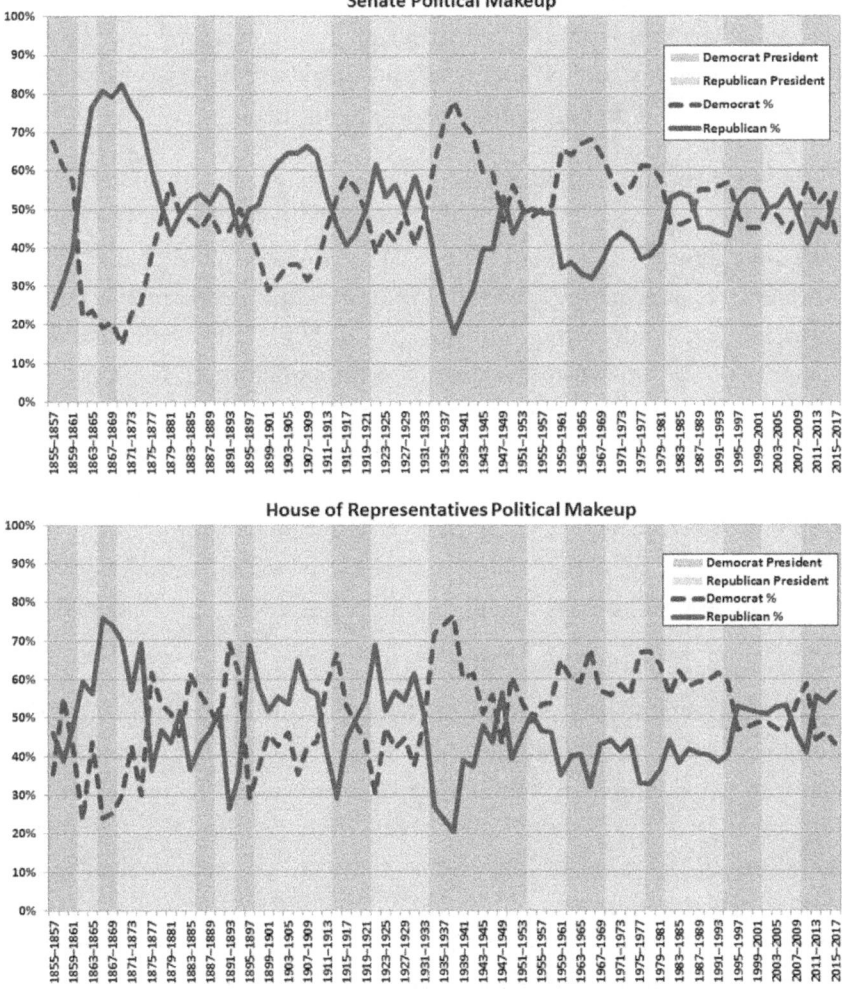

Figure 1: Legislative Political Party Makeup[3]

façade protecting the single party solution managed by the State, this seemingly confusing operation becomes the explanation with the least amount of assumptions.

Each election cycle seems to produce fewer and fewer alternatives in the election booth. The names are different, but the positions are only 'nuanced' shades of pastels. As expected, the 2016 presidential election brings this contention to absurd levels. The political parties in reality are but the surface perspective of what's called a dry-dock iceberg. From the surface is appears there are two icebergs, competing for the same space in the vast ocean. But beneath the surface, these two icebergs are actually connected and quite content with their location.

On the surface, the United States political system is dominated by two main political parties, the Democrats and the Republicans. The biennial battle for representation pits contestants against one another for the right to a lucrative seat in the Capitol Building. This is where the patriotic representative would bring their legislation, build consensus, win a vote of approval, and send it to the President for signature. Once signed, it's the law, and only a new law or a Supreme Court decision can overturn it. That's what those of us old enough to have had a civics class would describe should someone ask. The reality for most of the country's history is actually much less attractive, combining back room dealings and quid pro quo agreements in what used to be called 'sausage making'. But things appear to have changed recently and the reality is just a bit different.

While the political parties have always controlled who they wanted to nominate, there has been a noticeable drop in quality over recent cycles. It's been most apparent on the Republican side. It seems like the Democrats are fairly consistent about only allowing establishment candidates in the competition. Some may say the only real difference between the Republicans and the Democrats are that the Democrats are honest about their corruption. That may be, but the parties themselves appear to no longer have battles over principles. They are fighting to have the contestants they want to be on the ballot, regardless of the will of the party base.

Introduction

The Republicans are fighting to keep the nomination from going to an outsider, while the Democrats have so controlled the primaries that the only challenger for the Democratic nomination isn't even a Democrat. The establishment is now fighting for its life, as the country is no longer run by three co-equal governmental branches. The inter-branch collusion has gone public as the Judicial and Legislative are manipulated and threatened by the Executive, which is the seat which manages the fourth unaccountable branch of government, called the Administration, or referred herein as the State.

The elections may often select those who may have good intentions, but once in office, rarely maintain their stated convictions. It's as if they learn something shortly after they assume office, which results in their alignment with the State's agenda. A good example would be the current Speaker of the House, Congressman Paul Ryan. So convincing were his claims that he was doing the best he could before his Speakership, given the house leadership which constrained his conservative desires. He was seen as a fiscal hawk and a brilliant man with the budget, and as the Chairman of the House Budget Committee, the 2012 Vice Presidential nominee and Chairman of the powerful House Ways and Means, he had the experience to 'get things done'. With the ouster of the Speaker of the House, and his selection, he would have his chance. No longer was that horrible and duplicitous John Boehner in his way, he would take command of the Power of the Purse, virtually abdicated by the Republican leadership since reacquiring the majority in 2011.

Instead, it would be a swift and decisive rejection of the character he had spent years nurturing and developing, as he immediately had the House approve a blindingly irresponsible budget he was given. Was it that Paul Ryan was stymied and outmaneuvered, resulting in passage of this bill, or could it be that he now was in position to challenge the State, and he believed he had no actual power? Was it that he understood he would only have his comfortable existence as long as he played by the rules? And these were the State's rules. But he also was part of the establishment, willing to maintain the charade while he had the opportunity, prepare for the inevitable transfer of power, and the start the cycle all over. And that will happen as long as the establishment maintains control of the State. But what if control of the State was not intended to be relinquished; what can be done? Nothing, as this was once a game of managing power behind closed doors. Enter the Product.

Barack Obama would be raised unattached to American tradition and values. Spending his early life in Indonesia, and Hawaii, being passed between his on-again, off-again Mother and her parents; he would grow up fatherless in a moral-neutral environment. His father did exist, but from all accounts was there mainly for conception, and then would later meet his son one time at the age of ten. "Barry," as he was called into his college years, would find mentorship among Hawaii's anti-American elite, as he developed through a not-so-unusual adolescence of drinking, drugs, and an all-around aimless existence.

He would meander through the first couple years of college, attracted to the various counter-cultural groups he would come into contact with, but it would be during that time where he would find his interest. It would start as an inner struggle to self-identify his place in the world. He would be in search of belonging. Growing up in possibly the most racially diverse point in the country, he was aware of his black heritage, but his sense of his own 'blackness' would only be from the pages of books he had read growing up. His initial efforts to define himself as the black man he wanted to be led him to New York, and then Chicago, where he decided he could 'do some good'.

Never lacking in self-confidence, Barack, as he now wanted to be called, had decided he would be the one who would solve the problems of the people he was to beg for acceptance. And it was his old mentor, Frank Marshall Davis, who had provided him the philosophical foundation which would give him direction. The Alinsky-based training he received would make him a formidable foe in the inner-city shake-down tactical battles which define community organizing. He would become a lawyer, marry into 'blackness', and go into politics. But his road to politics would need some help. He couldn't get elected as Barry the pot-smoking choom gang member from Hawaii. There was a long list of other people struggling to get control of the lucrative community projects as well.

Although his public achievements were pretty scarce on his resume, he would be the first black editor of the Harvard Law Review. That got him some attention. He used his promise, and a great advance, to write a book about the experience, but he instead wrote an autobiographical novel in an attempt to invent himself for a political career. The book was initially weakly received, but would become a best-seller when he finally made a name for himself nationally. As a Harvard-educated lawyer, he could've made quite a comfortable life for himself and his family, but that wasn't where his heart was at. He wanted to become the man his father could only boast about. But like his father before him, Barack's family would take the back seat in his life. The tension would build over his disregard for his family's financial situation and it would almost end in divorce. Barack was really never motivated by money, and his own personal ambitions would always take front seat to his family.

He would serve virtually unnoticed in the Illinois State Senate, make a failed attempt at a U. S. House of Representative seat in 2000, but would win his U.S. Senate Seat in 2004. He would be virtually absent for the remaining time in the Senate, as he was preparing the battlefield for his presidential run. Elected in an embarrassing display that was counter to the dignity of the office he was to assume, he would immediately discard the traditions and values of those who preceded him, and begin his prolific destruction. The hope and change the country was promised was probably different than what was expected; he was transforming the country. He built a shadow cabinet, unanswerable to the people, and set about assaulting virtually every element which had made this country great.

The assaults were international and domestic. On the international front, he would go out of his way to diminish the greatness which much of the world relied upon, creating a less stable world. Domestically, he has attacked the energy industry, the banking industry, the currency, the military, law enforcement, and the citizens themselves should they disagree with his Marxist agenda. He even was effective at possibly destroying the envy of the world, the American medical system, by the government takeover of the entire industry, approximately one sixth of the country's economy. So thorough was the transformation, that there was virtually no part of American enterprise that had not been adversely affected during his first 4 years. The numbers horrendous, the debt unprecedented, but the Republicans wouldn't even put up a fight. They would select the one candidate who had perhaps the worst resume to contrast with the current office holder. Was it an accident? Hardly, and it seemed like even Barack Obama was surprised at the election win. However, a funny thing happened on the way to the show.

The once co-equal executive branch of the United States government had completed its transition to the single source of power and control. It had effectively transformed the legislative branch into its financial support wing, where the judicial branch had been bullied into submission to the will of the State, and the presidential appointees numbering in the thousands had taken control of every major seat of any import within. This sudden and illegal seizure of power may not have resulted through violence, but the ends remain the same. The Obama Residency has resulted in a coup d'état over the constitutional government that had been in place previously. As the nation watches, there appears no action which will cause the Legislature to take notice. The country's elected officials will run to the media outlets to feign indignation when an overreach is executed, but they will retreat from any substantial confrontation. They seem to all be in on the little secret that most Americans and the rest of the population have been carefully shielded from. The State is now in control, and the Democratic and Republican wings of The Party are vying for the right to sit atop for the next four years.

It's not a mistake that the Parties take turns at wielding power, as the electorate rises every few terms to oust those in control in the hopes of a different result. As it turns out something different had occurred during the last transfer of power. The election of 2008 was to be the Democrats' turn at the wheel. But the primaries pitted the establishment candidate against this outsider, the community organizer with the Chicago machine, and he would win against the presumptive next President, the first woman, the former first lady to the 'first black President'[4], the darling of the media, Hillary Clinton. But he would not just take his turn at the wheel; he would take the opportunity to spread throughout the administration those of a like mind, those true believers, the radical left, limiting the establishments ability to participate as they had expected. And in 2017, their time will have finally come to an end, and the seats of power will finally be returned to those who feel it is rightly theirs, the establishment. Or will it?

An American finds the situation, a result of the unethical and unconstrained abuse of the power entrusted to those elected over the past 25 years, unbelievable. The damage is a fire, and unquenchable. The American is tired of cheap distractions such as 'compromise'. Compromise between an American and a Progressive can be described through a simple metaphor of an arsonist. The Progressive, which is the arsonist (of course,) is hell bent on burning the American's house to the ground. Compromise is where the Progressive makes a deal with the American and pledges to only burn down the American's garage. But the Progressive is not finished; the objective is still to burn the house down. The American is told to once again compromise, allowing the barn to be burned. And still the Progressive is still not finished. The Progressive is like the Terminator from James Cameron's famous series. The Progressive "absolutely will not stop, ever, until [America is] dead!"[5]

It's difficult for an American to understand the radical's obsession for destruction of the country which has provided abundance the like of which has not existed prior to the United States. But as is described by a self-described recovering radical, David Horowitz, in *Barack Obama's Rules for Revolution*, it has little to do with America, but a mental deficiency of sorts which demands "heaven on earth", and compared to this, "America is Hell."[6]

The American must reevaluate their frame of reference, for the time is near. The Praetorian Guard media complex is inundating the aware with information at such a frenzied pace, it's understandable that few have taken time to consider what is really happening. And for those who are blissfully unaware, they will not matter anyway. It's time Americans reevaluate their assumptions, consider their frame of reference, rediscover that lost critical thinking skill, and ask the following questions:

Three hundred years ago, this grand experiment we call the United States was not even a thought in young Benjamin Franklin's head. Do you think this country will exist three hundred years from now? That would be longer than the Roman Republic existed. No other system of government had lasted for that long. It's hard to imagine ours would not see a similar fate. Isn't it?

About a hundred years ago, the Progressive movement found their way into the White House, and brought with it the fondness for European socialism and affected the removal of state participation in governmental decisions. Do you think this country will exist in one hundred years? The country's government is already in the early stages of bankruptcy. It can't continue along its current path for long. Can it?

About fifty years ago, the government had transformed from the protector of the citizen's liberty to the provider of the citizen's needs, resulting in the justification for out-of-control spending, while it developed a learned helplessness among many sectors of society. Do you think this country will exist in fifty years? The current rate of increase for core entitlement programs alone is projected to eclipse total revenues before then. There appears no serious effort to curb spending in Washington D.C. It seems like the train is heading to the cliff and no one is going to be able to stop it. Doesn't it?

Seven years ago the country witnessed what George Washington identified as that element that separated "this country from every other country in the world," which was the peaceful transition of power. We are anxiously waiting to see one occur again next year. Or will we?

I NEEDED A RACE

Dunham

> *The liberties of our country, the freedom of our civil constitution, are worth defending at all hazards; ... We have received them as a fair inheritance from our worthy ancestors ... [they] transmitted them to us with care and diligence.*
> *-Samuel Adams*[1]

At an early age, she "taught him to disdain the blend of ignorance and arrogance that too often characterized Americans abroad."[2] This fellow traveler started developing her own counter-culture positions before he was even born; Stanley Ann Dunham's opinions would be remembered years later, as friends and faculty recalled her days at Mercer Island High School, near Seattle. Studies included Marx and Mead, resulting in community uprisings and "mothers' marches" due to the outrage[3]. But Ann was attracted to the subversive message, and remembered for challenging the status quo: "What's so good about democracy? What's so good about capitalism?"[4] And her son, Barack Hussein Obama II, was clear about her influence, "The values she taught me continue to be my touchstone when it comes to how I go about the world of politics."[5] But as the autobiographical novel *Dreams from My Father* eludes, family history was also critical to his formation.

Ann's father, Stanley Dunham, was the closest thing to a Dad he had as he developed into an adult. Stanley grew up in the depression era Midwest where his family would find work primarily around the booming oil businesses. As many Americans, he was yearning to be his own man, make his mark, be the captain of his own destiny. Sneaking off with his high school girlfriend, Madelyn Payne, to secretly get married after the prom, he returned her to her home where she tried to keep her secret[6]. But that secret wouldn't last long. The family was heartbroken, not for the scandal, rather because [grandma] repeated what was frankly a family tradition. But 18 months later, World War II would be thrust onto this young couple as they started their new life. Soon after, and in the nation's turmoil, Stanley "Ann" Dunham would be born.

Madelyn would find herself an inspector at the B-29 factory in Wichita, Kansas, which was one of four plants building the thousands of *Superfortresses* which would provide the necessary reach to finally bring the Pacific conflict to a close[7]. Stanley would enlist, supporting proudly in the 9th Air Force during D-Day, and then in France later. He would return safely to renew his family, and acquaint himself with his daughter, now about 2 years old. The B-29s that Madelyn's plant would produce would get no closer to the European theater than carefully planted threats by intelligence services as a ploy to help divert German resources[8]. This airplane was the most advanced and threatening piece of war materiel on the planet at the time, but it would be unleashed half a world away.

The Boeing B-29 development, initially championed by Charles Lindberg prior to the entrance of the war, was to become a critical enabler of the pacific victory[9]. The size of this single development program dwarfed past efforts. At over ten percent of the entire United States Federal revenue for 1939, this program was kept under wraps. But the President, Franklin Delano Roosevelt, and his administration knew what lay ahead and made the decision to prepare for what was the inevitable conflict over the horizon. This airplane would make the difference.

The introduction of a pressurized cockpit allowed much higher operating altitudes, allowing longer ranges, and faster ground speeds. The rapid development demand coupled with the limited resources available for this secretive, unproven aircraft required immediate solutions. There was no time for research, a solution was demanded, but no engine existed which could pull this beast into the air. The quick solution was to combine proven engines front to back, in an attempt to increase the power necessary. The dual radial engine concept proved to be capable of providing that necessary horsepower, but was prone to failure due to overheating. This problem would never be solved, resulting in many losses, including the crash of an early prototype into a Seattle meat packing plant, killing all on board[10]. But by this time it was 1943, and this military reach was not only required for victory, but critical to avoiding the loss of hundreds of thousands of additional American lives. America would provide the plane, but it would be an unreliable and risky platform[11]. By the time the B-29 was operating in the pacific theater, the problems had not been solved, but the Army Air Corps knew they were the critical link in the chain that would win the war.

The tyranny of distance was to provide the American leadership the choice none would wish. Would they continue to sacrifice the brave and determined Navy and Marine forces through a continued attrition-based assault across the myriad of island fortresses on their way to a future invasion of the Japanese mainland, or would they use this new force of air power to take the war directly to the homeland of the enemy?

The engine problems described previously resulted in a strategy that has repercussions even today. While the aircraft had 4 engines, and was capable of traveling thousands of miles, these miles would be over the Pacific Ocean. Should an engine fail or catch fire, which was a common occurrence, the aircraft would need to land. A chain of islands between the air base and the target area provided several emergency landing areas, but a large part of the journey would afford no safe harbor.

As it turned out, there was an island with a runway capable of supporting the B-29 in the area, about half way to Japan, but this island was heavily defended and critical to their own defense as it served to provide Japan early warning of the strike missions. The enemy too knew the criticality of this airstrip, for without it, many B-29s would be lost. The Japanese were virtually defenseless to this aircraft operating at about 30,000 ft., far above where its fighters could fly. But the B-29 would rarely be attacking from that altitude, and the distance was too far for fighter escorts. They would go into the target area undefended. And they would have to attack at much lower altitude in order to place their cargo where it was needed. The accuracy was far too poor at that time for high altitude bombing. Even though they were then much more vulnerable, less than half of the aircraft losses were due to enemy fire, it was a very risky mission. This isolated island perfectly situated halfway from the air base and the target would become one of the most critical battles of the entire war. There would be no alternative. This objective would be won, at any cost. And the enemy would hold it, at all cost.

While the Navy was preparing for the invasion of Okinawa, they took the opportunity to remove the enemy from this island. Although they were skeptical of the one week estimate for the operation, they were not expecting the fight that lay ahead. Approximately 450 American ships, about 60,000 U.S. Marines and 2,000 Navy Seabees were planning to make this a quick and decisive victory. The enemy, who had been preparing for this battle for almost an entire year, would have other plans. Even though the Army had been bombing this island for seven months, it ultimately had little effective impact, because the American force was unaware of the labyrinth of tunnels which provided the enemy safety[12].

Each warship was assigned a region of the island and, two days before the amphibious assault, opened up a partially successful bombardment campaign necessary to weaken the island defenses. The frequent weather complications would result in only about a third of the desired preparatory offensive, but the invasion would occur as scheduled. The invaders quickly realized the island fortifications were much stronger than expected, the enemy even more determined than expected, and as a result, the casualties far more than expected. Of the over 20,000 Japanese on the island, only 216 would be captured, the rest either dying in battle, or by suicide. The bare island provided no cover, but the tunnel complex was so extensive that the final two Japanese soldiers would be able to avoid detection and finally surrender in 1949.

The battle lasted for five weeks, but only 13 days after the battle began, with the airfield under American control, the first B-29, Dinah Might, would land there, having not enough fuel to make it back to the Marianas. Under enemy fire, Dinah Might, the first of over 2000 B-29 landings, would be refueled and depart to make is safely home[13]. As the aircraft began to safely begin to separate itself from the mayhem, the crew would be able to see the small flag on the top of Mt Suribachi, on the southwestern tip of the island, where many of the 6800 American lives would end.

Iwo Jima would become the most iconic battle of the pacific theater and would provide America with the ability to end the war. The scene of some of the most horrendous fighting in the war was seen by the President as a necessary objective, and the future of the nation depended on it. He knew many Americans would not come home from that barren rock, but his primary responsibility was the prosecution of the war to its successful conclusion[14].

The last B-29 would roll off the line in October 1945, and Madelyn and Stanley would be reunited to once again start their life together, along with young Stanley Ann. The family however, would not stay in the Midwest. Stanley was not to return to a dead-end job; coupled with the rebelliousness of his youth, he carried with him the hope and enthusiasm which became the trademark of the 'greatest generation'. He would finally drag the family to Washington State, where he found he was a good salesman[15]. One can envision the stereotypical salesman, boisterous and cocky, speaking a little louder than he should, slapping the shoulders of a client, and inserting stories on whatever subject seemed to interest the client, as he coolly zeroed in on the kill. He would be a successful furniture salesman, and was a solid provider for his family as his daughter made her way through high school. For unclear reasons, the family would relocate. The story would be that the opportunity to change his surroundings and the excitement of a new challenge was too much to deny, so the family would move to the country's newest state, Hawaii. Madelyn would leave her successful career as a bank vice president as Stanley would be able to get in the Hawaiian market early[16]. The timing was right, as the distance from the mainland to Hawaii had been shortened by another Boeing aircraft in 1959.

The war that Stanley and Madelyn had just participated in may have ended, but those totalitarian regimes that were defeated weren't the only entrenched empires of the day. The Soviet Union, while severely damaged during the war, quickly became America's adversary. The communist ideologues which oversaw the slaughter of millions of their own people in the name of their utopian agenda, was hell-bent on world domination. With the remainder of Asia and Europe utterly destroyed, Africa centuries or in some ways millennia behind in social and cultural development, and South America firmly in the hands of despotic minor players, only the North American and Australian continents would have the ability to provide any resistance. And America was the only real threat to their calculations. America had, in the midst of a four years' war, transformed from the land of liberty into a military superpower.

But a standing Army was not an American tradition, nor could the country afford it. As the world would return to peace, America decided to quickly divest of her strength and return to the American ideals which made her great to begin with. But her innocence was shattered; she would no longer be caught unprepared.

The Soviet Union, having successfully cleansed its populace of most dissent through terror and murder, was under complete control of the elite Politburo, who would maintain their position as long as they supported the General Secretary, Joseph Stalin. America ended World War II by demonstrating the most fearsome and devastating weapon ever created, the 'atom bomb'. The power of such a device was thankfully not well understood as it had only been used against two targets: Hiroshima and Nagasaki. These relatively small devices were quickly eclipsed by larger and much more powerful versions making the mere contemplation of nuclear war seem ridiculous. But in the aftermath of the war, the Soviets embarked on comprehensive espionage campaigns which resulted in 'their' designs of this most powerful class of weapon.

America wasn't surprised they weren't the only country trying to crack the atom; the Soviets as well as the Germans were intent on creating such a weapon. But the war was now over and America could return to the land of liberty. Within a few years the free world would be rocked by the news of the nuclear explosion on the other side of the world. On August 29, 1949, the Soviets detonated their first atomic bomb, extremely similar to the American "Fat Man"[17]. Their overconfidence would ultimately be their downfall, but in 1949 they were an existential threat. World domination was the goal, and America was the target. But America had learned a hard lesson. The leadership of the free world came with it the responsibility to maintain vigilance. America would not start a conflict, but we would use our might to reduce threats, and if it should occur, America would be ready this time. While the threat of nuclear weaponry was beyond historical context, it was clear the adversary was threatening such a conflict. Could America assume the 'hammer and sickle' was bluffing? The ability of a single weapon to decimate an entire city changed the game. But this game goes both ways.

The American bomber had been a decisive element in the defeat of the most dominating enemy force ever assembled. It allowed the ability to reach out and apply the necessary military effect from a relatively safe operating location far from enemy influence. America needed to demonstrate it had the capability to not only withstand the threat, but would be prepared to take the fight to them in such a way as to ensure they know they would have no safe operating location. America was already building a new bomber that could deliver its payload anywhere on the planet. Where the B-29 was the plane of the future in 1939, the B-52 *Stratofortress* would be the plane of the future in 1945. This top secret airplane development was to produce 744 aircraft from 1952-1962, but it could only fly a few thousand miles, not that much further than her grandfather, the B-29[18]. What the Air Force needed was the ability to refuel her while the air, virtually extending her rage indefinitely. At the time, the main air refueling aircraft was propeller driven, providing only limited improvement in overall capability. What was needed was a jet power refueling aircraft. And Boeing would deliver.

Boeing had developed a "Dash-80" prototype aircraft using a third of its profits, in the hopes of enticing the government into a production contract. The aircraft had four jet engines, was 128 ft. long with a 130 ft. wing span, with a gross weight capability of 160,000 lbs. So successful it was, one week after its first flight, the Air Force made its first order. But this plane had other interests as well. Four months later Pan Am would make their initial order of a modified version, designated the Boeing 707[19]. It was in 1959 that Pan Am began air service to Hawaii using their Boeing 707, the same year she would become the 50th state in the United States of America. This dramatically reduced the travel time, but also the cost of the trip. The island up to this point had been relatively undeveloped. Stanley was going to get in on the ground floor and ride it to the top.

Seeds

> *My identity might begin with my race, but it didn't, couldn't end there. At least that's what I would choose to believe.*
> -Barack Obama[1]

Stanley "Ann" Dunham, an impetuous girl, seemingly enamored with exotic cultures prior to meeting the visiting student from Africa, found herself seventeen and pregnant at the beginning of her first year at the University of Hawaii[2]. She said the father, Barack Hussein Obama, was one of the first Africans sent to the U.S. as part of our government's plan to improve his continent through education. Barack appears to be the first in the family line to break the barrier between the tribal nature of the Kenya in the early twentieth century, and western civilization. When presented with the question of whether to let Ann marry, the Resident evaluated the situation with "The fact that my grandparents had answered yes to this question, no matter how grudgingly, remains an enduring puzzle to me"[3]. His lack of empathy could be clouded by his narcissist nature. Whether his mother and father ever actually married is still a mystery, but their time as a family would be short, if it existed at all.

It appears Ann was unaware that Barack had left a child and a pregnant wife in Kenya. But she decided to have her baby, Barack Hussein Obama II, and marry the father. Little more is known of the family as they virtually disappeared after the birth. There may be only one picture of Barack II with his father, and that was in an airport when he was ten. No-one seems to remember the young family at all. The story goes that Ann had met Barack and quickly fell in love. Barack had met the family, and the two of them quietly went away for the family tradition of a secret marriage. There was some limited evidence that the two had possibly lived together in Honolulu, but no one even remembers them at the house. If you struggle to stitch together the mosaic created, what appears to have happened, is that Ann was infatuated with the exotic nature of Barack, he was happy to oblige, and she found herself pregnant. She would then convince Barack to marry her, although there appears no record of the happening, and then something happened and the family dissipated[4]. It's quite possible Ann was not willing to return to Kenya with him.

Ann (with or without and Barack II) appears to have moved to Seattle to attend the University of Washington shortly after his birth, while Barack completed his studies in Hawaii. Barack II would not see his father again until he was ten[5]. If Barack was to be an important man in Kenya, he would not have time for this second wife and third child. And what is apparently a family tradition in the Obama family, the families belong in the back seat.

Barack Obama's collision with western culture was cataclysmic in the end. If you consider "Barry's" description of his father and the life he led, as written in his own words, he would be portrayed as a righteous figure that would go to his death a champion of his country's well-being. The reality is that his father was more of a con-man than a statesman, moving from one scam to another. Spawned from a tribal culture most Americans only could imagine through the pages of National Geographic magazine, he was to be one of the chosen to bridge between the new world and his own country, in many ways relatively unchanged for millennia. Deeply desirous of meeting the challenge, he was ultimately unable to break free of his heritage and brought his cultural norms with him into the society which had long since discarded them.

Although there seems to be no direct evidence of the specific reasons for the newlyweds' abrupt separation, Barack's uncanny self-destructive nature and predilection to abuse of others around him could surely provide an explanation, or at least insight. His third wife, Ruth Baker, whom he met while a student at Harvard shortly after leaving Hawaii, and brought back with him to Kenya, has been very forthcoming about the harshness of her treatment. Possibly a cultural norm, Barack's own father "the old man" has been made famous through memoirs and biographies for his abusive nature[6]. But Ruth was soon to be pregnant with another child. At one point she finally had the courage to leave and found her way back to Boston, only to have Barack track her down and bring her back three weeks later. The attempt to resist return was a plea to her parents, who responded "You made [your] bed; you have to lie in it."[7] It would be years later before Ruth could finally free herself from the prison of Obama. Anguish and destruction seems to be what was left along the trail of Barack's chain of women, marriages, and children.

After Barack left Hawaii, Ann was safe to return to (or with) Barack II. At this point, back under her parents' roof, she quickly sought a solution to her predicament. She was to get married again to another foreign student, this time from the island of Java. Soetoro Martodihardjo, going by the name Lolo Saetoro, would become Ann's second husband after she was able to secure the divorce from Barack Obama. Conveniently for Lolo, he was able to connect with Ann shortly before his J-Visa was to run out[8]. Avoiding deportation initially by finding employment, it would not save him for long. He was finally required to return to Jakarta, and Anne and young Barry would follow 16 months later. Lolo himself, would turn out to be quite the womanizer as well, bringing woman back to their house when Ann was away. As the unravelling of their marriage seemed to begin, Ann found herself pregnant again, with Barry's sister Maya Kassandra Saetoro[9].

As a six year old, Barry was whisked off to Indonesia with no knowledge of the language. That would be dramatic for any child. The next several years he would integrate into the Indonesian culture, learn the language, and experience the exotic nature of the county in the midst of governmental instability during these most critical formative years. But the schools were poor and the environment dangerous for young Barry[10].

Barry's education would provide the core of his mother's focus for quite some time. He would be sure to receive the four "R's": reading, writing, 'rithmetic, and the cultivation of the soul which would be drawn to radicalism of the day. Ann's counter-cultural proclivities are apparent through her life and career choices, and seemed to make Barry's education a high priority, placing him at better schools while adding english lessons herself to make sure he was afforded the best foundation she could provide. But instability would be the consistent element in this family. As the family disintegrated in Indonesia, Barry's grandparents in Hawaii were able to gain him the opportunity to attend the prestigious Punahou School near their home in Honolulu[11].

Barack seemed to be raised around, and exposed to, many religions, but does not follow religion himself. He grew up in a household where "the Bible, Koran, and the Bhagavad Gita sat on the shelf alongside books of Greek and Norse and African mythology"[12], and developed a sense of moral equivalence when it comes to religion, indifferent to the actual manifestations which must be found beyond those pages. His mother seemed to be securely in the camp of the 'secular beings' which were indifferent to such things. He had however identified the importance of religion, or churches to be more accurate to the citizenry he would decide would be his followers. Collecting any and all relevant references to the culture he planned to infiltrate, his account in *Dreams* provided a Chinese menu of religious and social ideologies. He would find out later that this sense of indifference toward a higher power would need to be carefully managed.

It was a national crisis. Only 71 days earlier the nation had awoken to the most devastating and "cowardly" surprise attack on Pearl Harbor. The country was now at war. As a result, the western edge of the United States would feel vulnerable and expected a mainland invasion. With virtually absolute power seized over the previous 9 years, President Franklin Delano Roosevelt believed he had authority over America and Americans. To reduce home-grown threats by people of Japanese ancestry, they would be 'excluded' from 'military areas'. The areas included the State of California, and much of Washington, Oregon, and Arizona. Anyone who was Japanese, American citizen or not, would be notified of their situation and had to relocate outside of the military area, or would be removed. It was done under Executive Order 9066[13]. As is often the case, when a President cannot win support by the weight of his argument, he will resort to unilateralism. He too had a "pen and a phone", should congress not act. Given that there was only a single elected official who challenged this unconstitutional act, Colorado Governor Ralph Lawrence Carr, it's quite possible it could've been accomplished differently, but FDR had long since discarded the notion that the Executive was a co-equal branch of the government[14].

A young journalist, with community organizing in his future, would find himself in San Francisco when the Pearl Harbor attack occurred. This recent graduate from the University of Georgia grew up in Hawaii, a 'Nisei', or child of a Japanese immigrant worker and an American citizen. It would be in San Francisco where this aspiring journalist, Koji Ariyoshi, would become connected with the International Longshore and Warehouse Union (ILWU). A United States citizen by birth, but designated a threat of espionage or sabotage because of his ancestry, he would become one of over 120,000 sent to internment camps at the beginning of the war[15]. But Koji would be luckier than many, as he was able to volunteer support for the country, his country, the country that had imprisoned him because of where his parents were born. While at the Manzanar Ware Relocation Center in eastern California, he decided to support the Army as a language specialist, and was sent to various locations throughout Southeast Asia where he became more attracted to the communist movement spreading across the globe. Other Japanese volunteers would serve in the European theater as part of the segregated 442nd Regimental Combat Team. It would be these Americans of Japanese ancestry which would liberate at least one Nazi concentration camp, a part of the infamous camp at Dachau[16].

Kori would finally return to Hawaii in 1948, and start a newspaper called the Honolulu Record, which would be the voice of the local communist movement, "consistently supported by the Chinese Communists."[17] This was before statehood, and the 'community organizing' projects at the time included various strikes, in cooperation with the ILWU, on the many industries controlled by the "White Republican aristocrats." In 1949, a dock strike would freeze all shipping in Hawaii for 177 days. As a result, the territorial legislature requested the House Un-American Activities Committee investigate, which resulted in the prosecution of what became known as the 'Hawaii 7', seven major organizational leaders which included Charles Fujimoto, the chairman of the Communist Party of Hawaii, and Kori Ariyoshi[18].

Ariyoshi's paper, the Honolulu Record, would be found to be "a front for the Communist Party" in 1950, but would continue to be published until 1958. Another fellow traveler would arrive the same year Kori returned to Hawaii, and would provide prose for a weekly column titled *Frankly Speaking*, in the Honolulu Record, beginning in May, 1949. The column, which "defends Communists and attacks capitalism with the same vigor as columns appearing regularly in the Daily Worker [published by the Communist Party USA in New York City]," would be authored by one Frank Marshall Davis.

In addition to his mother, Barack seems to have an uncanny ability to collect coincidental acquaintances that just happen to find themselves at various levels in the who's who of radicals. A central character in young Barry's development would be among these, as much has been said and implied about his friendship with the old 'poet' Frank Marshall Davis; Barry, at times, implying he was just someone who his grandfather knew[19]. But would you go out of your way to seek advice from someone who was just an acquaintance of your grandfather from years past? It's pretty clear there is more to the story here than just what is portrayed in the autobiographical novel *Dreams from My Father*. There are plenty of other theories, from reasonable to full-blown tin-foil hat, but they are all theories resulting from the clear obfuscation provided for character definition during his self-marketing days.

An American would find it an interesting coincidence that the family had built a solid, stable living in a strong community in Washington State, and then suddenly decide to uproot themselves and make such dramatic changes. As it turns out, there would also be a significant level of communist and anti-communist activity in the Seattle area during the timeframe they lived on Mercer Island. Ann was not subtle in her support for the anti-capitalist nature of the times; in fact many of the interviews later reveal people remember about her primarily for her outspoken radical positions. Within a very short period, this family experienced the graduation of their daughter, who would end up pregnant at seventeen, a seemingly erratic set of circumstances which landed them in Hawaii living a relatively spartan lifestyle with the coincidental family friendship of a famous member of the Communist Party USA, who gained notoriety for his activities in Hawaii and Chicago. The family would never regain the lifestyle they once had when in Washington.

Regardless of these coincidences, his own description of events, true or not, provide insight into the mind of Barack Obama. His identity-based descriptions of those who come in and out of his life begin with race. Most people he meets aren't 'gentleman', or 'lawyer', or 'supporter'; they are 'white gentleman', 'black lawyer', or 'black female' such and such[20]. This is presented not only in his books, but across his public speeches as well. He grew up, not on the south side of Chicago, where the color is mostly 'black', nor did he grow up in the rural mid-west where the color could be claimed 'white'. His implied depiction of the racial friction during his school years in Hawaii was a fabrication. One of his teachers, Eric Kusunoki, was surprised and provided his own perspective: "In Hawaii, ethnicity is blurred."[21] And fellow student Constance Ramos felt "betrayed" by the portrayal[22]. It was clear this story was developed to support the production of the public figure he wanted to be.

Blackness

> *I was trying to raise myself to be a black man in America*
> *- Barack Obama[1]*

His childhood was spent in one of the most diverse areas of the world. He grew up in Hawaii, where the only place where 'white' was the majority was probably under his grandparent's roof. It's true there weren't many black people either, but there were many other shades, colors, creeds, etc. Hawaii was a true 'melting pot', but his time there was split with a few years in Indonesia. Again, the racial 'injustice' attitude would really need more time to find root. But that didn't stop Barack from planting the seeds of victimhood he knew he needed in his attempt to claim his chosen cultural heritage.

Where he was able to gain some perspective to the real struggle going on in various areas of the country was through the reading material his mother provided. Concerned with the same issues any single mother with an only son might be, she would appear tireless in her attention (when she was there) and made sure her son's development included descriptive histories of his black heritage, and texts chronicling the 'black experience'.

The 'black experience' can trace its roots to before the founding of the country, before the mayflower compact, in fact, to a period long before America was discovered, before Christianity[2]. The colonies, representing European values and practices at the time, brought with them the scourge of slavery. Slavery was legal in all 13 colonies prior to the American Revolution; the Republic of Vermont would be the first to partially ban the practice as early as 1777. Shortly after the Constitution was ratified, abolitionists were successful in ending legal slavery in the northern states (1804), followed by the banning of importation or export through international trade (1808)[3]. It's clear the effective purge of slavery in the colonies was due to the creation of the United States of America. But as is the case with major cultural movements, it would take more than a "pen and a phone" to eradicate. It would be decades of internal struggle that would finally be settled by the Civil War. But this country's battle was only one chapter in the world-wide effort to cleanse this blight on humanity, and in some places on Earth, laws have still been necessary to outlaw the practice as late as 2007 (in Mauritania)[4].

While the institution of slavery has existed in recorded history as far back as 1760 B.C. (Code of Hammurabi), it had become integrated into the Muslim culture and codified within Sharia Law; early records indicating the capture and enslavement of Chinese paper makers, which helped spread the use of paper across the Middle East, Africa and Europe[5]. Half way around the world this anti-Christian ideology had been struggling to come to grips with slavery as the rest of the world was; the Ottoman Empire having outlawed white slaves in 1854. The slow but steady world-wide abolitionist movement would move south along the African east coast around Cape Horn and up the west coast, where at one point the only safe ports for the slave trade were the eastern shores where slaves would be traded by the warring tribes, including the Luo tribe, ancestors of Barack Obama[6]. Whether conversion was by choice, or for survival, his Islamic family would probably be a reason his father was able to reach America as a free man, while many others from Kenya and Somalia would only reach America as slaves[7].

Through this period, Christian abolitionists would be relentless in the cause for humanity. The American southern states would find themselves increasingly isolated from western culture. What had become a major industry in the 16th century, took root in America in the 17th century, found the seeds of its own destruction being sowed in the 18th century, resisted its conclusion in the 19th century, and would find a new home in the 20th century. It would not be the legalized slavery of the past, nor would it be the indentured servitude the Irish, Chinese, Italians, etc. had to endure as they integrated into this country. It would become the dependency class with members holding virtually no individual power, but as a group, would grow to dominate the political landscape as targeted voter blocs. And for those who could play the game, there would be benefits.

But to young Barry, his mother was teaching him about his 'noble' heritage. Not just the uplifting black history of Martin Luther King, Jr., but that of the radical Malcolm X as well. And that education would also include the fabricated history his father as a great man from Africa. He knew only 'of' his father, having not even met him until he was ten, when he was on a short visit to Hawaii. As Barry progressed through adolescence, much has been made about his drinking and drug use, the choom gang, smoking pot for maximum effect, searching for a sense of belonging. This is hardly surprising as he was on his journey to find where he belongs, unmoored from family and tradition. As a child, he was lacking the consistent parent figure, being passed back and forth between his own mother and grandparents. He found family in his ring of friends as do many Americans. He wasn't a great athlete, but seemed to be a great enthusiast. His love of basketball would be kindled and provide him internal satisfaction for years to come. Being of average ability, he wouldn't play much, but he never gave up hope he could perform as his basketball idol 'Dr. J', Julius Erving. Where he did start to separate himself from the crowd, was intellectually. What would serve him well throughout his early life would be his apparent insatiable appetite for study. This didn't translate to his classwork, however; he was quite the average student as well. "He was a B student," noted Eric Kusunki, his High School homeroom teacher[8]. But this didn't dissuade his plans for college.

Although the family seemed to have little money, and Barry only an average high school student, he would secure a position at Occidental College in Los Angeles in 1979. Frank offered a little mentoring support, "Leave you [sic] race at the door", and provided a warning, "They'll tell you so good, you'll start believing what they tell you about equal opportunity and the American way and all that shit. They'll give you a corner office and invite you to fancy dinners, and tell you you're a credit to your race. Until you want to actually start running things, and then they'll yank your chain and let you know that you may be a well-trained nigger, but you're a nigger just the same."[9] Not unexpectedly, his first year of college would be very similar to high school. The academic performance was uninspiring, his partying, more intense. He would spend most of his time in a more bohemian lifestyle.

Barry would find he fit in with the students who had "middle- to upper-middle-class backgrounds", David Mendell would note[10]. Don Terry, a writer for the Tribune, would characterize him as a "California black", more laid-back, less 'urban'. But this is where his behavior would illuminate the hole within himself. Possibly subconsciously, he began to assert his own desire for "blackness". His awkward interactions whether calling someone a "Tom", or greeting a friend (who obviously already knew him) with a seemingly innocuous "What's up, brother?", only to receive a "Huh?" But he was still an intellectual, in his own mind.

He managed a collection of friends who he would characterize as "foreign students, Chicanos, Marxist professors, structural feminists, punk-rock performance poets"[11], once again describing his surroundings as balkanized groups. But as the 'intellectual', he began to be attracted to the positive feedback he would receive from the group of like-minded people he would begin to preach to. The counter-cultural, anti-establishment nature of early college experiences would resonate with his childhood development and provide validation as he began to develop his own sense of self. He also seemed to realize the power of mystery when it comes to the perspective others would have of him. As David Maraniss described his Oxy years, one gets the sense that Barry's friends would describe a caricature of Barry, rather than maybe the more realistic character[12]. This projection of what people want to see onto this future politician would generate strong feelings, both positive and negative, later in life, resulting in extreme opinions about the nature of this person's values. But in reality, he was the average college student, balancing his studies with the unencumbered social life the college experience can provide. He would spend his first year focused on being cool, being accepted, trying to belong to his group.

A year down, but still directionless, Barack returned home for the summer. While at home his 'white' grandmother Toot would be "bothered by a panhandler," a black man, while she was waiting for the bus she took to and from work each day. She was very upset, implying it was more than just being "bothered," and the situation affected him deeply as well. During a mentoring session with 'Frank', he brought the subject up and it seemed clear Barack was unprepared for the tone of the response: "black people have a reason to hate."[13] He had been provided the indoctrination material, but still hadn't been able to integrate it. This event seemed to have a profound effect on him as he returned to 'Oxy' with a newfound sense of purpose. He realized he was on the wrong path; failure was the only thing at the end of this road. He was now determined to find the black person that was supposed to be inside of him.

He developed the 'big fish in a small pond' perspective which would feed his ego and give him the desire and confidence to strike out for a bigger venue. At the same time he was showing more signs of his own sense that somehow he was different than others, although this was not the difference Americans understood or valued. He was separated from Americans, a sense of identity and belonging that placed him outside of American society, and eventually above it. He would begin to project this separation as he asked to now be called 'Barack'. For the past dozen years, he was known as 'Barry', a less exotic name. But he was now to start creating his own identity, not the identity others had given him.

His previous 'lame' attempts to claim 'street-cred' were comical, but now he would start a self-improvement program with the purpose of building his credibility as a black man. During an organized protest of South African Apartheid, he was given a minor scripted role where he would have his opportunity to speak to the crowd. His "There's a struggle going on..." speech spoke to the crowd yearning to be participants, and the response was electric[14]. Barack could connect to those looking for a leader. He also knew he could write.

Already an intellectual in his own mind, Barack would begin to develop his writing talents. He would attempt to get published in the Oxy student magazine for poetry and short stories, but he would find initial rejection was waiting. Later, he would have two poems published about the two most influential men in his life to this point, his grandfather Stanley, and his mentor, Frank Marshall Davis. But Oxy would be "too claustrophobic" and unable to provide him with the insight into the "black experience" he was yearning for. Fashioning himself as a writer, maybe a journalist someday, he chose New York City, and Columbia

University. Surely he would be able to find his "blackness" if he could immerse himself into the culture, which at this point remained foreign to him, learned only through the experiences of others. He "just needed a bigger pond to swim in." The summer between these two cultures would be an opportunity for "travel and adventure", as his Mother had secured for him the funds for a 16 stop Pan Am trip around the world.

Ann appeared to have finally matriculated to a self-sufficient adult working for the Ford Foundation supporting the various causes in Southeast Asia. Barack would travel to Jakarta for a reunion with his mother and sister, where he interestingly was able to secure his New York apartment for the following school year as a result of some incidental contact during the visit. He would remember his time in Pakistan above all, and would avoid the African continent during this trip through the third world. He was now a "man of the world" as he made his way back to the blessings only America can provide.

As Maraniss describes, a roommate, Phil Boerner, would 'liken' Barack to the main character of the Walter Percy novel, The Moviegoer, "where you're not participating in life, but you're kind of observing, one step removed."[15] This keen insight into the ability to remain at arm's length from the activities in his midst would also become a characteristic of his leadership style of "leading from behind". The knack of never really considering himself responsible for the events under his watch would become the rule, rather than the exception.

His transfer from Oxy provided his first opportunity to effectively claim oppression. He would be forced to live in a very low quality apartment off campus, as his status as a transfer student didn't provide him with on-campus housing. But as he will demonstrate throughout his public life, his 'glass is half empty' perspective always gets in the way of accepting the gifts his life would provide. Partly because he was becoming more serious about his own future, and probably also because he had less money, he started to reduce his partying and became more disciplined. But with so little mentioned in his 'over-indulgent' autobiographical novel, it appears his academic period at Columbia was either uninspiring, or he just felt it would be inconsequential, or conflicting, to the portrait of himself he was trying to paint.

But Barack was not the racialist we see today. He was still the student of the movement, not a participant, or even a believer. Boerner would later comment "One of the things that surprised me when I read his book was that he wrote about the black student world as the rest of it...I wasn't aware of him looking at things in such racial terms."[16] No one can see inside a man's heart, but the portrayal he would develop in *Dreams* would appear to be hyperbole used to provide structure to his fictitious character development.

Consumed with the effort to find himself, he would spend his Columbia years virtually anonymous. Maraniss would note "At Occidental everyone knew him; at Columbia he had almost been an apparition." While he would graduate with a Political Science degree with career ambitions, his roommate for his second year, Siddiqi, only knew he wanted to become rich. But other than an escape into a short relationship with Alex McNear whom he knew from his time at Oxy, he mainly focused on completing his degree. Alex seemed to realize there was little room for others in Barack's life, and the relationship withered away.

After graduation he would once again have the ability to travel leisurely. He would make his way to Jakarta to rejoin his Mother, but he would realize this part of his past he no longer belonged to either. "I can't speak the language anymore. I'm treated with a mixture of puzzlement, deference, and scorn, because I'm an American. My money and my plane ticket back to the U.S. overriding my blackness."[17] The victim begins to emerge.

As he returns to New York, he first mentions his initial foray into the real world. He is trying to find employment. It's hard to believe he hadn't had any meaningful employment to help support his schooling and extensive travels to this point, but he hasn't volunteered this in his product development literature. He would work for Business International Corporation as an editor and research assistant in their international financial information division. He proved to be adequate, but unenthusiastic about the "coldness of capitalism" he would be studying. Some temporary jobs managed to keep him afloat, but he already had decided during the last year at Columbia he would go into "community organizing."[18] He mentioned to Alex in a letter, the income was "too low to survive on,"[19] but he was drawn to the opportunity to prove his blackness by getting involved with Harlem and Brooklyn boroughs as a Community Organizer.

During this period he would meet Genevieve Cook, a woman three years his senior, who would be drawn into Barrack's sphere[20]. Common connections through her Australian roots, and his mother's network of acquaintances, they would provide the conduit for attraction. Genevieve would prove insightful into the inner workings of young Barack, describing the 'veil' he maintained between himself and the outside world[21]. Nothing could pierce that veil without his "double checking, inwards and outwards." She would also identify the drive within him. "He said he would never keep a job just for the security."[22] While most college students graduate with the goal to find their place in the world and integrate into the society, Barack was straying in the other direction. He was not interested in integration into a country he didn't understand and felt like he didn't belong. Genevieve's school teacher career, the core of the American childhood development, was becoming more at odds with Barack's developing vision of the problems in society. The cohesion once felt between the two was deteriorating as they drifted apart. But as he was just drifting at this point, searching for direction, juggling his own ambitions, he gets a phone call from Jerry Kellman.[23]

Kellman was looking for a prospect to work the Roseland neighborhood of the South Side of Chicago. He needed a community organizer. The Developing Communities Project needed an African American for the job, and placed ads in several papers around the country in search of a candidate. Obama had a solid background indicating he would have the desired "outsider sensibilities," but he had a fairly comfortable life to this point. Kellman would be concerned over his ability to push through failure, as a community organizer doesn't expect to win many battles, and would be relentless in championing change. But Obama wanted it. The more Kellman would describe how bad things were, the more

Barack wanted the job. He had his man. He was promised a $10,000 salary, and a car allowance. He packed up his blue Honda Civic and left for Chicago.[24]

THE PROPHET

Direction

> *There is another class of coloured people who make a business of keeping the troubles, the wrongs, and the hardships of the Negro race before the public. Having learned that they are able to make a living out of their troubles, they have grown into the settled habit of advertising their wrongs — partly because they want sympathy and partly because it pays. Some of these people do not want the Negro to lose his grievances, because they do not want to lose their jobs....There is a certain class of race-problem solvers who do not want the patient to get well, because as long as the disease holds out they have not only an easy means of making a living, but also an easy medium through which to make themselves prominent before the public.*
> *- Booker T. Washington[1]*

It would be Frank's "black people have a reason to hate" moment which provided the spark to the fuse. Barry returned to Oxy in 1980 with a newborn realization of what he saw as his destiny; he would become a 'great man' for his people as he believed his father was in his country. He would follow in the footsteps of his mentor, but despite his studies, he was ignorant of the black culture. His second year saw a dramatic change in his focus. Although he had always seen himself as an intellectual and was well-read, he was to start to take his grades seriously for the first time. There was a noticeable reduction in his social life, only because the time available had been reduced. Barry was beginning to awaken as the results of the 1960's civil rights movement were taking shape. The Civil War may have defeated the state-sanctioned institution of slavery and the Reconstruction Amendments applied the legal foundation for abolition, but it would be a tumultuous journey of transformation for the adolescent country.

They called it the "Three-Fifths Clause" (Art I, Sec 2), a compromise resulting from negotiations surrounding the development of the United States Constitution. At the time, before the industrial revolution would transform the northern states into the dominant force of the late 19th and early 20th centuries, the power of commerce resided in the southern states. Coupled with the "Fugitive Slave Clause" (Art IV, Sec 2), the institution of slavery was allowed. The abolitionist contingent wanted the elimination of slavery, but they also realized a need for a strong government. The southern states had the economic power at the time. The ratio of free men to slaves in the southern states was dramatically lower when compared to the northern states. If the northern states accepted slaves to be counted for representative purposes, the balance of power would surely shift strongly toward the south, and the hopes of abolition would be lost. The south on the other hand, realized if representation was only based on the population of free men, they would no longer have any say in the direction of the fledgling federal government, only a concept at this time. The result would have been at least two separate countries. The divisions probably would have resulted in the reintegration of territories into the various warring foreign powers at the time. The United States would not have existed.

The growing abolitionist movement would have their day, but it would not come soon enough. Article IV protected property, and was used by the Supreme Court to stifle the efforts of those dedicated to human decency with the famous Dred Scott decision which provided legal precedent for future challenges[2]. But the slave industry was being attacked from all sides at this time. While this landmark case provided cover for the specific slave owner at the time, much larger tectonic shifts had been occurring. The wave of world-wide abolition started to gain momentum while our nation was born. Across the globe, the institution of slavery was being defeated. In England, the Sommersett case would become the landmark event for the beginning of the removal of slavery from Great Britain (1772)[3]; Russia would start to eliminate slavery in the Crimea (1783)[4], Upper Canada in (1793)[5], France (1794, but would be reintroduced by Napoleon in 1802)[6]. The dominoes we're beginning to fall in the New World as well with initial legal movements to eliminate it in the original colonies: Vermont (1777), New York (1799), and New Jersey (1804). New northern states would immediately include abolishment clauses into their constitutions as they became new states, but as new southern states would be considered for inclusion, the Civil War would start. Not on the battlefield, but in Washington.

The California gold rush had begun, and Washington wanted in! It was not a state at this point, and the battle would bring the issue of slavery to the forefront. The south, already seeing the writing on the wall, needed to maintain some pro-slavery balance in the federal government if it were to maintain what it saw as its right to have slaves. The strong Democratic control of the legislature would squash the attempt to make the territory free. President Polk recommended a compromise, allowing slaves below the 36 degree, 30 minutes latitude, and making the northern section free[7]. This line is roughly a line running east to west at the northern borders of South Carolina, Tennessee, Arkansas and Texas. Luckily for California, congress did not support this. It was the lame-duck session awaiting the new President Taylor to take office, and the Democrats were convinced he was a "states' rights" advocate which would support their cause. But the old General outflanked them, pressing California to submit for statehood, bypassing the territorial connections with congressional oversight. California would be free! But the South and the Democrats still controlled the federal legislature and were feeling increasingly threatened as new president was on the offensive, pressing New Mexico to become a state. Jefferson Davis proclaimed "For the first time, we are about permanently to destroy the balance of power between the sections."[8] If the federal government would be able to increase the number of "free states", the senate would bend toward abolition and ultimately strangle the remaining slave states. But the northern section was dominated by the Whig party at the time, and there were scant signs of party unity to take the issue on directly. They preferred a carefully calculating approach, as it seemed less risky to the comfortable elites at the time.

The Democrats realized they were being cornered, and the Whig Party, weak as they were, would go on the offensive themselves. The battle was almost bloodless, as the Democrats were in an all-out fight for survival of their most cherished economic system of slavery against a party which was more interested in the status quo and keeping their position and standing. The result was the collapse of the Whig Party and the birth of the Republican Party. Fiercely abolitionist, this new party quickly gained support and claimed their first major victories in Ohio during the 1854-1855 elections, and would take control of the House of Representatives the next year. But it would be in dusty Kansas that the spark of the final removal of legal slavery would occur.

Kansas would have competing territorial governments, each recognized by partisan groups in Washington. The freemen of Kansas would find themselves at war with the attacking mobs sent from Missouri. It was gang warfare on the prairie. The south demanded Kansas be a "slave state", where the north would not allow it. The Republican controlled house would not pass a statehood bill allowing slavery, and the Democratic controlled senate would not pass a bill without it[9]. It's good Presidents Pierce and Buchanan (Democrats) didn't have a pen and a phone. This was the backdrop of the rising national popularity of a staggeringly brilliant and inspiring leader who would travel the country to champion the abolitionist cause.

Abraham Lincoln, a "free soil" Whig, had spent twelve years as an Illinois State Representative before he would be elected a Unites States Congressman, serving only one term, as he had promised, as the only non-Democrat in the Illinois delegation. His government service would end as the new administration only offered him a position as secretary or governor of the Democrat dominated Oregon territory. He wisely declined and returned home to resume his legal career. It was the pro-slavery Kansas-Nebraska Act which brought him out, once again, into the political forum in 1854. His attempt to win the United States Senate seat that year narrowly failed, and two years later he placed second in the Vice President voting for the Republican candidacy. But it would be the campaign for U.S. Senate in 1958 where he would forge the future of this great country.

Democrat Stephen A. Douglas was the senior Senator representing Illinois, and Abraham Lincoln was selected to be the Republican challenger. He entered the race with clear convictions: *"A house divided against itself cannot stand. I believe this government cannot endure permanently half slave and half free. I do not expect the Union to be dissolved—I do not expect the house to fall—but I do expect it will cease to be divided. It will become all one thing, or all the other."*[10] The importance of the Lincoln-Douglas debates would quickly rise to almost mythical heights. Lincoln was a steady abolitionist, knowing right was on his side, and that the answer, in the end, was simple: "All men are created equal." Douglas however was a seasoned politician, standing by the Freeport Doctrine, which allows the territorial people to decide for themselves what the future of the state's slavery laws would be. On the surface, this would be acceptable; except that the populace really wouldn't get an honest opportunity to decide. As has been the strength of the Democratic machine for its entire existence, they would be controlled through intimidation, threats, bribery, and outright murder. And that was what was happening in the Kansas territory. The democracy which Democrats find most appealing is the democracy where they control the vote.

This 1858 Senate race became the most followed at the time. National headlines would be made at every encounter. This was the front line of the battle for the livelihood of the southern institution. While the Republicans would win the popular vote and seats in the state legislature, in the end, it would be Democrats that would win more seats in the Illinois Senate. And the Senate selected the Illinois senator; Douglas would return to Washington victorious. Lincoln however was now a major player in the new Republican Party. And both would meet again to battle for the presidency in 1860.

The spark that had been ignited in Kansas only a few years earlier, was accelerating along a fuse throughout the campaign. The animosity between the various forms of "free soilers" and "state' rights" forces was growing without bound. The election was as polarizing as could be imagined. Lincoln would win only 2 counties (out of 996) in the south, garnering not a single vote in 10 of the 15 slave states. But he won more Electoral College votes than all other candidates combined, and was to be the 16th President of the United States.

But the country was already at war; it just didn't realize it. While Lincoln found slavery personally abhorrent, he fundamentally believed in the Constitution and through it the solution would be found, as he seemed accepting of minor pro-slavery legislation being proposed. But the Democrats and the south believed otherwise. The assassination of Lincoln was already being defended against even before he was sworn in. He arrived in Washington for the inauguration, but had to travel in disguise. He even flatly reiterated his previous positions "I have no purpose, directly or indirectly, to interfere with the institution of slavery where it exists. I believe I have no lawful right to do so, and I have no inclination to do so." This may have been true, but the South was already in a battle for its own survival, and the balance of power had shifted, making the days of slavery numbered, nonetheless. It would be only 39 days later that Fort Sumter would fall, initiating the Civil War.

The chain of events was to occur quickly as the southern states would claim succession, but the President would not accept it. At the outset, the South would win the initiative, but in the end, the industrial might of the North would crush their hopes, and the institution of slavery, but at the cost of over 700,000 lives. The destruction of the south was virtually complete. Not only was slavery now outlawed, creating a societal collapse, but the economic system was crushed. Reconstruction would attempt to recover the region and reintegrate the states into the Union, but it would be a long, hard road which in many ways is still not complete.

In 1862, while the south asserted their independence and did not participate in the United States legislative branch activities, the North quickly passed the Confiscation Act[11], banning slavery in all federal territories. As the Copperheads predicted, this would be serve up a serious problem relative to reunification. In fact, it caused the winner-take-all nature of the escalating conflict. The South knew that without victory, it would become another historical footnote. But Lincoln had declared what some may claim extra-constitutional authorities as he thought necessary as commander-in-chief implied in the war powers under the Constitution. The Emancipation Proclamation was coordinated only amongst his cabinet, but would be added to the country's foundational documents. And even before the conflict had ended, Constitutional changes were placed in motion.

Regardless of progress, the community organizer will always press forward. But much like a dog which finally catches the car, it doesn't have a plan for that eventuality. The community organizer's sole purpose is to instill discontent and generate friction between the competing elements in order to claim victories. It turns out the community organizer was really only a tool for larger, more powerful elements which collect the rewards of action, leaving the victim unsatisfied. This is precisely the objective, as it reinforces the need for more confrontation. It's quite the opposite tactic as chosen by the great Fredrick Douglas who was a champion for integration of the "black man" into society. But today, there is an army of racialists reaping the rewards of the current situation, and find financial benefit in reinforcing the fiction that the struggle is still on, at least outside of the community itself.

The 'Reconstruction Amendments' were crafted in an attempt to correct the language of division initially implanted in the Constitution. Although some would claim the southern states, at the time, were not members of the Union, and weren't needed to ratify the amendment, the 13th Amendment was finally ratified December 6th, 1865 with southern state participation, dissolving the institution of slavery from the United States and wherever it may hold jurisdiction. It should be noted that the southern state legislatures were confederate prior to the war's conclusion. Reconstruction saw the implanting of Republican legislatures in each state, which made the process much easier, but would sow the seeds for future conflicts as well. The 14th and 15th Amendments would follow in short order, ratified on July 9th, 1868, and February 3rd, 1870, respectively.

What would become known as the "magic" amendment for its use by creative judicial activists as a basis for their expansion of extra-constitutional activities was, in fact, created in order to more clearly define the scope of the removal of slavery. Much to the dismay of megalomaniac politicians, just stating that people will act a certain way, or creating a piece of paper somehow will change the person's heart just doesn't happen in the real world. Substantive changes will only occur if the change is beneficial to those it's imposed on, or ultimately, at the end of a gun. The "magic" 14th Amendment was fiercely debated, but ultimately clarified the protections granted to the emancipated slave. The 13th Amendment may say there are no longer any slaves, but a significant portion of society was not about to treat each other differently. Through this amendment, the Citizenship Clause would identify them automatically as United States citizens, as well as citizens of the State they were in, overruling the Dred Scott decision. The Privileges and Immunities Clause dictate to the States that they will not infringe on these rights. The Due Process Clause states no State can deprive someone "of life, liberty, or property, without due process of law." This basically imposes the elements in the Bill of Rights on the States themselves, a substantial alteration of the scope of the original document. The Equal Protection Clause would be used as the basis for Brown vs Board of Education almost 90 years later.

The second section eliminates the Three-Fifths element of the constitution and allows apportionment of representation only to be based on the number of eligible voters, a lawyerly way to motivate the states to allow "male inhabitants…being twenty-one years old" to vote in national elections. The third section requires two-thirds of each house to allow a participant in a past 'insurrection or rebellion' against the United States government to again hold office. The fourth section states that any debt incurred by the Union during the Civil War would be paid, but debts by the Confederacy would not, and that no claim for loss of property (slaves) will be honored. While this amendment was clearly to enhance and reinforce the emancipation of the slave, it would magically find its way into virtually any social experimental legislation argument for the next 150 years. The 15th Amendment clarified the confusing language of section 2 of the previous Amendment. It unequivocally provided the right to vote to the emancipated slaves. It would be over 40 years before another amendment was ratified, and the racial friction in the south would continue, often enflamed by the Democrats not willing to reject their old prejudices.

Even though the Republicans would be inserted into the legislatures in the south, it was only a matter of time before the electorate would recover, replacing them with Democrats. Democrat institutions such as the Ku Klux Klan and legislative tricks identified as the Jim Crow laws continued to restrict and threaten black Americans for decades to come, and Democrats would only be able to provide two Presidents during the Republican domination (1861-1933).

Grover Cleveland was the only President to serve non-consecutive terms, winning the popular vote three times (1884, 1888, 1892,) but losing the Electoral College in 1888, to Benjamin Harrison. This very popular, former New York State Governor was attractive due to his stance against corruption, which the Republican candidate in 1884, James G. Blaine, seemed to have issues with. A solid Constitutionalist, but confronted with a Republican congress, Cleveland vetoed more bills that any President up to that time. Although a Democrat, he did nothing to further encroach on the black person's liberties fought for and won 40 years prior. It would be the next Democrat which would once again fertilize the seeds of conflict.

Almost 50 years after the Civil War, the Democrats would finally win control of both Congress and the White House in 1912. Woodrow Wilson, an intellectual academic, convinced America it was his staggering intellect which would solve the problems of the day. When referring to the Constitution, he clearly discarded the historical precedent that the document was a blueprint for the management of the government and defined what the federal government was permitted to do, with the concept that it was some sort of ticket to wherever you might like to go, stating the presidency "will be as big as and as influential as the man who occupies it."[12] His proclamation that the president can define the extents of his own authority would become a recurring problem over the next century. He felt that his own opinion of what might be responsible would be the guiding principle of his administration. He was the original 'Pen and a Phone' president. Another interesting parallel was the tumultuous 1912 Democratic convention, where Wilson decided to let things work themselves out, and remove his own interference…by going golfing[13]. In addition, possibly because of the lack of interest being shown by its ultimate victor, it took 46 ballots to finally declare Wilson their candidate.

Seeming sure that he was the smartest person in the room, his solution to all major issues was some form of international diplomatic agreement. Regardless of the outcome, it was the publicity he garnered which seemed to satisfy his own measure for success. But his half-hearted efforts combined with isolationist statements regarding World War I, would leave the country years behind when the decision to enter the conflict was finally made. He would proclaim our independence from the carnage only long enough to get reelected, when he miraculously changed course and demanded we participate. But he would not commit until he had assurances his League of Nations would be supported[14]. That would certainly be a fine legacy. He would be the leader of the entire world. But as an unabashed racist, he, along with his party, refused to denounce lynching, and re-segregated common areas in buildings. Befitting his pompousness, he would demean protesters, "segregation is not a humiliation but a benefit, and ought to be so regarded by you gentleman."[15]

Booker T. Washington and W.E.B. DuBois would be towering champions for the "black man" during this period. Washington, president of the Tuskegee Institute during the early years of the 20th century, believed the path toward effective integration was first through education. The "black man" needed the tools to compete in the industrial world which was leaving them farther behind with each passing year. DuBois believed Washington to be an apologist for the problems afflicting the black man, and the battle for control of 'their people' was intense.

After over four decades of fruitless struggle, DuBois didn't believe in the integration into society that the great Fredrick Douglas had promoted. On the contrary, he would come to believe the community should not integrate. He believed capitalism was the cause of racism, becoming an outspoken champion of socialism. It was during this period that the black culture started to realize its power as a voting bloc. With insufficient support from President's Roosevelt and Taft, the move from the Republican Party to the Democratic Party had begun. The 'community organizer' DuBois would ultimately be recognized by the leadership of the socialist world, winning of the Lenin Peace Prize in 1959[16]. The award was presented to several people from 1957-1990 for their notoriety as prominent Communists or supporters of the Soviet Union.

The Civil War was over 50 years past, and there was still little change in the heart of man. It would take another 50 years for the next major attempt at correcting the injustice still infesting the establishment.

"I have a Dream" would become a call for humanity once again to look into their own hearts and find the strength to break from the establishment. Martin Luther King Jr's advancement of civil rights using nonviolent civil disobedience would bring about the most sweeping changes in almost a hundred years. From his Montgomery Bus Boycott in 1955, through the March on Washington in 1963, he was able to move the state of race relations from the back pages into the Oval Office. In 1964, he was awarded the Nobel Peace Prize for what he had accomplished, and it was the Civil Rights Act of 1964 that appeared to provide a sweeping framework for success.

It would not come easily, for the fight was epic, with Democrats leading a 54 day filibuster. But this would not be their day, the bill would pass. The President, Lyndon B. Johnson, however knew the victory would be claimed by the party that signs it into law, not those who fought to get it there. As a result, he famously stated: "I'll have those niggers voting Democrat for the next 200 years."[17] He knew the act may eliminate many elements hurtful to the black American, but he also knew it was setting up a monstrous social class which would become forever dependent on the 'generosity' of the State. And it would be the power of the State which would apply direct changes through rules and regulations.

Affirmative Action, as it would be known as, would enable many disadvantaged minorities to leap over other people to gain access to elements of society that seemed out of reach to prior generations. One area would be education. While it was shameful for schools to have discriminatory entrance criteria, it would become problematic to have reverse-discrimination policies creating animosity amongst new, yet unborn generations, who would be told to pay the price for the past. Or as recorded in Mark Levin's *Men in Black*, Thurgood Marshall would proclaim, "You guys have been practicing discrimination for years. Now it is our turn."[18] Regardless of the moral gymnastics necessary to justify these policies, the combination of entry-standard reduction, and education funding would make a quality education available for thousands of kids who may have never had their shot without it.

As Barack had discovered, being a competent student and a minority would provide additional opportunities many Americans would not have. Being of apparently limited financial means, and quite the average student through his Oxy years, it looks as if he was able to navigate his way through the education gauntlet with the help of student loans and grants. He moved to New York in the hopes that he could learn about what he was missing: his blackness. At the end of his Columbia time, he found himself inspired to get involved. Maybe he could earn his way 'in' by being the catalyst of improvement. He would insert himself into the culture he so much wanted to be accepted into, and as a community organizer he would earn his place as a great man he still thought his father was.

Chicago, famous for its historical segregation, would be the beacon on the hill for half a million black Americans who would flee the south's Jim Crow racism during what was to become known as the Great Migration. Chicago would become one of the nation's largest black urban centers and attract and produce giants in music, sports, and literature. Louis Armstrong, Mohammad Ali, Oprah and Michael Jordan would bring fame to the Windy City. But for Barack, he was just another person searching for direction. He would spend the first few nights with his Pakistani friend, Beenu Mahmoud, who was interning at Sidley Austin, an elite Chicago Law Firm that will appear in future scenes along Obama's story. Mahmoud was staying in the Hyde Park area, which was where Barack decided to settle.

Community Organizer

> *If there is any ideological fanaticism in American political life, it is to be found among the enemies of freedom in the left and right—those who would sacrifice principle to theory, those who worship only the god of political, social, and economic abstractions, ignoring the realities of everyday life.*
> *- Ronald Reagan[1]*

Hyde Park, being a bridge between black and white worlds, was one of the most integrated neighborhoods in Chicago. Barack's granduncle, Charles Payne would live only a few blocks from him at one point. But Hyde Park would also be the home of Jesse Jackson, Baptist minister, former follower of Martin Luther King Jr., and candidate for Democratic Party nominee for president in 1984, and 1988. It would also become the home of some of the most anti-American radicals, and domestic terrorists, Bill Ayers and Bernardine Dohrn. Bill Ayers was leader of the Weather Underground, responsible for bombings of the United States Capital, the Pentagon, and others. At one point Dohrn would be on the FBI's Ten Most Wanted List[2], but would also find herself employed by Sidley Austin[3]. Bill Ayers would become faculty at the University of Chicago. Both unrepentant, and their continued comfortable existence is a testament to the greatness of the country they live in.

It seems like it was very long ago when a man who fancied himself as a writer, a poet, an intellectual, would achieve a respectable education, whose writings would be widely-read, would operate in the shadows to mask his true intentions, was adept at dividing the classes, and would be tagged a radical. No, the subject of this review is not our Resident. This man would never become the leader of a country, but would provide the inspiration to some of the most infamous and destructive leaders over the last century. They would ultimately earn their fame not for the improvement they brought to the world, or even their own country. They would earn their fame through belligerent behavior, bringing about wars as well as the mass-extinctions within their own borders, in the name of a better social construct. The man was Karl Marx, and would become the name most-often associated with socialism.

Marx was born with a silver spoon in his mouth, a product of a wealthy family which provided him the comfortable upbringing which allowed him to explore his own path[4]. His non-religious father was an attorney, a product of the enlightenment, interested in developments like Kant's philosophy of universal democracy. Marx seemed to reject society as it was and spent his life participating in planning the overthrow of the bourgeoisie. Graduating from the University of Berlin, he found his way to where like-minded liberal thinkers could be found. In 1844, this would be Paris, where he would meet his lifelong comrade Friedrich Engels[5].

Over the next several years, he would be kicked-out of several countries, as a result of his subversive writings. He would use his pen to phone out the criticisms in support of the secretive League of the Just. First banned by all German states at the time, the French government would then expel Marx at the request of the Prussian King. Marx would then drag his wife and kids to Brussels, where he would write his *Communist Manifesto*. Surviving on loans and being able to publish articles from time to time, he was able to scrape together at least a pauper's life. This was the period where the League of the Just would come out of the shadows and become publicly recognized as the Communist League.

The *Communist Manifesto* made the case for uprising against the concept of historical materialism, the German Ideology. He would forever change the political language we all now take for granted. He championed the class divisions, real or not, which could lay the seeds of discontent. He believed the utopian communist economic model was achievable, but only after initial imposition of socialism which would wither away at some point. The critical spark to start this mass movement would be the simultaneous uprising of the proletariat, the overthrow of the bourgeoisie, and the substitute of socialism for capitalism. The bourgeoisie were the 'wealthy capitalists', and the proletariat was the 'industrial working class'. Naturally, the governments of the countries in place at the time didn't think much of this concept, and ultimately forced Marx into exile. Marx would land in London, and ultimately live out his life there providing a long list of publications espousing his ideas on the problems with the capitalist economy. Marx, the ideologue, was unable to see the weakness of his own conviction.

Those that cite Marx as an influence include the creators of history's most homicidal tyrannies such as Lenin, Mao, Castro, and Tito. What Marx didn't take into account was what the United States Constitution did. It was that men can't be trusted. Power was too intoxicating, and once tasted must be constrained. The leaders of the socialist economies took total control, and used it…mercilessly. It's been estimated that the 20th century has seen the extermination of over 100 million citizens at the hand of their own governments[6]. It doesn't sound like a worker's paradise to an American.

It's the Marxist ideology which generates the justification for class warfare, and that has seeped into the corners of society wherever a community organizer can implant it. But before Barack had decided he would be the hope and change the black community needed, the true giants had come before. Booker T. Washington championing the strength of the individual through self-improvement and achieving success would represent the American values defined in his three pillars of education, self-reliance, and entrepreneurship. In addition, Allen West would identify a fourth pillar, Christian Faith[7], as he presented the contrast between Washington and his ideological competitor, W.E.B. DuBois, a giant in his own right, who believed the Marxist approach would be more effective.

Co-founder of the National Association for the Advancement of Colored People (NAACP), he would spend his life organizing those with a sense of oppression into a powerful bloc which could use their strength in numbers to influence positive results. Many of the reforms he had campaigned for throughout his life would finally become law in the Civil Rights Act of 1964, the year after he died. Now 50 years later, the effectiveness of these reforms should be considered. Much like communism, they may have been seductive to those wishing for a just master and still sound worthy of merit. But remove the hype and what remains is that little has changed, other than the increased frustration of the groups which were intended to be saved by legislative action. That's not to say that there aren't plenty of people who've enriched themselves along the way, much like the politburo in the U.S.S.R. Socialism is for the people, not the rulers who are in power. This is probably why it's so attractive to the criminal mind.

A fellow progressive, born about 40 years later, would be one Saul Alinsky. Educated as a teenager who literally infiltrated the Al Copone gang in Chicago as a part of a school project, Alinsky would become the most effective community organizer of the times, at least until 2008. Alinsky would die a rich man in a beautiful part of the California Coast, Carmel-By-The-Sea, and would not live to see the magnificent result of his most effective disciple. To date, he has one 'descendant' living in the White House, and another convinced it's her turn to move back in. Dedicating his benchmark book *Rules for Radicals* to Lucifer; he clearly was uninterested in being a moviegoer. He would manipulate events and impose fear into his targets in order to get change. His philosophy separated the Haves from the Have-Nots[8]. In true Marxist fashion, he would work at separating groups and instilling hate between them.

He didn't really operate in the shadows either. He gave seminars which anyone could attend. His rules had become extremely effective organizational principles for use when you are confronting others with more to lose. Whether it's a business or a political office, the 'non-violent' tactics Alinsky applies can result in devastating effects on the target. The result is usually at least partial agreement, to remove the immediate threat. But the target will remain the target until the 'organizer' achieves their goal. Studied and praised by none other than Hillary Rodham (Clinton) during her school years, Alinsky was not only a community organizer himself, but also as a teacher and trainer of others. One Jerry Kellman comes to mind.

Kellman was Obama's supervisor and trainer in the Developing Communities Project (DCP), and assigned him to the Roseland and West Pullman neighborhoods in the South Side. Providing insight into the community, Kellman described how they had low literacy, were financially poor, and distrustful of authority. But Kellman decided Obama was somewhat of a natural. "All I had to do was to teach him not to be idealistic and he did the rest."⁹ As the migration of blacks into Roseland as late as the 1950's increased, the white population would slowly but surely depart. But the black middle class developed and strengthened, until the local industrial base declined in the 1980's, leaving "real divisions in a community—and I'd even say a sense of division within the race", said Pat DeBonnett, executive director of a nonprofit group dedicated to improving the South Side neighborhoods.¹⁰

Kellman had keen insights into his young protégé, however. He realized the moviegoer was on duty, with his notebook and pen. He told him "You can either change stuff, or you can write about it."¹¹ But Barack was apparently just one of many aspiring subversives. His grand uncle, Charles Payne, would comment "Community organizing didn't mean a thing to me. And yet, Hyde Park seemed to be full of them."¹² He also became recognized for his ability to keep cool in stressful situations, as 'taking the high road'. But his behavior often bordered on passive, although in time the ability to remain out from underneath confrontations would allow the bridge to be crossed later.

The DCP was ecumenically funded, aligned in the tradition of Saul Alinsky, and is still there today. The Alinsky model is to have the leaders operate in the background, spend many hours listening to the residents, decipher what the community needs are, and understand what can realistically be achieved. But everything is based on Power, how to get it, and how to use it. Obama would write "Once I found an issue people cared about, I could take them into action. With enough actions, I could start to build power. Issues, actions, power, self-interest, I liked these concepts. They bespoke of sentiment; politics, not religion."¹³ But Obama would need to connect to the people of the community.

Obama was assigned 20-30 interviews a week. Initially they were weary of the young man, but over time, they warmed up to him. Kellman assigned Obama to the Altgeld Garden housing project.¹⁴ Its location was near a landfill and sewage plant; it was just as bad inside. His favorite story had to do with a time when he would learn that there was an asbestos problem in the building, and went on the attack in order to fix the problem. He persuaded the alderman, Bobby Rush, to hold hearings. The meetings were explosive, but the result was a community organizing success; the city would pay to have the asbestos sealed. It reads as a minor event, but because so much weight is placed on that event in Obama's writings, as well as others, it was either a bigger deal, or there was little else to claim. But by all accounts, Obama worked hard and was on a mission. He was going to make a difference; he was going to earn his "blackness" and his way into the black experience one way or another.

Ever the pragmatist, he knew the center of the culture was the churches. He needed to search out connection with the churches. Early, he would connect with Reverend Alvin Love, pastor of the Lilydale First Baptist Church[15]. Reverend Love would provide enormous support for the local organizing Obama was focused on. But when he set his sight on the bigger picture, it would be another church where he would find his connection.

He attended several as he searched, but ultimately ended up at the Trinity United Church of Christ[16]. The now famous (or infamous) pastor, Jeremiah A. Wright would become his religious mentor for two decades. Wright spoke to the heart of his congregation, and it was a Black Liberation Theology which was preached: the social gospel which could be used to sooth an aching heart or enrage the inner demon. Obama felt if he could get a consortium of these churches to work together, great things could be accomplished. But he quickly realized the leaders in the churches had egos that challenged the size of his own and each felt they themselves had the keys to the kingdom.

Before Jeremiah Wright, James Cone would define what Black Liberation Theology meant and why it was important. He felt the "White Church" should not be followed because it was a supporter of the oppression of the black race. As Barack had found, Cone declared "Being black in America has little to do with skin color. Being black means that your heart, your soul, your mind, and your body are where the dispossessed are."[17] Obama would struggle with this demand to be separate, but at the same time demand that they are not. And another "teacher" at Trinity, along with Jeremiah Wright, is Dr. Dwight Hopkins who more clearly stated "People are poor because they are victims of others."[18] Obama would have to come to grips with the cult of victimhood if he were to bridge the gap from where he was and where he wanted to be.

Although Barack seemed to realize he was starting to fit in, he also knew he was also reaching the limit of what he would be able to accomplish. He would never become great along this path, and the jury was still out on whether or not he was even successful as a community organizer. He learned there was a limit to what you could do as a normal person on the streets. To make a difference, you needed the law behind you. Or better said, you needed to move the law with you. He would leave his community on the South Side and head to Harvard. But before that, he would finally visit his father's side of the family in Africa.

Stopping for a few weeks in Europe on the trip to Kenya, Barack found he had even less in common with the culture there; he was happy to leave, and find his way to Nairobi. He reports that Kenya was where he felt at home. From the welcome at the airport, to meeting his father's other wives and children, his encounter seemed very warm. It was more than he expected. "[He] had relationships there, people who cared deeply about [him] and that [he] cared deeply about."[19] Returning to Chicago, he would remember bringing gifts for the many friends he had made, but only stayed long enough to throw his belongings in his blue Honda, and depart for Harvard.

The early 1990's saw significant racial strife on the campus of Harvard. The students would demand more minority representation on the faculty, and a group even sued the school over the matter. Obama, always careful not to get too close to the fire, avoided any entanglement. This is also the period where the Progressive activists would impose pressure on the system, and as a result, national reputations of leftist thinkers like Alan Dershowitz and Lawrence Tribe would be won. Tribe, Obama's mentor, later would be remembered stating: "He's a guy I hope will be President someday."[20]

Barack was going to return to Chicago, but he now knew how difficult it was going to be to become accepted into the black community he so wanted to be part of. He would not be able to work his way in. He needed to find another way. During his first summer break, in 1988, Barack would return to Chicago and intern at Sidley Austin. This was the last year when Bernardine Dohrn had been an employee at the firm. Dohrn had never been accepted to the New York Bar Association, but then again, it would be difficult even for the legal profession to look the other way when it comes to accepting an unapologetic former domestic terrorist. She was able to find employment through her father-in-law's, father of Bill Ayers, friendship with the head of the firm, Howard Trienens[21]. There was also another young lawyer, Michelle Robinson, who would be assigned his mentor. Smart and attractive, she would become his path to validation. Obama, never short in the self-confidence arena, decided he was going to marry this woman. Michelle, it turns out, was not quite so smitten. He was relentless and would finally win her over. But during their early life together, she would quickly separate herself from the high-brow legal path, and become instrumental in helping various community support groups.

Michelle's family was as American as "Ozzie and Harriet," with her hard working father, the provider, raising adults in the middle of the country. Her mother only started to work outside the home once the kids reached high school. It was the polar opposite of his foster-like upbringing in the Pacific. But Barack knew he needed to transform himself into the type of person his community was made of. Even though her family seemed to embody the philosophical traditions of the Booker T. Washington wing of the movement, by lifting themselves up by their own bootstraps, Michelle would slowly but surely be turned to the W.E.B. DuBois frame of thought where the individual becomes entitled due to past oppression. But this sense of entitlement would not appear overnight; it would surface later as the enticement of power would overwhelm the Obamas.

It was winning the position as editor of the Law Review which would be his crowning achievement to this point. Highly coveted with a long list of truly extraordinary predecessors, he was also the first black person to win the seat. He performed well, handled the pressure-packed selection of members with grace, and won overall praise from his staff. He was going to be a lawyer, and was planning on returning to Chicago, maybe to be mayor one day. He still believed he could have an impact. It was during this time that he began to see that while his original intention may have been noble, it would also provide only limited returns. As a lawyer, he would be able to open more doors and provide more support for the community, but he finally realized it was the politicians who controlled those doors. He began to see politics as the true source of power, and that would be where he would make his mark. But he also knew he needed to maintain his radical ties as well. He would maintain his close relationship with Kellman, paying visits when he was in town.

Barack finally returned to Chicago a graduate of Harvard Law. He had married Michelle, and they began their life together. But she was only a part of her husband's strategy. He was provided a little money to write a book championing himself as the first editor of the Harvard Law Review, but he would instead delay progress for six months as he supported the upcoming 1992 elections; it would take a few years for *Dreams* to finally be published. He took a position directing what was called Project Vote, a voter registration and education campaign with the objective of boosting participation of Chicago's low-income black communities[22].

Project Vote was very successful, registering over 100,000 Democrat voters to support the presidential campaign of Bill Clinton, and the senatorial campaign of Carol Moseley Braun. Never far from his deeply rooted Alinskyite tendencies, he created the catchy slogan, "It's a Power Thing," which was broadcast over the radio waves and plastered across brochures.[23] But with ambitions overshadowing responsibilities, the home front would become stressful. Barack didn't experience the stable family structure most Americans would, so it would be up to Michelle to not only raise their kids, but her husband as well.

With the elections over, Barack would then find the time to secure stable employment. With serious Harvard bona fides, he would have many opportunities to choose from. Davis, Miner, Barnhill & Galland would be his choice; the civil rights and discrimination specialization was right up his alley[24]. But for all the proclamations of his experience as a lawyer, not to mention the ridiculous notion that he somehow was a constitutional expert, Obama had a law license for nine years, and had not handled a single trial. He was careful not to get out in front. His Alinsky training had become internalized, he would operate from the background.

Politics

> *It is the true believer's ability to "shut his eyes and stop his ears" to facts that do not deserve to be either seen or heard which is the source of his unequaled fortitude and constancy. He cannot be frightened by danger nor disheartened by obstacles nor baffled by contradictions because he denies their existence.*
> *- Eric Hoffer*[1]

He wouldn't have to wait long for his first opportunity for political office. He would use administrative trickery to get his opponents removed from the ballot, leaving himself virtually unopposed. He walked right in to an Illinois State Senate seat with an apparent landslide, even though it's hard not to win a one-horse race. This would now thrust him into the spotlight, and as a result, the public would get their first taste of his rhetoric: all promise, no direction. On one hand he would state that he "could bring church and community leaders together easier than [he] could as a community organizer or lawyer."[2] But on the other, during the same interview, he would project the same century-old class warfare language laying blame on "society" which would become his trademark appeal. He would be a good politician, validating personal and community oppression, while maintaining a safe distance from the responsibility to make actual improvement through the power of his office.

It was during this time he also once again would retrace the footsteps of Bernardine Dohrn, as he became a part time lecturer at the University of Chicago; a former Harvard Law Review editor on the staff would be a valuable asset for the institution[3]. He would allow his handlers and public relations army to inflate this position to one of academic importance, but in the end, it was a convenient opportunity for some extra income with little effort.

His time in the State Senate would become contentious as he would find himself an outsider there as well. He was doing everything he could to be accepted, but it just wasn't enough. While he was a Harvard indoctrinated lawyer, teaching night school, and marrying into a respectable Hyde Park family, he would find it difficult to gain acceptance into the Black Caucus. The leader, Emil Jones, didn't give up on Barack however, and assigned him a mentor, Dan Shomon[4].

Shomon would have some respect for Obama's idealism, but "didn't really like the guy that much."[5] Shomon and Obama decided to tour southern Illinois in the hopes of gaining insight into the current "racial equation."[6] The Central and Southern portions of Illinois had been hotbeds for racist activities in the past, and they were going to evaluate the current state of affairs. They would "spend a week playing golf", but in between rounds, Shomon would see that Obama had the ability to cross racial lines with ease, although noticing his tendency toward elitism could cause problems.

As though it was becoming his trademark, during his eight year reign in the General Assembly, Barack would accomplish little. At least that would be the impression one would have if successful legislation would be the measure. He would quickly claim his own oppression as a member of the "minority party" during his first six years. This would also be an early sign that while he could work a room of differing agendas, he would find himself unable to bridge the gaps and develop real solutions. He continued to be the spoiled child who would rather take his ball and go home. As his time in the State Senate would drag on, he would begin to lose interest in the drudgery. Finding the environment unsuitable for his talents, he saw the opportunity to run for Unites States Congress in 1999. He would challenge the sitting representative, Bobby Rush.

Rush, absolutely part of the community, won his bona fides as a member of the Black Panthers and parlayed that 'street-cred' into a successful political career. Obama, overflowing with self-confidence, could not see that the man he decided was a tired, old, worn out man (even though he was only 53 at the time) was instead the fighter he had always been. Another competitor best stated the perspective the political wing of his community with "Barack is viewed in part to be the white man in blackface in our community. You just have to look at his supporters. Who pushed him to get where he is so fast? It's these individuals in Hyde Park, who don't always have the best interests of the community in mind."[7] The race card was pulled and put Barack in his place. In the end, it was a spirited campaign. But Obama was trounced by thirty points.

He would return to his position, and was said to be able to not hold grudges that others could easily have developed during the nasty campaign. But he was in financial trouble. Never really too interested in money, beyond what he felt he needed to do what he wanted, he found himself "broke". He and Michelle were still paying off Harvard student loans, and Barack had maxed out his charge cards for the campaign. Even though the poor destitute family was reporting roughly $250,000 annual income, they found themselves underwater.

Back at his job as a State Senator, Shomon would continue to mentor young Barack. But Obama was gaining attention based on his lack of participation. Shomon would continue to stress the issue of his voting record. It was not that Obama was voting 'incorrectly', but that he wasn't voting at all. Shomon would continue to press Obama on the subject, but Obama, always staying in the background around contentious issues, would avoid voting. One critical bill would present itself while the Obama's were on their annual vacation in Hawaii. His daughter miraculously came down with a cold, and Barack would fail to appear and support the critical legislation. But by this time, Barack had already set his sights on bigger venues than the Illinois State General Assembly. And his opportunity would present itself.

The Democrats were able to win a majority of the Assembly in 2002. They selected Barack's political "Godfather", Emil Jones, as their leader. A couple months later, Jones remembers, "He said to me, he said, 'You're the president now, and with that you have a lot of *pow*-er.' And I told Barack, 'You think I have a lot of *pow*-er now?', and he said, 'Yeah, you got a lot of *pow*-er.' And I said, 'What kind of *pow*-er do I have?' He said, 'You have the *pow*-er to make a United States *Sen-a-tor*!' I said to Barack, I said, 'That sounds good!' I said, 'I haven't even thought of that.' I said, 'Do you have someone in mind you think I could make?' and he said, 'Yeah. Me.'"[8] It was the careful selection of legislation, controlled by Jones, and given to Obama, that provided all the claimed success he would have during his time in the Illinois General Assembly, often at the expense of others.

Young Barack went from being a back-bench participant, to the chosen one. Leader Jones would direct over eight hundred bills through Obama as sponsor. But at the same time, Jones deflected controversial bills to insulate him form the more problematic issues of the day. And Jones was helpful at scheduling the Assembly's business around Barack's campaign schedule.

Obama had such grand illusions about what he could accomplish when he arrived at the State Senate. But his inability to build consensus, coupled with his desire to work in the background, left him with a sense of failure, once again. But it wasn't Barack, it was the system. He would need to move from the farm team to the big leagues, as he had tried with the Rush challenge. The U.S. Senate seat was to become available, and he was going after it.

THE SAVIOR

Stealing Senate

> *You can fool all the people some of the time, and some of the people all of the time, but you cannot fool all of the people all of the time.*
> *- Abraham Lincoln*

The country is finally becoming more aware of the type of politician Barack Obama represents. The initially naive 'do-gooder' who is motivated to change society at an early age, believes he and those around him are the solution. With little practical experience, their vision is what's needed. So convincing they were; the voter fell for it. It was not so long ago that someone like Barack wouldn't be considered. Although he would claim this would be due to the color of his skin, in reality it would be due to his lack of experience and minuscule collection of accomplishments. A review of several biographies would highlight a single, seemingly insignificant event in young Barack's life where he was benched as an average, but self-assured high school basketball player who challenged the authority of his coach[1]. The implication which rises out of the pages is that this event somehow provides insight into the experience he would bring to the highest office in the land. The authors struggled to support the image of a seasoned competitor with a valuable background which prepared him for the office he was bidding for. But it was this background, devoid of substance, which would provide the actual strength to his campaigns. No one could really think two steps ahead and ask whether this ability to 'lead from behind' would become more of a weight around the country's neck. By having an uncanny ability to avoid inclusion through his life, the observer could project onto him the characteristics they wanted to see. He didn't have a voting record which could label him, other than the taboo subject of abortion support. He hadn't been embroiled in a past controversy, which could stigmatize him, other than the questionable electioneering shenanigans; again, apparently taboo. He arrived at a time when people were looking for what they wanted, and he was the blank canvas that allowed them to create their own candidate.

In 2003, the siting US Senator, Republican Peter Fitzgerald, had low ratings, and was ripe for the picking. It also looked like there would be no substantial challenger on the Democratic side. Barack decided the seat would be his. But he had no money; he would need to collect a lot of donors, and quick. If he could build a ten million dollar war chest, he proclaimed, "I guarantee you that I will win."[2] But money would only buy the team; he needed to assemble the team. The most critical member would be David Axelrod, who had previously held a small fund-raiser for him during an earlier campaign. 'Ax', however tried to dissuade Obama from running at all; suggesting a wiser direction might be the expected opening after Chicago Mayor Daley retires. But Obama had already decided what his objective would be.

The target was obscured for a time, however. Carol Moseley Braun, who had been the first black Senator, had lost the very same seat to the incumbent, Fitzgerald, and she was sending out messages indicating she might run for it again. Obviously in the political game of victims' rights, Braun would present a major obstacle. The fact that she would consider another run at it, after her previous ethically-challenged reign, is a testament to the corrupt nature of the profession, in general. But she had nothing better to do. The Obama campaign even tried to find her employment, and failed. Where else would an unemployable person go, but into politics. And she felt entitled.

As the campaigns were beginning to take form, Barack took a trip to Washington to meet with the Black Caucus. Whether it was just an attempt to collect some self-incriminating evidence on him, or that is was a description of the normal activities the Caucus engaged in, he was "in shock". The women and "booze" gave him a rude awakening[3]. He would return unwavering, however. But Braun finally did waver, and decided not to run. Axelrod would be Barack's first call hearing the news.

Being courted by both Obama and his competitor, multimillionaire Blair Hull, Ax would be turned off by Hull's lack of seriousness and join the Obama camp. Intelligent and shrewd, Axelrod was masterful in his ability to create advertising spots which could reach into the hearts of the voting public. Borne of family tragedies, he would put his focus in his work, and part the waters for his latest product[4]. Axelrod would throw large annual Christmas parties, famous for the list of attendees, the elite of the left in politics and media where others would recognize, "he was belle of the ball." And Barack was his new date.

As it turned out, the ever-aware Axelrod would uncover in Hull a critical flaw, which would bring down his campaign. He didn't know the details, but could sense Hull had personal demons which would prove disastrous in the face of public opinion. His intuition about Hull and his private issues would manifest themselves later, but at the time Hull appeared the major Democratic challenger. And with over one hundred million dollar personal bank account, he was to be reckoned with. There is nothing to indicate whether Ax had any participation in the events which would unfold and crush Hull's chances. But it happened. The hatch just blew.

In the meantime, Obama needed to get on the national radar. He decided to take a position against the recently instigated Iraq War, making arguably his first political position on a national issue. Standing virtually alone against the enthusiasm of the vast majority of the American public, Barack Obama challenged the "dumb war"[5]. But his base would love it. At the outset, he would identify the problem with the current plan of "undetermined length, at undetermined cost, with undetermined consequences."[6] This was true, and it would take another leader years later, on the field, to right the ship. But in the end, the Senate candidate who identified the "dumb war" rose from obscurity to see General Petraeus turn the expected defeat into resounding victory while he was a Senator, and would himself when in the Oval Office, turn that victory into defeat. But at the time, it was calculated to appear courageous and provided initial insight into the person making the statement. Because he would be the only top-tier candidate making such a bold claim, he quickly became the darling of the anti-American left. His momentum was building, and he could feel it. But he was still a significant distance from the top of the Democratic contenders. He would need some help.

But that help wouldn't come from his old partner Dan Shomon. Whether or not he felt Obama had destiny on his side, Shomon was not up for the "grind". Mendell would conclude this was a blow to young Barack, who believed he was "a special person since childhood…unaccustomed to being left at the alter."[7] He would start collecting supporters from his main targeted constituency groups: Representative Jan Schakowsky, representing the Northside lakefront crowd, and Reverend Jesse Jackson Sr., fellow Hyde Park resident, and leader of the Rainbow/PUSH organization. The family ties would include the fact that Michelle, as a teenager, had been babysitter to Jackson's daughter. The coalition was building. Although the campaign was moving in the right direction, he was still far from the top of the heap. But Ax was just beginning. Obama, without the normal baggage of an actual life of experiences, was also a blank canvas, and he would paint a masterpiece.

The competition would resurrect the previous whispers of "Barack is not black enough", and campaign photographer David Katz would emphasize his elitist tendencies by explaining him away, "…you know Barack, he just can't help himself."[8] But in the end, it would be an awkward defense of her husband, "Barack is a black man," which would be remembered as more of a plea for the world to accept him. In the end, Barack had chosen wisely. Michelle would be the key to the legitimacy he wished for. But before he would gain acceptance, he expanded his rhetoric. His claimed plan was now to find a way to reverse the self-destruction deeply rooted in the community he decided he would save. From the damage wrought by drug usage to the disenfranchisement which could be affected by ex-offender legislation, he was going to find the solutions his people were yearning for. But he would soon capture his biggest endorsement, providing the presumptive front-runner, Dan Hynes, his first tactical defeat of the competition.

Obama, with the help of his Godfather Emil Jones, would win the support of the Service Employees International Union (SEIU), which would become a strong ally in his future efforts as well; over a hundred thousand members in Illinois alone would become active members of the campaign.

But the coronation was far from secured; Hynes and Hull were still out there. Hynes had secured another major union endorsement with the AFL-CIO, but campaign finance irregularities would further weaken his position. Many believed Barack would be the inconsequential third in a three way race at this point; Hynes and Hull seemed to focus primarily on each other.

Early in the campaign Hull would gain unwanted attention as a woman was found dead at his home (while he was not there.) The fury surrounding such an incident was handled well, and would dissipate over time. But his personal life would turn out to be his undoing. Although his divorce papers had been sealed by the courts, the media would win a challenge and gain access. What was uncovered was the story of allegations of spousal abuse, and the feeding frenzy would doom his campaign. In what would again present the media's double standards, he would be pressed to admit decades-old cocaine and alcohol problems, which he had since overcome[9]. But at the same time, the candidate who proudly proclaimed these activities in his youth wasn't even considered as Hull would find his past on trial. At this point Hull was down, but Obama needed him in the game; he would be useful by pulling the down-state white votes away from Hynes.

As the election neared, Obama would snag another key endorsement. Former Senator Paul Simon was a giant among the Illinois Democratic Party, and his daughter decided to provide her support, "Paul Simon stood for something very special—integrity, principle and a commitment to fight for those who needed a voice. Barack Obama is cut from that same cloth."[10] The resulting media campaign was moving, as the candidate would fill the frame, "I'm Barack Obama and I'm running for the United States Senate to say, 'Yes, we can.'" No one ever really considered what 'we can' means, but it was catchy and served its purpose as the product who now claimed to be "bipartisan" with the myth that he would somehow bring about change. In the end, both main competitors ran clumsy, self-destructive campaigns; Obama would win with over fifty percent of the vote, and would claim the right to be the Democratic challenger.

But the incumbent, Republican Peter Fitzgerald decided not to seek reelection. Obama's competitor would be Jack Ryan, "Hollywood handsome and independently wealthy," and the contrast could not be greater as Ryan was a dedicated capitalist, and Barack, a leftist big government liberal. Obama's campaign now had attracted national attention, and the media enterprise would provide uncompensated campaign advertising. Where reporters would lose even the appearance of professional independence, detractors would be muzzled for fear of being labeled racist. And those who were afraid not to be part of the product's claim of a historic event began to get in line.

Moving to the middle for a leftist is unnatural and resisted, as it means you would increasingly acknowledge more positive American core values in order to attract the American voter. And, as expected, this would not be a comfortable move for Obama. He would, for the first time, be in a contest where he would have to find that bridge which allowed him to convince the majority of the voters that he would represent their best interests. Fully indoctrinated into the leftist philosophy, he would be very attractive to those who would claim oppression for their own missteps, using statistic realities to somehow claim bias, such as laws providing stiffer sentences for gang-related crimes, claiming it unfairly targeted minorities. This could present a problem as he tried to seduce the Fraternal Order of Police (FOP) for their support. But the FOP was a union and not the individual officer on the beat, so it would be rationalized away. But those who knew him understood where his political leanings really were, a Republican cosponsor of one of his bills labeled him "to the left of Mao Tse-Tung."[11] He would not be able to hide when the gloves come off in the general election. He would need a miracle.

But for Obama, who appears to be only a pragmatic Christian, he would be granted another miracle along his road to Washington. In a repeat from earlier in the year, Barack's opponent had a sealed divorce file which magically found its way into the public arena. In this case, his ex-wife, famous actress Jeri Ryan, claimed he would take her to sex clubs and pressure her to have sex with him in front of others. This was quite the sensation, but Ryan was not part of the Democratic Party, so he would be held to a different standard. His candidacy was crippled and he would finally relent and back out altogether, for victimhood is not accepted amongst the Republicans. To add fuel to the fire that was under the Obama campaign, John Kerry and the Democratic National Committee decided to give Obama a nation-wide platform at the national convention. His momentum was only increasing.

His Tuesday-night keynote address at the convention would be dubbed "The Speech." His speech would draw on the themes of his Progressive predecessors. The tale of two cities and the red versus blue divided country would be intertwined with the acknowledgement of each critical voting bloc that he hoped to collect would be mentioned along with his heroes, like Martin Luther King, Jr. But King spoke to the people; Barack would speak to the democratic base. The sycophants would praise his moment, while many Americans would see through the mask. His follower's response was electric, and he began to think bigger than the Senate. But his immediate goal at the moment must first be achieved.

The pace continued to grow, as did the crowds, and the campaign would be tireless. He would try to balance the neglect to his family with the ambition he had to be a great man. It would be a strain on his young family. But the GOP would implode with the collapse of their star, Jack Ryan. In a last ditch attempt to find victory, they had to look for another. Ex-Chicago Bear Mike Ditka was considered for short time, but the party decided to go outside of the State and court the famous conservative Alan Keyes[12]. But it was far too little, and far too late. The momentum of the Obama campaign was not to be reversed and in the end, Barack Obama would win in a landslide. He would be elected United States Senator.

But even before he was sworn in, "The Plan" would begin to be formulated. In a carefully choreographed sequence of events, Barack Obama would be elected the next President of the United States[13]. But for the time being, he would have to fall in line with his party, and bide his time. In his first year, he would prove a party loyalist and would avoid publicity. He did happen to come out momentarily to make a commencement speech at the small Knox College in Illinois. The speech was his opportunity to highlight the Alinksy 'have versus have-not' theory of social Darwinism, an attack on capitalism and the society which had provided him his mythical rise to prominence. But his other appearance provided indicators as to how the media would treat his involvement, which would show the partnership he would use for his future plans.

It was to storms what the Gulf War was to military operations. The media coverage was a voyeur's dream. America had unprecedented coverage of not only the storm, but the aftermath. The storm would be the costliest in the history of the country. It would be one of the strongest storms on record and would take a direct hit on a prized seat of the country's cultural heritage. Katrina was devastating, not only to New Orleans, but to hundreds of miles of the American Gulf Coast. States of emergency would be declared all the way to Florida, and a satellite picture of the storm would show it the size of Texas.

The eye of the storm would trace itself right through New Orleans, with the 27 foot surge causing damage a state away in Mississippi, reaching 6 to 12 miles inland. Americans would watch in horror as the Democrat controlled State and City leadership would demonstrate their impotence to actual crises and to the power of Mother Nature. But that wouldn't keep the media from picking up their fumble and carrying the case of Republican oppression to the ignorant and gullible. To put things in some perspective, the storm wasn't expected to hit New Orleans only a couple days earlier. As the storm changed direction, and moved west toward the Crescent City, the incompetent administration was overwhelmed. Although many evacuations were called for, there wasn't transportation for many residents. In addition, many residents had been through hurricanes before, and what is not uncommon, decided they would just stick it out. By the time the storm hit, it was far too late to change their minds.

As the storm's effects built, the remarkable system of levees which had previously protected the neighborhoods, which in some areas were actually below normal water level, began to fail. Entire sections of New Orleans would be submerged, and many people would find themselves in the Superdome searching for shelter, but without power and necessities. The media had the story they were after, and they would blame the

President. Many would not hear that for a hundred miles in all directions were effects from the storm. Little attention would be paid to the rest of Louisiana, or the total destruction of the Mississippi Gulf Coast. It was the racialists who would once again win the day.

The incompetent and irresponsible preparation and response by the City and State administrations would be virtually ignored as the Democratic public relation firms, known as the major media outlets, would do whatever they could to attach blame to the federal government. But in the midst of the carnage, the self-proclaimed social leadership would see the wounded animal and attack. To the racialists like Al Sharpton and Jesse Jackson proclaiming the response was withheld because it was the black person who found themselves in need, the media was attracted like bears to honey.

Barack had to come out from hiding for this event. But his response was constrained and surprisingly responsible; in the heat of the racially charged event being inflamed by the radicals and supporting media, his speech wouldn't attack the federal government. The reaction by the racialists and the media, rather than attacking everyone else who provided a similarly responsible statement, would be to excuse Barack, and find a way to explain to the followers 'what he meant to say'. Even when he didn't line up with the radicals, they would find a way to excuse his apparent missteps. Dan Shomon would say "People have always had a tendency to give Obama a pass. It's like no other politician I've seen. They feel like he is on this important mission. And maybe he is."[14] Less than two months after taking the oath of office as the newest U.S. Senator for the State of Illinois, Barack Obama, on the steps of the Old State Capitol in Springfield, Illinois, would declare his candidacy for the office of the President of the United States.

As a United States Senator, he would prove to be a strong party supporter; he voted with the party 95% of the time. In 2007, the National Journal named Barack the most liberal member of the Senate[15]. That was quite an achievement since he had tough competition with socialist Bernie Sanders of Vermont. Assigned to many subcommittees, he would participate as necessary, missing many hearings. But in the end, as a

Senate aide would say, "He was so bored being a Senator." He would keep himself busy with things he was interested in, like Barack. He would write another book, travel, and fundraise. He had a penchant for raising money.

He would be able to complete his second book, *Audacity of Hope*, which earned him a comfortable stipend with an advance from Crown to cover *Audacity*, a children's book, and a third, yet to be determined. With the book out of the way, he could make time for a trip to several African countries, where he would receive a hero's welcome. His family, aides, and the rest of his entourage were not prepared for the magnitude of emotion which exploded on the continent, especially in Kenya[16]. But the reaction was candy to the media, providing just the enthusiasm which would further bolster his name as they prepared for his next campaign.

And he attracted the rich and famous, always wanting to be part of whatever the big thing is. He could call on Steven Spielberg, Oprah Winfrey, George Soros, etc. He would attract thousands to events. His political-action committee, Hopefund, would build a war chest to help colleagues, but also himself when the time was right[17]. And the time was now.

Serendipity

> *We are the ones we've been waiting for*
> *-Barack Obama[1]*

She was supposed to be the chosen one. The once first lady during the previous Democrat presidency and New York Senator, Hillary Rodham Clinton, had the establishment machine behind her. She would be the first woman presidential candidate from a major party, and because it was 'her turn', she assumed she would win the election. But serendipity would not be on her side. She was the presumptive winner, even though she never held a lead throughout the race. While Barack Obama had made a career, however short it had been to this point, out of others making excuses for his foibles, Hillary would not be so lucky. She was unnatural, unbelievable, and unlikeable by all but her own set of groupies.

The beginning of the end for Hillary would be the first caucus in Iowa. It wasn't because she came in third where she was supposed to win. It was because the main stream media left her the instant it appeared they might not be on the right side of history themselves. Disgustingly transparent with their lack of integrity to their claimed profession, she was an afterthought from that moment on, only included as a means to camouflage their Obama-monomania. But in the end, it was the un-Democratic processes which did her in. Yet, it would be especially entertaining for those Americans who continue to hear how the Democrats like Mr. Global Warming himself, Al Gore, would claim his own election in 2000 was stolen.

The complex set of rules controlling the party candidate nomination process is comparable to the tax code they are battling to take control over. Two major factors would result in her losing the nomination. The first would be that two critical states, Michigan and Florida, decided to hold their elections before the required first state, eliminating their results from the contest. The other would be the method for counting the delegates. The Democrats decided to move away from the winner-take-all delegate results historically in place in many states, in order to provide a method to better distribute the delegates based on relative proportion of the vote itself. Combining this with the establishment's gimmickry of super-delegates to ensure the correct candidate becomes the nominee, if it was still winner-take-all, she would've won her party's nomination.

But, as it turned out, it was not Hillary's turn after all, and thanks to the media's lack of interest into the new chosen one's past and political leanings, it would be Barack's. It's convenient rationalization for the Democratic Party that their candidates really don't have to appeal to them anyway, as long as they deliver when they get in office. And Barack had already been able to do so even as a junior Senator. It would just be fortuitous again that his own family would collect the windfalls as a result of favorable legislation. Or maybe it was the other way around. For example, in 2005, poor Mrs. Obama was struggling to make ends meet with her own salary of $121,910 when coincidentally she would get a little raise: a raise to $316,962. It was just a coincidence that Barack would create earmarks for her employer[2]. It seemed like Obama was the stereotypical politician, willing to make the sausage in Washington, but never failing to bring home the bacon. And through either incompetence or collusion, the Republican Party would do their best to ensure the historic opportunity for the first black President would materialize.

The Republican primary process was not quite as controversial. Prior to the primaries, it appeared as though former New York Mayor, Rudy Giuliani, would be the one to beat. But Senator John McCain would win, even though the 'experts' wrote him off early in the year. John McCain was an American hero, spending five and a half years as a prisoner of war in North Vietnam, and permanently disabled as a result of his treatment; he will always be remembered fondly by Americans. As a Senator however, history may not be so forgiving, should he be remembered at all. But while he could hardly be counted on to toe the party line, he was rarely the cause of actual conflagration. Making a name for himself in the 1990's as someone who would challenge the establishment, he would give way to a more predictable, if not controllable Senator who had developed more affinity for his friends in the Capitol building than the Americans he would represent. He may have claimed he was his own man, but in reality he was the process, and it was him.

While he was a safe selection for the Republican Party, his selection for Vice President came out of nowhere and would inspire vitriolic hatred from the left and their public relation front, the mainstream media, the likes of which hadn't been seen before or since. Alaska Governor Sarah Palin was an unapologetic American and a fiery personality which would be attacked viscously. She was the polar opposite to John McCain, and would be a great choice when the objective may have been to deflect attention from the struggling main candidate. While the venom was unrelenting, Republicans understand this is how they are treated. What they didn't expect was the nationwide ground game of questionable activities which just happened to aid in the election of the candidate from the Democratic Party.

Possibly more a result of his predilection to obfuscation, Obama's ties to the Association of Community Organizations for Reform Now (ACORN) would be veiled, but this organization would provide nationwide get-out-the-vote support. Without success, the McCain-Palin campaign would accuse them of "massive voter fraud."[3] A long relationship between Obama and this organization had laid the foundation for challenge due to irregularities uncovered during the voter registration drives. But by 2010, long after their deed had been done, this organization had lost their support and finally filed for Chapter 7 insolvency.

More interesting may be the case of the Service Employees International United's (SEIU) support for the Obama campaign. It was stunning that a single organization of 'volunteers' would spend $85 million on his election[4]. They would also become the collector of unverified contributions from locations such as "Nairobi, KY", and citizens by the name of "Donald Duck," "Bart Simpson," and even "King Kong."[5] Virtually unverifiable, the campaign accounts were open and receiving more money than they could spend. And spend it they would; but an audit of SEIU would be as realistic as an investigation into the New Black Panthers.

While hardly a case which would turn the election results, it would be the opening salvo from the Civil Rights Division of the Justice Department which would set the tone for this most racial administration. They may have been miscreants, but they meant to be dangerous miscreants. And when a group of thugs were pacing outside a polling station carrying billy clubs, shouting racial slurs to voters on Election Day, the message of intimidation was unmistakable[6]. While it wasn't apparent why local authorities didn't intervene and no formal complaint was ever made, it would be the offensive lack of concern from the racialist Attorney General which made Americans angry. Rationalists like these could provide support as a result of the look-the-other-way attitude, resulting in an increased sense of validation for their anti-American activities, and things could spiral out of control. It might one day turn into an actual movement resulting in deaths to police officers called something like 'Black Lives Matter'. Oh, and it did! But it would be only the initial salvo, for Americans would be stunned by the racial nature of not only the so-called Civil Rights Division, but by the senior administration officials themselves. It would be candidate Obama's actual positions which would foreshadow conflicts to come.

His own sense of superiority and invincibility would weaken his controlled persona, and would result in the exposure of the Alinskyite inside of him. Ridicule would be his modus operandi when dealing with others not considered True Believers. "Ridicule is man's most potent weapon," is rule number 5, and would be the showcase attack method for his tenure[7]. With the pressures of a presidential campaign stretching him to his limit, it was only a matter of time until his disregard for American values would find its way into the light. The pattern of disrespect for anyone who disagrees with his position is demeaned, if not outright attacked through ridicule.

Rather than accepting that there are a lot of people who still believe in the American values inherent in our society, he would attack their character, "*And it's not surprising then that they get bitter, they cling to guns or religion or antipathy to people who aren't like them or anti-immigrant sentiment or anti-trade sentiment as a way to explain their frustrations.*"[8] But this would be during the Party nomination push, where he would be speaking to a majority of like-minded Democrats. By the time the general election was in full swing, the Praetorian Guard media had already decided to treat these exposures as 'old news'. Their main opponent was the Republican candidate anyway, and style over substance was the controlled message as the media itself appeared afraid to confront the candidate's radical and un-American background and principles for fear of being casted as racially motivated.

Obama's promises of 'universal healthcare'[9] would go unexamined, as would whatever 'full employment' might be. His consistent message that America was not respected would never be challenged. This may have been more the pot calling the kettle black in an effort to distract the voter from his own lack of capability, but true to his roots, he would "push a negative hard enough…[and] it will push through and become a positive," in accordance with Alinksy's 11th rule[10]. It was his constant insulting message to Americans which wore thin. Somehow laying blame for the 1300 year old anti-Christian cultural practices of an ideology, which declared war on his county, at the feet of his own country was such hyperbole it was difficult to find reason. He would play to his base, which would be the 'blame America first' crowd. But that wouldn't be enough, as Americans still barely held the majority in the country.

He needed to add voters to his cause. While there is plenty of evidence that voting 'irregularities' exist, it's unclear whether they have actually changed an outcome. The plan required motivating more voters to participate if he was to succeed. And he did. By generating the fiction that the Bush administration was responsible for the barbarous activities in the Middle East, the housing collapse, even the weather, he could motivate those willing to be led and those still gullible enough to fall for the snake oil sales pitch. He would put fear into the minds of those reliant on the State, as well as those young people who had yet to integrate into society as independent, self-reliant citizens. The entitlement class would always strongly support the socialist agenda as, whether through their own action or inaction, or sometimes due to events outside of their control, they would find themselves reliant on the variety of support programs developed over decades to keep them in their own designated section inside the ranch they had been assigned to. But the Democrats are always careful not to cause their followers to question their leadership as once the man behind the curtain is discovered, the jig may be up.

Young people would overwhelmingly support the Democrat agenda as they had not the experience to understand the lies which were be flung from the podium. They believed the government somehow creates jobs, and should provide for the most basic need, healthcare, which they didn't care about anyway. The Republican camp appeared unable, or unwilling to challenge the Marxist agenda on public display. The media would run interference for the Democrats and would not press for an explanation, as if they knew the answer would ultimately be a threat to their own place at the table.

The government primarily performs two functions: it takes money needed to perform a duty, and distributes it as needed, or it imposes regulations controlling what people can do, effectively causing similar results. The first method in no way can create a job, for it is stealing the money from another, causing a reduction of a job to begin with. The second method could release constraints on the economy, resulting in increased job demand, but that is counter to the prevailing nature of the establishment, for reducing constraints means returning power to the people. Combine the job creation lie with the healthcare lie and there should've been ample opportunity to unmask the agenda of the candidate and his team.

Healthcare is fundamentally products and services available to improve the life of the individual. What Obama was after was not healthcare, but the money in the healthcare system. The money itself wasn't the objective, but what the money would buy: Power. And control of that money supply would be managed through the massive health insurance sector. Either the media surrogates were in the tank with the Obama machine, or they were proven intellectually-challenged by equating the two. Long a goal of the anti-American socialist movement, the "single payer" system in no way provides healthcare; it only provides control over your healthcare, and ultimately your life and how you choose to live it. Young people would fall for the scam, and provide Obama the push needed to claim victory. But it was also in no small part a result of his choice for Vice Presidential running mate, the 'brilliant' Joe Biden.

There would be no better evidence of the shill the media had become than their treatment of Joe Biden. Elected Senator six times by the state of Delaware; he never met a tax he didn't like, or a pro-life effort worthy of his support. He was a perfect candidate to represent the Democratic Party. And much like his running mate could not shield the public from his own inner character when allowed to go off-script, the gaffes would be enlightening in their racist nature. But he was a Democrat, after all. In an off-script moment in 2006, CNN would record one of his most famous 'Biden-isms', "You cannot go to a 7-11 or a Dunkin' Donuts unless you have a slight Indian accent.... I'm not joking." A sense of humor to be sure, but it's always at the expense of others mixed with the Democrat's perspective of identity-politics.

The most striking example of the media's look-the-other-way attitude when it comes to their team would be when Biden commented on the chosen-one himself, "I mean you got the first mainstream African-American who is articulate and bright and clean and a nice-looking guy. I mean, that's a storybook, man." And it wasn't even just the media; you couldn't even get a rise out of the scion of the racialist wing, who was clearly just identified as either non-mainstream, inarticulate nor bright or clean, or nice-looking, Rev. Jesse Jackson, as he could only muster that it "could be divisive."[11] It's always party first! But what Joe did bring to the ticket was much more valuable than his stinging wit and unbounded intellectual capabilities. It was precisely these distractions that would provide necessary insulation as Americans tried to figure out who this Barack Obama was and what he was all about. The goal was to win the election, not get caught out of the sheep's clothing.

The momentum was created by a massive ground game, and sustained by the media. But the victory would not come cheap, a foretelling of his administration apparently. The presidential election bid would cost Obama/Biden twice as much McCain/Palin per vote ($10.94 vs. $5.78)[12]. However this was of little concern as the Democrats dominated among young people and lower income brackets, winning 60% of those under 40, and those making less than $50,000 annually[13]. The result was predictable, yet shocking for Americans who witnessed the country seduced by promises only possible at the end of a gun held by a police state.

Myth-Building

> *The great enemy of truth is very often not the lie—deliberate, contrived and dishonest—but the myth—persistent, persuasive and unrealistic. Too often we hold fast to the clichés of our forebears. We subject all facts to a prefabricated set of interpretations. We enjoy the comfort of opinion without the discomfort of thought.*
> *- President John F. Kennedy* [1]

She had strength and resolve few could imagine. Accompanying her husband one last time, still in her blood-stained dress, she would ensure his life would go down not only in history as the 35th President, but as the Once and Future King. The dashing World War II hero of PT-109, heir to the throne of American aristocracy, Massachusetts Congressman and Senator, John Kennedy would be elected President at the young age of 43.

His Presidency was short, with a mix of failures and successes. Whether it was the humiliation of the Bay of Pigs, his steadfast resolve during the Cuban Missile Crisis, initiating our commitment in Vietnam, creating the Peace Corps, or inspiring the moon landings, he would forever be remembered favorably. It was an assassin's bullet, from a communist and admirer of Fidel Castro, which ended his life. But it would be his epilogue which made him a legend.

It was but a week since he was killed, and the grieving widow would call upon a trusted journalist to create their story[2]. Theodore White would create the mythical aura about this young family which would splash across the country inside the pages of Life magazine. She explained the fondness they had for King Arthur and Camelot, and the story would come to life. She would explain, "There will be great presidents again, but there will never be another Camelot."

But that was not how the Obama campaign saw it. There was to be another Camelot, and this time they would create it. The similarities were striking, youthful families striving for the top, yearning to "do good". "By God, he is Jack Kennedy all over again," was heard from Chicago lawyer, Newton Minow, and the machine went to work[3];

initiated in a shroud of secrecy because Barack had been very vocal about his desire to live up to his promise to Illinois and the Senate seat he had just won. But he wouldn't take long; he would announce his candidacy the next month.

Historic events should happen in historic places, he concluded. It was a cold day in Springfield, and the Obama team had decided the announcement would be on the steps of the Old State Capitol building where, in 1858, Lincoln began his Senate campaign. But the skeletons would need to stay in the closet if they were to create the illusion they were hoping for. And the first skeleton would be Obama's pastor, Reverend Jeremiah Wright.

Wright, being a friend, a mentor, the man who married him to Michelle, was also a powder keg of controversy. A recent Rolling Stone magazine article provided more than enough ammunition which could be used to derail his campaign before it even got on the tracks. One of Wright's sermons recorded, "Racism is how this country was founded and how this country is still run!"[4] Barack and his campaign would manage the uncontainable egos in an exquisitely amateurish fashion, but in the end, would find enough supporters to provide enough excuses to help the fiasco blow over. The issue of how to manage the kaleidoscope of racialist personalities wrestling for a piece of the action would take determined effort. The "radioactive blacks", known as Jesse Jackson Sr. and Al Sharpton would need to be isolated, while more moderate personalities, like Henry Ford Jr. and Jesse Jackson Jr. would prove more palatable[5]. Race was critical to the campaign, but needed to be carefully managed; otherwise the package may not be sellable. All the while, his primary opponent, Hillary Clinton seemed to do whatever she could to make the road a little easier.

Where Barack was carefully balancing the "first black" presidential candidacy, his challenger would become comical in her demeaning condescension of the black culture. Her embarrassing stereo-typical caricatures of the people she was trying to reach out to would be blatantly racist; it would be hard to imagine anyone else getting away with it, even her husband. But she would maintain a solid ring of supporters like Vernon Jordan, past president of the National Urban League, and Andrew Young, advisor to Martin Luther King Jr, mayor, congressman and U.N. Ambassador[6]. But while the media would try to make everything about race, it still came down to who people thought was a winner. As David Remnick noted in his book, *The Bridge, The life and rise of Barack Obama*, "In 1984, [Jesse] Jackson had struggled to get support from African-Americans who didn't think he had a chance."[7] But the Democratic Party wasn't just about race, even though it was built on racism. It had fundamentally transformed. It was now about victims, and it had built its constituency by piecing together a mosaic as a result of its balkanization. What Hillary may still not have realized is that as a result of building a party of groups wanting to get something from the government, the candidate still needs to be able to inspire them. They needed to believe in her. They wouldn't be enthusiastic just because it happens to be her turn.

But the rhetoric was extremely racial. How could it not be? Here was the chance for an entire section of America to finally have a chance to feel accepted. They knew nothing from the day they were born except that they were black, and that meant they would be treated as less, that they should learn to expect less, that they were less. This would come not from America, but from their families, churches, and communities. Here was hope that change was possible. And his opponent was a terrible candidate, and unlikeable as well. He could win, and the entire party started to take notice. But the old Democrats just couldn't help themselves. Most Americans would watch the circus unfold, and wonder how such a big tent of malcontents would find achievement like this.

The storm was building around his old pastor Jeremiah Wright. Both Obama's and Hillary's campaign made claims that with all the background checking, they never considered his pastor's explosive sermons. While it would be easier to believe that the race card would shield the Clinton campaign and that the Obama campaign would hope it would not become an issue, they both claimed ignorance when it blew up. And blow it did; threatening to derail his already shaky campaign. Wright's tapes have him calling the country then "U.S. of the K.K.K. A", and shouting "Not God Bless America. God Damn America!"[8] If

Barack wasn't careful, the country would realize his claimed ignorance was laughable since he spent 20 years at Trinity listening to Wright's sermons. The solution would be a speech, carefully tailored to bridge the divide with the help of the media.

On March 18th, 2008, he delivered "A More Perfect Union", summoning the great Fredrick Douglass' 1952 Fourth of July speech where he called on the country for the end of "the injustice and cruelty to which he is the constant victim." He would "borrow the language," although most Americans could see it was only words to Barack. But he also chastised Wright. It was his attempt to show he could rise above the racialism of his community. His competitors wouldn't buy it, but as was the case for all of his incongruities, his posse would manage the dissent and build an apologetic front, explaining what he meant to the supportive and malleable media protecting the candidate. But this would also provide another sign of what lay ahead: the candidate's inability to cooperate with anyone with a different agenda. The petulance would become his scarlet letter 'P'. But in the end, Hillary would fall. And that was the first objective. It was just icing on the cake that, as a Clinton aide would characterize; they felt that they "took those fuckers down. [They] retired the Clintons to the trash heap of history."[9] But this battle was not among respectable competitors; it was between people who were both 'chosen' and had little respect for the other. The wounds would be deep, and would never heal. But that would be dealt with later; his immediate concern would be his Republican opponent in the general election.

The Republican establishment had chosen John McCain. In 2000, he would make a respectable run for the presidency, only to be out-played by the establishment's choice at that time, George W. Bush. As Remnick noted, McCain would be so distraught, he considered "joining the Democrats, creating a third party modeled on Theodore Roosevelt's Bull Moose party; and in 2004, even joining his friend John Kerry on the Democrat ticket."[10] But true to his nature, he chose the easier route; he remained a Republican. And in 2008, he would finally win his party's nomination. But even with the energetic and magnetic personality of Sarah Palin as his vice presidential running mate, the campaign would be tepid, trying to generate public concern over Obama, his character, and his ring of friends. What McCain had in 2000 when he was going after the establishment's chosen one, Bush, was media support. What he seemed not to understand was the lack of support this time through the gauntlet. For a seasoned beltway bandit not to understand the proclivities of the media in how their first and foremost support will go to the most Statist candidate, his befuddlement was curious. But he soldiered on.

The Obama campaign was 'historic'. There was more talk about how the country could have its first black president, than who the man who would be elected president was. Obama was managed very well, and seemed to be the right person at the right time. Not burdened with actual life experiences and accomplishments, there was little meat on the bone for researchers to really delve into. His positions and arguments would be vague and unmemorable, but his campaign would be brilliant at its ability to carefully add detail to his featureless plans which both provided insight to those who were willing participants, and assure separation from criticism by those who would challenge him. But he was still trying to take his Chicago operation nationwide. He would be collecting the valuable support of the entertainment and media sectors along the way, but needed a credible endorsement. The conga line of elitists who would fawn over him would be extremely valuable to maintain the emotional appeal, and he was assured the Democrat vote from the collection of hundreds of special interest identity-based voting blocs, but he needed more to bridge over to the American vote. And that bridge would be General Colin Powell.

George W. Bush's Secretary of State, the retired Chairman of the Joint Chiefs during Desert Storm under his father, George H.W. Bush, Colin Powell was in many ways the opposite of the presidential candidate. He had a life of achievement, rose to greatness, and deserves the honors he's received. In fact it was fairly clear to those observing his chess moves that he was planning on becoming the 'first black president', or more precisely the president "who just happens to be black." He almost ran in 1996 as a Republican, but decided against it. Because of this, many assumed he was Republican, but Powell was a professional soldier, and appeared to never have any passion for politics. By the time Barack was on his way, and much like John Lewis, he did not want to be 'on the wrong side of history'. Powell would conclude his support speech with, "*He is a new generation coming into the world, onto the center stage, onto the American stage. And for that reason, I'll be voting for Senator Barack Obama.*"[11] It would be the preceding comments which foretold more than he may have expected:

> "*I come to the conclusion that because of his ability to inspire, because of the inclusive nature of his campaign, because he is reaching out all across America, because of who he is and his rhetorical abilities—and we have to take that into account, as well as his substance; he has both style and substance—he has met the standard of being a successful President, being an exceptional President. I think he is a transformational figure.*"
> -General Colin Powell[12]

It's easy to become caught up in the emotion of an event, and want to be part of something bigger. But it is the exceptional person who can temper that emotion and provide the leadership others would rely on. At the time, many Americans would scratch their heads and wonder why they didn't see the same thing he saw. And many would be swayed. But as with presidential legacies, they can't be written in present tense. It is that test of time which solidifies actual accomplishment. And this statement illustrates how even men of great accomplishment and character will, at the end, be just as human as the rest. Powell claimed he was misled by Bush and Cheney during the build up to the Iraq invasion. Time will tell whether he will claim he was setup again, should he decide to once again explore the political battlefield.

Selecting the Vice-President appears to follow a fairly consistent calculation. Political labeling is a game of relative positioning. You are left or you are right; you are liberal or you are conservative; you may be a Progressive, or you may be an American. But the name of the game is to portray yourself as a mainstream candidate when you hit the general election. Whatever label you are afraid the President will be stuck with, it seems the approach is to select the Vice-President to lean MORE in that direction. In this case you select your old racist ex-competitor from Delaware who seems to be a few cards short of a full deck, and voila, you are the smartest guy in the room. In fact you are the most forgiving and compassionate guy in the room. And most importantly, when you are facing impeachment threats, you are the only guy in the room.

But true to form, the media would ignore crazy Uncle Joe Biden and provide focus of laser-like precision onto McCain's running-mate. Sarah Palin didn't speak to the establishment, which was McCain's duty. She spoke to the American, she spoke to the average family, and she spoke to those feeling the rigged-game of electing representatives could not be changed. Whether she was a good choice at the time can be questioned, but the unbridled attacks she would face during and after the election should shame the establishment and their public relations apparatus called the main stream media (MSM).

The original and still most successful transformer would not be the person elected to be the 44th President of the United States. Nor would it be the 16th President who shepherded the initial transition from the original republican roots as a result of the Civil War. Nor would it be the 28th President who saw the permanent removal of the states from a representative seat at the federal government's table. It would be the 32nd, Franklin Delano Roosevelt. Toward the end of his reign, while the country was completely engrossed in World War II, he would proclaim his 'Second Bill of Rights'[13]. Nothing professed by a President would be more anti-American before, or since. A result of eleven years as President, accepting for the government, the responsibility for the well-being of its inhabitants, witnessing the raw American might that would win the war, his elitism was uncontainable. His state of the union speech contained:

"This Republic had its beginning, and grew to its present strength, under the protection of certain unalienable political rights -- among them the right of free speech, free press, free worship, trial by jury, freedom from unreasonable searches and seizures. They were our rights to life and liberty.

"We have come to a clear realization of the fact, however, that true individual freedom cannot exist without economic security and independence. Necessitous men are not free men. People who are

hungry, people who are out of a job are the stuff of which dictatorships are made.

"In our day these economic truths have become accepted as self-evident. We have accepted, so to speak, a second Bill of Rights under which a new basis of security and prosperity can be established for all -- regardless of station, or race or creed.

"Among these are: The right to a useful and remunerative job in the industries, or shops or farms or mines of the nation; The right to earn enough to provide adequate food and clothing and recreation; The right of farmers to raise and sell their products at a return which will give them and their families a decent living; The right of every business man, large and small, to trade in an atmosphere of freedom from unfair competition and domination by monopolies at home or abroad; The right of every family to a decent home; The right to adequate medical care and the opportunity to achieve and enjoy good health; The right to adequate protection from the economic fears of old age, and sickness, and accident and unemployment; And finally, the right to a good education.

"All of these rights spell security. And after this war is won we must be prepared to move forward, in the implementation of these rights, to new goals of human happiness and well-being.

"America's own rightful place in the world depends in large part upon how fully these and similar rights have been carried into practice for all our citizens. For unless there is security here at home there cannot be lasting peace in the world. One of the great American industrialists of our day -- a man who has rendered yeoman service to his country in this crisis -- recently emphasized the grave dangers of 'rightist reaction' in this Nation. Any clear-thinking business men share that concern. Indeed, if such reaction should develop -- if history were to repeat itself and we were to return to the so-called 'normalcy' of the 1920's -- then it is certain that even though we shall have conquered our enemies on the battlefields abroad, we shall have yielded to the spirit of fascism here at home."

Stunning how these new 'rights' would cost Americans their original rights "to life and liberty," for to produce these rights, someone will have to be the provider. Is it possible he spent a little too much time with Stalin as they strategized the demise of the Third Reich? What had been birthed by President Wilson, and been nurtured by FDR, would have to gain more control if it were to provide. The State had defined its objective, but the wheels had been put in motion years before.

He would take office during what would be called 'The Great Depression'. Initiated by the collapse of the United States stock market in 1929, it spread across the globe. It would help foment the instability in Europe which would lead to World War II, but at home it would the opportunity for the State to emerge. FDR's predecessor, Herbert Hoover, who's Smoot-Hawley Tariff Act in 1930 would exacerbate the economic catastrophe by choking international trade, was considered a great business man. He could make things great again, and knew how to create jobs. Hoover's approach to the internal struggles would be a comprehensive infrastructure plan. It's quite possible that the country would've found its way out of the depression sooner had the tariff act not been implemented, but by 1932 the damage was far too great, and FDR would win by a relative landslide.

He would bring the 'New Deal' to the country. Where Hoover would try to build the economy by creating employment opportunities surrounding great government projects, FDR would begin to take over the industries he felt were causing the problems. He would start with the banking industry pushing the 1933 Banking and Emergency Banking Acts in an attempt to stabilize the system. The Securities Act of 1933 would put controls in place to hopefully prevent another market crash. The Federal Emergency Relief Administration would provide direct financial support to cities and states, and the National Recovery Administration was created as a forum to eliminate "cut-throat competition" which resulted in collusion and price-fixing; it would later be found unconstitutional. But with all the government largesse, little improvement could be claimed. In a prequel to events 75 years later, the answer to poor government results would be more government.

The next wave of New Deal legislation would again attempt to correct the failing economy. But this time, it would start to 'invest' in the public more directly. The Wagner Act would institute the labor union as a major manipulator of national politics and create the National Labor Relations Board (NLRB), which would become the arbiters of conflict between the unions and employers. The Works Progress Administration would basically double down on the earlier Civil Works Administration effort to provide work. But this time, the government would take on the responsibility to literally build communities: parks, schools, courthouses, hospitals, even zoos. But it was the National Housing Act, which created the Federal Housing Administration (FHA), which was put in place to stem the tide of home foreclosures in the late 1930s, which would provide the opportunity for future disaster.

The government was now able to provide financial support to the banks, who felt the pressure to foreclose, by creating a secondary mortgage market under the Federal National Mortgage Association, known as Fannie Mae. In 1968, Fannie Mae was split into the current Fannie Mae and the Government National Mortgage Association, which is known as Ginnie Mae. The loans protected by Ginnie Mae, such as Veterans Administration (VA) or Farmers Home Mortgage Administration (FmHA) insured mortgages would remain backed by the 'full faith and credit of the United States government,' which could loosely be translated into 'guaranteed by the tax payer'. In 1970, the Federal Home Loan Mortgage Corporation, Freddie Mac, would be created with the purpose only a Washington insider could justify, to compete with Fannie Mae. Fannie Mae and Freddie Mac would now become partners in the social science experiments managed by the new Department of Housing and Urban Development (HUD).

Over the next 4 decades the authorities and procedures which were originally put in place to help control the real estate market would instead be used to create more and more lucrative arrangements for investors. In 1992, Congress would declare that they "...have an affirmative obligation to facilitate the financing of affordable housing for low- and moderate-income families" and set the target goal that 30% of this category of mortgages would be financed. At the end of the ruinous ride in 2007, the level would rise to 55%[14]. In 1999, they would be directed to increase their portfolio holdings in 'distressed inner city' areas. These decisions even produced a 1999 New York Times warning predicting the future need for "government rescue."[15] But that was immaterial to those in control who knew they will not be held responsible for these irresponsible decisions.

The point man during this period was the former Director of the U.S. Office of Management and Budget for the Clinton administration, Franklin Raines. In the next five years, before he would accept "early retirement," Raines had been paid $90 million for his apparently superior capabilities as the CEO[16]. But he wasn't "too big to fail", and the government tried to at least recover some of the 'overstated earnings,' which for the average American means 'alleged' fraud. To rub salt in the wound, Fannie Mae was required to cover his legal costs as well. The foundation of the country's financial system was being undermined, and the collapse of the house of cards would not be an 'if', but a 'when'.

It was in 2007, when the instabilities resulting from sub-prime loans, zero-down-payment, and worthless properties would finally reach the limit of what the market could sustain; the resulting foreclosure rates would bring the facade of banking discipline to its knees. Many of the banks had been built on this scheme but would see the writing on the wall; banks were going to fail. This would not be allowed. There was an election on the horizon, and not only would the Republican party collect the blame, but it's possible the contributions flowing from the spigot would also slow to a drip if they were allowed to fail. The banks became "too big to fail". At least, that's what the American was told. There was no other option presented, they needed to be bailed out.

The Bush administration created the Emergency Economic Stabilization Act of 2008, which authorized the Troubled Asset Relief Act, or TARP. Originally providing up to $700 billion, later reduced to $475 billion, this was more than the entire Department of Defense budget request of $661 billion, which included the cost for the two wars. But TARP would allow the government to directly control the financial system, and ultimately stabilize the financial crisis. Again to translate for the

American, the country would provide vast amounts of money to bail out fraudulent practices that finally collapsed.

But as is usually the case, many Americans would wonder if the government solved *their* problem, while ignoring the country's real problems and creating a new precedent for government intrusion. It would become the gift that keeps giving throughout Obama's tour. "It's Bush's fault" would become the answer to any and all negative results during the next administration.

> "The problem is, is that the way Bush has done it over the last eight years is to take out a credit card from the Bank of China in the name of our children, driving up our national debt from $5 trillion dollars for the first 42 presidents — number 43 added $4 trillion dollars by his lonesome, so that we now have over $9 trillion dollars of debt that we are going to have to pay back — $30,000 for every man, woman and child. That's irresponsible. It's unpatriotic."
> -Barack Obama[17]

After eight years of Republican rule, the military still fully engaged in two wars, a banking system on life support, national debt through the roof, and a Republican candidate that couldn't even interest Republicans, the time was ripe for a change.

Of course Barack would win, and convincingly. His story, manufactured and carefully maintained, would give the country their historic moment. Not the moment manufactured after the fact like Camelot, but in that moment. The crowds were spectacular, the emotion contagious, and the expectations beyond even what was promised. He would be the next resident of the White House, but after getting there on a pathway built of racialism, could he find the skills in his toolbox never before demonstrated to actually lead those who may not see things the way he does. Only time would tell. How would a community organizer, who had spent his entire political career working for his next job, be able to apply that small radical skill set to the job of the presidency? He would not be able to sit in the background and create conflict in order to force the 'Have' to accept 'an offer they couldn't refuse'. He was now THE 'Have'. The country would see him perform, and if the Praetorian Guard media would be asked whether they could continue to protect him, the answer would be, "Yes we can."

"Remember the Maine!" would be the battle cry for a nation poised for war with Spain. That war would come, but fifty years earlier, to the day, the United States declared war for only the second time in its brief history, but this time on Mexico. The insatiable expansion of Americans westward had created the kindling for a short, but transformative conflict which ultimately produced the 28th State, Texas. The settlers would follow the call of Stephen F. Austin whose father, Moses Austin, had been granted a large amount of land by the original Spanish authorities over the region. It would also happen that in 1821 Mexico would have won its own independence, setting a collision course between American expansionism and Mexican nationalism.

By 1829, English speaking 'Anglos' would outnumber the Spanish speaking in the area. Through the next seven years, the embattled Republic of Texas would find inspiring defeat at the Alamo, and decisive victory at the Battle of San Jacinto, resulting in Mexico's formal surrender six weeks later, ultimately resulting in the recognized independence of the new state. But the border between the two states had never been settled. Texas would claim the area south to the present-day Rio Grande River, but Mexico maintained the Rio Grande in the treaty was actually the Nueces River, approximately half way to San Antonio.

With this dispute unsettled, Texas would be brought into the Union in 1845. In an effort to forestall hostilities apparent on the horizon, President Polk, responsible for the greatest territorial increase in United States history, had secretly offered to forgive the Mexican war debt of $3 million, and provide over eight times that to purchase the disputed land from Texas to the Pacific, including California, which was also becoming more unstable with resistance movements against the Mexican government. But the secret plea would be rejected. Polk, elected over a year before, won with a claim that he would settle the conflict in the disputed territory. Some would say he provoked the conflagration, but what transpired would be the Mexican-American War.

President Polk, a lifelong slave owner, would win his party's nomination over Martin Van Buren. Van Buren was against slavery in the new territories, and because of that fact, would lose support from his Democratic Party. It was the time of Manifest Destiny, and the push to the West was unstoppable. However, the southern states would feel their 'heritage' weaken with each new state admitted to the union. The southern slave states needed to maintain some balance in Congress, or their days were numbered. But the controversial Missouri Compromise effectively allowed slave state expansion below the 36° 30' latitude line. That would be mostly Mexican territory, and Polk and the democrats knew they needed to gain control of the Mexican territories in order to strengthen their 'institution' of slavery, as Mexico had long since abolished it.

The war was swift, and the great General Santa Anna would see defeat at his final battle. As a result, the United States and Mexico signed the Treaty of Guadalupe Hidalgo, where the U.S. assumed the $3 million Mexican debt, but paid $15 million for what would become the States of California, Nevada, Utah, most of Arizona and New Mexico, and parts of Wyoming, Colorado, Kansas, and Oklahoma, while further acknowledging Texas. But Texas was the only state at the time. The battle over "states' rights" to slavery would only be won during the Civil War. In addition, this war was also the first time the mighty power of the United States military would be used by the government in an offensive manner[18].

Fifty years later, the United States would declare war on Spain. President James Monroe had projected the Monroe Doctrine, stating no European government interference would be tolerated in the western hemisphere. But that was in 1821, and Cuba was not included within the sphere of control at that time. For almost four hundred years, Cuba had been a part of the Spanish nation. But by the end of the 19th century, revolutionaries from safe harbors in Florida would instigate uprisings, which ultimately won Cuba her independence in 1898. Nothing sold papers like war, and publishers Joseph Pulitzer and William Randolph Hearst sensationalized the conflict. At the same time however, the revolt was beginning to have a serious impact on trade, causing President McKinley to get involved and press for stability.

Just as the infant Cuba was beginning along its road to autonomy, the warship USS Maine would anchor in the Havana harbor as a show of strength to assure Americans of their safety. But on February 15, 1898, a massive explosion sank the mighty ship, taking 266 souls (of the 355 on board) with it. The semi-fictional drama in the press continued to play out as the furor of the American populace and Congress pressed McKinley to respond. Had Spain attacked the U.S.? It turns out it's much more likely the cause was an internal explosion, but the fuse was lit and Congress wanted war[19]. The "splendid little war" would be swift, with Cuba, Guam, and the Philippines relieving themselves of Spanish influence after only 10 weeks. But once again, the United States had used its might in an offensive fashion to achieve prized territories. The nation, just winning its third war with little resistance, began to develop the self-determined authority over the prospects of others. One of the biggest supporters for intervention would be a future president, but at this time Assistant Secretary of the Navy.

Theodore Roosevelt earned fame with the "Rough Riders", memorialized for their involvement in the Battle of San Juan Hill, and would return to the United States a hero[20]. Although he had previously lost a bid for New York City Mayor in 1886, he knew he could now ride his wartime glory into office. But this time it would be as the Governor of New York, that same year (1898). Before he could make an impact and change things, those in control quickly moved him out of the way as he was nominated for Vice President to McKinley. It would be during his first year as Vice President, when President McKinley would be assassinated, and Teddy would become the youngest President in history at the age of 42.

He was bigger than life, the "cowboy" and the intellectual wrapped up into the model American president would begin to turn the government's outward sense of authority inward toward the states and the people. It would be called the "Progressive Era" and Teddy had the self-assurance necessary to proclaim the federal government's elite would be best suited to tackle festering social problems. The previous decades would be coined the "Gilded Age" by Mark Twain, and be the period where the U.S. would begin to see rapid expansion of industrial capability resulting in the creation of the world's wealthiest men, as well as a great many in abject poverty. The country was exploding and there was an opening for men who would do great things.

Presidents Roosevelt, Taft and Wilson would oversee the beginning of the transition of the federal government from that which was envisioned in the Constitution to the national government which we are witness to today. The problems were vast, and the solutions would change the fabric of the country as they knew it. Previous administrations, excluding the Civil War period, understood the power and responsibility for governing was "delegated" by the states, and that which was not enumerated in the Constitution was "reserved by the States..., or the people." But Roosevelt, Taft and Wilson proclaimed that the enemy was "corruption" in government, and they had the obligation to weed out this disease.

The source of this corruption would be identified as the political system itself, and the movement from the republican system of government toward direct democracy had begun. The seductive attraction of targeting "the rich" would drive many of the solutions. At the time, the richest American would be John D. Rockefeller, first person to amass $1 billion, and that was in 1916. The brilliant industrialist would be remembered by the envious as one of the "robber barons", along with Carnegie, Ford, and many others which the country would also be indebted to for its future. To put things in perspective, Rockefeller's wealth alone equaled the entire annual budget of the federal government at the time. But it was the poor, the proletariat, which had been gaining attention as the European intelligentsia had been infusing the populace with the promises of a worker's paradise.

Clearly forecasted throughout the election, Obama would go after the rich. After all, his predecessor showed him the way. Crisis relief can produced unimaginable sums of money with little required justification. There just wouldn't be time to describe the purpose, just that it was needed. Obama's first priority would be the economy, or at least that was what was announced. His solution would be the American Recovery and Reinvestment Plan, or "the Stimulus." As a candidate, he would proclaim "Only the government can break the viscous cycles that are crippling our economy,"[21] as he more famously began his mythical projections of promised successes. He was going to "save or create at least three million jobs over the next few years."[22]

While his predecessor would institute the unconstitutional TARP program, which ultimately cost the tax-payer $475 billion, he had grander plans. He needed an immediate infusion of $767 billion to stem the tide. What was it for? He claimed it was for "shovel-ready" jobs. In the end, the spending had been stopped at $862 billion. But that was money the government didn't have, and so Americans would also be paying interest on that spending spree. And on top of that, no one could point to where the money went as claims of success were even difficult to conjure by the government media appendage. It would be the Resident himself who ultimately admitted that the "shovel ready projects…were never shovel-ready."[23] By 2012, the tab was estimated already to be over $940 billion[24]. For those that can still handle a little math, this is about $3000 per person, more than quadruple that if you only take into account actual tax payers!

Did the media take notice? Not a chance. The Stimulus was a miserable failure, but their mission was to protect the incompetent otherwise it would reflect poorly on them as well. And an inquisitive American might wonder if it's quite possible that the very press guaranteed their freedom in the Constitution might also be the recipients of much of the payola. There were several party-line squabbles, but America was overwhelmed with a system drunk with money. In true statist fashion, the solution would be "Stimulus 2.0". The outright theft had risen to such a staggering scale; Americans seemed to find it unbelievable. It's quite possible the administration was also finding the ease at which they had been able to accomplish their initial attack to be astonishing. But these were short term targets. If he was going to have a lasting effect on the system, the State needed to get control of the banking industry itself.

And there just happened to be two institutional corruptocrats who were ready to serve it up.

Congressmen Chris Dodd and Barney Frank had spent their career protecting the institutions which brought about the 2008 financial crisis, Fannie Mae and Freddie Mac. And in another worn-out tradition, it would be the inmates which would provide the solution for the asylum. The Dodd-Frank Act of 2010 was more of a framework than a law, allowing the administration over the following years to develop the rules they themselves felt they wanted in order to "guarantee 'systemically important' banks created by the Consumer Financial Protection Bureau…and imposed hundreds of new regulations which make compliance very costly for small community banks."[25] The government was now inside the boardrooms of the financial system and picking winners and losers, without public oversight. This framework approach would be the method to take over other sectors as well.

Prior to World War I, the Progressives hadn't yet cast the Constitution away, as four more amendments were ratified as part of the effort to correct the country's social maladies. The 16th amendment provided the authority to impose the income tax. Promised to only afflict the 'rich', it would not take long for its tentacles to reach into all American's pocketbooks. Government programs would not be cheap, and there would be a need for revenue to support them. The federal government would begin to create the departments and agencies necessary to control the population and resources once the purview of the states themselves.

The 17th amendment would fundamentally transform the relationship between the federal government and the 'several states'. Some Americans may think it effectively eliminated state authority. This amendment took the Senate seat selection away from the State and required the result to be by popular vote.

This critically injured the balance of power within the federal system by basically removing the state's participation in the federal system by creating a single representative block beholden only to popular sentiment, and at the same time by leaving their six year terms in place, they became virtually untouchable. Senate duties, once important as a cooperative agreement mechanism between the State governments and the Federal government, such as Treaty ratification and judicial consent would forever be changed.

While the 18th amendment would be repealed only 14 years later, the purpose of this amendment provides insight into the self-righteousness of the elite a hundred years ago. While alcohol had been a social problem, the federal government decided they needed to "do good". They needed to outlaw behavior through the imposition of a constitutional amendment. This single act alone illuminates the omnipotence which moved the elites of the day.

The 19th amendment would be the victory of the suffragettes. Even though the country was roughly 130 years old, voting rights had experienced dramatic swings and were used regionally to control the electorate. The voting rights up to the Civil War had been predominately a state affair. The state had the responsibility and authority to define what requirements a voter must have. Much to the dismay of many now, race and gender was not an exclusionary characteristic in America when it was founded. Not directly, that is. Voting rights were mainly connected with land ownership, and as such there were black Americans and women who voted in early elections. But as voting became a right of all Americans, the exclusionary nature of the rules across the country would require federal government involvement. This was changed initially with the 15th amendment, and then further with the 19th amendment, removing any restrictions "on account of sex."

These four amendments were a statement to the societal problems of the day. While one was to eliminate the disenfranchisement of half of the citizenry, the others marked a transformational shift in the role of the federal government. The Constitution was at least partially recognized by the establishment of the day, but the euphoria of power and the righteousness of superiority would begin to provide the nutrients for the newly developing State. But it was the beginning of extra-constitutional powers which started the country down the road to perdition.

Roosevelt believed in the authority of the government over the people and the land, creating five national parks, 150 national forests, and dozens of preserves and monuments with the federal government providing environmental protection over an area almost the size of Texas and New Mexico combined[26]. While the beauty of these grand expanses brings awe to those who visit, it could hardly be argued that the intent of the framers was to provide the federal government authority over land within sovereign states. Article VI, Section 3, Clause 2 of the Constitution provides the government authority over territories. But once the state was formed, those properties should have been turned over to the state. As an example, the federal government now 'owns' almost a million square miles, and an average of over 58% of the property in ten western states[27].

President William Howard Taft, a good friend of Teddy's, would take up residency as the next President. He would continue with the trust-busting agenda of his predecessor, would be the first to require departments to present their budgets to the cabinet for review, spearheaded the 16th amendment fight for the income tax as a method to balance the tariff problem of the day, and held the "southern policy" of not hiring blacks into offices where race friction could be expected. By the end of his term, Teddy wanted back in. But he had burned too many bridges in the Republican Party, and decided to run third-party; he started his own "Progressive Party" or the "Bull Moose Party". The results were that he split the Republican vote, and a catastrophe for the country as it allowed the Democrats to once again win the office[28].

President Wilson would be elected on a commitment to keep America out of the war is Europe. Wilson provided his 14 Points which were to be the foundation for an armistice and succession of hostilities which would ultimately claim over 30 million lives, over half of them civilian. The treaty at Versailles however, would betray the promises made earlier and place all blame on Germany. It would not be enough to just blame Germany; blame would be placed on the German people directly as Wilson states, "A people are responsible for the acts of their government. If their government purposes things that are wrong, they ought to take measures to see to it that that purpose is not executed."[29] The result would be an animosity which would birth the Nazi movement.

Little mattered to this prototypical Progressive President; he would remain focused on his legacy, and his crown jewel was to be the League of Nations. Leave alone the fact that the United States never joined, and it proved impotent to any actual global conflict, the ideologue would not be dissuaded. His call for self-determination was also only for some. While the humiliation of Germany set the stage for the next world war, he also showed callousness to a young representative of a nation half way around the world who wished to speak at Versailles and make a case for the liberation of his small country from the domination of the French. He would be turned away, only to find a supportive partnership with the communists in Russia. The United States would meet this spurned patriot in another war, although never officially declared by Congress. He would be the leader of his people by that time. We would confront Ho Chi Minh in Vietnam four decades later[30].

A politician to the core, Wilson was at his 'best' when identifying fault in others, but more than willing to look the other way in his own backyard. The same person, who would victimize all German people for the war, would also be the southern democrat willing to allow the re-segregation of the federal government and excuse the Ku Klux Klan. It was his self-assured superiority which would remove restraint. He would believe the executive should not be an equal branch of the government, but the superior. He would collude with congressional leaders to ensure his progressive agenda would have support, and in 1913 would be the first President since John Adams to address a joint session of Congress. He would use the theater of it to project his own sense of aristocratic authority over the representative branch. And he was all about reform, reducing tariffs through the Underwood-Simmons Act, which would be offset with the initially small, graduated income tax. Banking reform would be tackled through the Federal Reserve Act, creating the current system of reserve banks and the Federal Reserve Board, which was hoped to provide the country with a stable currency. Finally, the Clayton Antitrust Act would be his nod to labor and farmers, excluding them from the Sherman Antitrust Act of 1890.

Progressive thought of the time however believed the individual was not born free, rather that freedom must be granted upon them. It would be the government that would be the granter of that freedom and their liberty. This was, and is, a complete rejection of the concept of unalienable rights as stated in the Constitution. And this would become the underlying authority felt by the establishment as the State would develop and devour the Republic.

In many ways Wilson's philosophical cousin, Barack would also see the office as a blank check for his own personal intuitions and the election as a validation of his desires. Reminiscent of the Wilson omnipotence, the Resident would also project authority over the American.

Residency

> *The militant man of words prepares the ground for the rise of a mass movement: 1) by discrediting prevailing creeds and institutions and detaching from them the allegiance of the people; 2) by indirectly creating a hunger for faith in the hearts of those who cannot live without it, so that when the new faith is preached it finds an eager response among the disillusioned masses; 3) by furnishing the doctrine and the slogans of the new faith; 4) by undermining the convictions of the "better people"–those who can get along without faith–so that when the new fanaticism makes its appearance they are without the capacity to resist it.*
> *- Eric Hoffer[1]*

Barack Obama's election was celebrated as 'historic', and it surely will be. But many Americans are becoming aware the significance will not be due to some superficial label based on skin tone, but due to the superficial seriousness which he has applied to the oath of the office. He won what may go down in history as the last 'free election' for the presidency of the United States inspiring hope and promising change. The party most aligned with the progressive movement would once again take the reins and continue to drag the country toward its 'utopian' end. The public would be insulated from his extreme positions, because for the Progressive it was time to 'dance with the date that brung ya'. But in the end, his actual agenda was vague, and much of his public projections would be uninspiring.

His administration was going to be the "most open and transparent in history."[2] He had a reform agenda which would tackle the leviathan and improve its efficiency and integrity. In his first year he promised to close Guantanamo Bay and enact immigration reform. Given his lack of experience, not only in government, but in any venture outside of campaigning, it was not surprising he would fall short. To list several of the promises made, and as we'll see, broken often without a hint of good intentions[3]:

- Curbing Lobbyists and Special Interest Groups
  ◊ Two year wait for lobbyists to move into government positions.

- Modernize the Financial Regulations
- Make Government More Effective
  - Create a new Chief Performance Officer who reports directly to the president.
  - Reconfigure OMB Program Assessment Review Tool (PART).
  - Implement consequences for success and failure.
  - Move workers from bloated bureaucracies to the frontlines.
  - Eliminate wasteful redundancy.
  - Streamline government procurement.
  - Protect whistleblowers.
  - Increase the use of technology.
- Cut Wasteful Spending
  - Line by line review of the budget.
  - Slash earmarks.
  - Sunlight on corporate tax loopholes.
- Fix Government Contracting
  - Cut federal spending on contractors by at least 10 percent.
  - Restore management and oversight capacity.
  - No federal contracts for tax delinquent companies.

He was an ideologue with little appreciation or patience for competitive viewpoints. He had no record of consensus building, and what few successes he would claim have would be as result of good old cronyism. The era of hope and change would have to somehow find root in the Chicago-style backroom bartering which got him to where he was. But before anything could be accomplished, he would need to bring in his team to replace the 'Bushies' who had control of the levers of government for the past eight years.

The Obama administration would not get off to a smooth start. He would find that the collection of malcontents and ideologues which would follow his 'real' agenda would have a more difficult time gaining acceptance once the specifics of their backgrounds moved into the light of day. The amateurish staffing escapades alone could fill a book all its own, and it has in Michelle Malkin's book, *Culture of Corruption*[4]. He would immediately demonstrate his ability to redefine terms to serve his purposes as he 'qualified' the meaning of the word 'lobbyist' in order to bring in several of his chosen team. It quickly became a joke on the Internet, "What is the difference between Obama and Jesus? Jesus could actually build a cabinet."

While much focus is on the cabinet selections, few Americans know that there are over a thousand presidential appointees which need Senate approval, not to mention the many more that do not rise to that level of scrutiny. But even with just the cabinet members, the Obama team would bungle. Not only did they select people wholly incompatible with the responsibilities of those positions, it became clear the administration didn't even perform their own background checks prior to submittal. Then, there would be the czars. Presidents have had czars for the past century, but they would normally be assigned a specific issue to provide the president a mechanism to affect some change through an independent actor. In Obama's White House, this seems to have expanded dramatically. When confronted with the question as to why he needed over 30 czars, the answer would usually entail some form of 'Bush did it.'[5] But one would have to go back 70 years to find another president before Bush which had more than ten, and FDR had only eleven czar positions during his reign[6].

The original czars for issues such as Director, National Drug Control Policy, or the Director, White House Office of Faith-Based and Community Initiatives would remain. But a new breed of czar would emerge. These would effectively create a shadow cabinet, insulated from the pesky oversight the Legislature was responsible for. One example would be Carol Browner, former EPA chief under Clinton, and Obama's Assistant to the President for Energy and Climate Change, or Energy Czar. Another would be Nancy-Ann Min DeParle, another Clinton official, as Director of the White House Office of Health Reform and Counselor to the President, or Health Czar[7].

As we have seen, the United States Constitution originally limited the authority of the federal government to those things the states could not do for themselves. The new government would have responsibilities substantial enough to warrant dedicated departments with directors reporting directly to the President. These mainly focused on international relations, and to manage the currency. The first cabinet would contain the Secretaries of State, War and Treasury. Shortly thereafter, the burgeoning Post Office system would be promoted into a new cabinet position. It would be over 50 years before another federal government role rose to a stature demanding of a presidential cabinet position. In 1849, as the federal government was beginning to expand with 'Manifest Destiny', it would need to create a department to manage the vast territories being consumed, and more importantly the natural resources it was apportioning for itself. Transferred to this new Interior Department would be the Patent Office, which had a strong Agricultural division clamoring for recognition.

As noted by Dr. Thomas Sowell in *Wealth, Poverty and Politics*, agriculture can be seen as the critical enabler of societal advancement. "Agriculture, perhaps the most life-changing advance in the evolution of human societies, came to Europe from the middle-east in ancient times."[8] And it was this ability for societies to live off of smaller and smaller geographic areas which enabled consolidation into cities, which would produce the technological advancements of the industrial revolution. And there was no other place on Earth like the American frontier to provide for the further development and enhancement of society.

It was 1862, and General McClellan would need the best for his men. The Civil War had just begun, and the Union had to ensure quality food and medical care was available. The Agriculture Division would separate from its parent and be elevated to a full cabinet-level position.

It would be interesting to many Americans that the executive branch had only five cabinet positions at the beginning of the Civil War. It would rise to seven shortly after the war concluded with the last addition before the twentieth century. Until 1853, the Attorney General was basically a part-time position. The United States Attorneys were under the Interior Department at that time, representing the federal government in legal matters. But in 1870, it was decided to create a Department of Justice, and raise the Attorney General to a full-time cabinet position, to oversee all U.S. Attorneys as well as the new Solicitor General office[9]. The next change wouldn't be until three decades later when the Progressives would begin the vast expansion of government authority into the lives of the people.

In 1903, it was decided the government needed to "create jobs, promote economic growth, encourage development and improve living standards for all Americans."[10] And, of course, the solution would be new government programs and an office of oversight, the Department of Commerce and Labor, which would absorb the original Bureau of Labor Statistics. In 1913 however, the Department of Labor would become its own cabinet level position, and the Patent Office would move once again, to the newly named Department of Commerce. Even the great Progressives of the first half of the 20th century didn't expand their cabinet. Wilson would be far too much of a micromanager and more interested in legacy and dreams of a one-world government with the League of Nations. FDR wouldn't expand his cabinet, but would create a wide range of agencies to directly manage the country's machinery like the Federal Security Agency (FSA), responsible for health, education, and social security, and the Federal Housing Administration (FHA), providing mortgage insurance to FHA lenders. But it would be FDR's successor, Harry Truman which would once again change the cabinet, but in a relatively minor fashion.

The Department of War was responsible for the operations and maintenance (care and feeding) of the United States Army and Navy in 1789. By 1798, the Navy Department had separated without executive cabinet level representation. The Army was limited to funding for no more than 2 years at a time, where the Navy, on the other hand, by Constitutional obligation, necessitated long-term investment and management. It would also assume leadership over the United States Marine Corps, and the United States Coast Guard, when directed by the President. The twentieth century would bring air power to warfare, where the Navy and Army would each use their own, sometimes redundant, air power to support their mission areas. It became clear during World War II that air power was far more than just an additional tool to either the Army or Navy toolset. This new dimension in warfare demanded its own doctrine, managed by the United States Air Force.

The Department of the Air Force was created in 1947, under the Department of Defense, as an equal to the Departments of the Army and Navy.

As the budget of the FSA continued to grow beyond that of several cabinet responsibilities, President Eisenhower would elevate the agency into the cabinet as the Department of Health, Education, and Welfare (DEHW). The DEHW would remain intact until 1980, when Education would become its own Department, and the Social Security Administration would separate into an independent agency. But before that would occur, President Johnson created two additional cabinet positions to support his Great Society. The Department of Housing and Urban Development (HUD) would become a cabinet position in 1965, assuming the FHA, Ginnie Mae, and many other community support programs. In 1966, the Federal Aviation Administration (FAA) had growth in importance and motivated the creation of the Department of Transportation. The Post Office would finally lose its cabinet level position in 1971, and it would be President Carter who in 1977 would consolidate safety, handling, and management of all things nuclear into the Department of Energy. But it would be under President George H.W. Bush in 1989, that the Veterans Administration was lifted to a seat in the cabinet as recognition for the sacrifices the country was morally obligated.

Let's review. This United States executive branch would have only 4 departments in the President's cabinet at the end of the 18th century. At the end of the 19th century, it would have but 7. But it would be the 20th century where the growth had doubled to a total of 14 departments, 10 of which are primarily responsible for the inner workings of the country. But the State was not through. The attacks on September 11, 2001, would be the opportunity for the government to consolidate over twenty agencies in order to "detect, prepare for, prevent, protect against, respond to, and recover from terrorist attacks within the United States."[11] The Department of Homeland Security would be born. The federal government had transitioned far from the protector of individual liberty, to something the founders would hardly recognize.

The power of the office provided both the mechanism to enlarge the country, and the authority to expand the administration. The founders knew this and were weary; hoping the separation of power between the branches would provide the needed balance. But it would be Manifest Destiny which would first set the country on its course of destruction. Much like the legal system, precedent will lay the foundation for further encroachment. The State would be nourished by the executive over the previous century as the seductive pull of legacy and riches pulled our country westward.

The seeds of the State started small, building on its authority over territories, and natural resources. The presidency was to become more than the overseer of the bureaucracy and executor of the laws of the land. It was to become the sole leader of the country. President Lincoln seized the power and met the confederacy on the field of battle. What was won was more than the reuniting of states into a more perfect union. It was the precedent of the Civil War which provided validation to the State. It was the superiority of the executive over the states. The executive would slowly amass power as it acquired territory. But it would be the Progressive century which would develop the state through adolescence.

The superior German educational system would find its way across the Atlantic in the late 19th century and with it the teachings of socialism, which would become the religion of the State, and its clergy, the Progressives. Justification would be claimed for authority and mechanisms of control. But it would be the intellectual progressives which would yearn to be accepted by the European establishment which would bite of the apple. The State would take over the responsibility of providing for the people. The State would slowly devour the states' authority and subsume all. By controlling the distribution of tax revenues it would lure the weak and bend the remaining states to its will. It would hide behind the three branches of government for as long as it was able, but it would only be a matter of time before it could no longer remain hidden and constrained. As a predator often waits until the prey is weakened, it would be the Great Depression which provided the first opportunity for it to feed. The first overt attack on the Constitution would be under the New Deal.

Unemployment had remained under ten percent for decades. But the market crash in 1929 resulted in sharp increases over the next couple years. It would be about 25% in many areas of the country when FDR took office in 1933, after about a 30% drop in the gross national product[12]. The banks had virtually shut people off from their deposits, and something had to be done. And what has become the standard response from the President; it would be decided that grand government programs would save the country. Or at least that was the plan. The blitzkrieg included dozens of new agencies, which would target the banking industry, securities trading, and suspended the gold standard. There was a vast array of public works, and make-work projects. This was also when mortgage lengths went from about 10 years to the current 30 year standard, allowing more people to afford home ownership. Some elements, like the Agricultural Adjustment Act, which virtually took over the industry by developing a system of domestic allotments controlling production and prices, would be ruled unconstitutional. The country needed a drink, and so they repealed prohibition as well. But this was not enough. By the beginning of his second term, unemployment had barely moved. The solution was obviously to be even more programs.

The unions would gain substantial power through the National Labor Relations Act guaranteeing collective bargaining, and if there was an issue, the government would be arbiter through the National Labor Relations Board. It made employment for individuals younger than 16 illegal, and 18 if the job was characterized as hazardous. That still didn't move the needle, so the government just hired them itself. FDR would then build on earlier programs such as the Food Stamp Plan, and create the largest, most damaging single program in the history of the country.

It seemed like the right thing to do. The Social Security Act created a system which would provide for the elderly, temporarily unemployed, dependent children, and handicapped. In 1935, the life expectancy of a man or woman would be 60 and 64 years, respectively, with approximately 6% of the population living past 65 years of age[13]. In 2015, it had risen to 76 and 81 years and over 12% of the population was over 65 years old. The retirement age is rising slowing, and will reach

67 years of age in 2027, but that will hardly make a difference. In 1937, 53,236 beneficiaries were paid a total of $1,278,000. By 2008, there would be 1000 times more beneficiaries, at a cost of over $600 billion (about 5 *hundred* times the amount per beneficiary.)[14] Throw in Medicare and Medicaid and it was almost $1.2 *trillion*, in just 2008. The entire Department of Defense budget, while fighting two wars, was less than $800 billion. But it isn't just the financial cliff which is accelerating toward us; it was the resultant damage to the American culture it had wrought.

As a prequel to today's socialistic executive theatre, the program was created from the same elitist attraction to European examples which seem to plague our elected officials today. It was said the United States was the only advanced country not to have a nationalized old age insurance program. Several states did, however. And with an echo of arguments to come 75 years later, this would be a tax. No, it wasn't a tax. It depends on who you are selling it to. At almost 150 years since the Constitution was ratified, the State had begun to absorb the seats of power, and there would be no turning back. But with every assault on personal liberty, there can be devastating collateral damage. In this case, it would be the American family.

The family would be the primary community of mutual support in America. But after a few generations of the government taking care of the elderly, families have slowly dissipated. The younger generation, once raised to respect the older generations through regular interactions and witnessing the  responsibility each generation has toward the previous, would slowly be separated from that responsibility. The family unit would begin to unravel. The parents no longer had to plan to take care of their parents; the grandparents would slowly disappear from the family unit; and the child would grow up detached from their family. The breakdown of the American family can be traced back to the institutionalization of the Social Security Program. And it would be this disintegration of generational ties which would provide fertile ground for disconnected and malleable voting blocs willing to bite of the apple.

"Facts are stubborn things," President John Adams once said. The structural problems developed over the past decades are a direct result of the overreach of elected oligarchs, supported by the peoples representatives, and provided cover by the well-maintained supportive media. The Resident brought with him the same failed policies which have produced the failures of the past, but he is unencumbered by rational reflection or the need to answer for his disastrous performance. It is the country that will be to blame.

Barack Obama Comes Out

> *The fanatic is also mentally cocky, and hence barren of new beginnings. At the root of his cockiness is the conviction that life and the universe conform to a simple formula—his formula.*
> *- Eric Hoffer[1]*

During the election he would be the most pro-abortion candidate in history. Far beyond the progressive 'pro-choice' mantra, he would win a 100% rating from the Illinois Planned Parenthood Council for his support[2]. While this subject represents a terrible choice a soon-to-be-mother may have to confront, it is possibly the best example of why the United States Constitution specifically limits government's intrusion into the lives of the people. But for a Progressive, the ability to control the decisions of the masses is too seductive to avoid, and Barack would go 'above and beyond', ensuring the rights of the mother were protected. In a Senate debate in 2001, he refused to support legislation which protected the living baby, which would sometimes survive these ghastly procedures, if it would in any way inhibit its free exercise. On the floor he would state his objection to the bill, "It would essentially bar abortions because the equal protection clause does not allow someone to kill a child, and if this was a child then this would be an anti-abortion statute."[3] It is a sad day when the person elected to the highest office in the greatest country the world has ever known values some manufactured right of the abortion industry over the life of a child. Many Americans would find it very ironic that the most steadfast protector of what was once called the 'Negro Project', aimed at 'reducing' the population of unwanted people, the progressive Eugenics Movement, part of the Progressive Movement, created by Margaret Sanger, who helped found Planned Parenthood, who has approximately three-fourths of their offices in minority neighborhoods, would be one Barack Obama.

As the real person began to emerge out from underneath the product's carefully developed image, it became clear that the Barack Obama was not what had been advertised. A promised healer and bridge between the various warring factions within the society would instead become the über-polarizing instigator of more discontent and derision. He would use his bully pulpit not to speak to the country as much as lecture those willing to listen on how the country was the problem. His inarticulate and pessimistic confrontational approach to those elements he found interesting, combined with his utter disregard to those items he did not, would begin to tell the tale of what the administration would be all about. He did not speak to the American values which built this peerless civil society, but to the other True Believers who yearned for the diminishment of the country.

Barack's disregard, or more accurately contempt, for the country's traditions and customs would be on display throughout his residency. It would begin with the public rejection of our bond with our heritage, as symbolized by the return of the Churchill bust, immediately upon transition. It's true that each president before would rearrange the Oval Office to best fit the environment they wanted to create. Barack would replace the bust with those of other great men, Martin Luther King, Jr. and Abraham Lincoln. What was the disgraceful example of his lack of class would be rather than placing it in another location, symbolizing our continued brotherhood spanning the Atlantic Ocean; he would return it to England.

But the most spectacular of affronts to the dignity of the office of which he fought to achieve would be the projection of aloofness and incompetence which initially could be viewed as just an acceptable period of amateurish behavior due the administration's inexperience. But after several years with no apparent improvement, it became clear to Americans that this wasn't an accident, but neither was it unacceptable to the administration; it was exactly how they planned to govern. The use of the media to deflect and distract the public with unending crises, real or manufactured, would eventually numb the observers from the actual activities taking place. In fact, there seemed to be more attention paid to the unending vacations which apparently became the centerpiece of the administration's agenda.

It would be early in the previous administration when President Bush realized the disrespectful nature of his golfing during the country's time of crisis. He would explain that, "I don't want some mum whose son may have recently died to see the commander-in-chief playing golf. I feel I owe it to the families to be in solidarity as best as I can."[4] This minor gesture to those sacrificing for their country speaks volumes when compared to the current Resident. He in fact would support Obama's golfing as an important method to manage the stress of the job. But you cannot transfer class from one person to the next. There is obviously a limit at which the optics betrays the intent. Prior to the 2012 election, Barack would have played over 100 golf games[5]. His annual Hawaii vacation that year alone was to cost taxpayers $4 million over two weeks[6]. Effectively a self-promoted aristocrat at this point, he would feel justified as he considered the presidential fleet of aircraft his own personal travel service. Realizing this, Alex Pappas would report in the Daily Caller that the country's overall bill for the Obama 'royal family' would amount to $1.4 billion in just 2011[7].

But the cost would only be an issue to the Resident if he had to pay for it himself; entitlement had all but become second nature to the first family. They couldn't even be inconvenienced with sharing the same government aircraft for a vacation trip. The 2011 summer vacation opportunity to mingle with the rich, famous, and contributing elite in Martha's Vineyard would be one such golf outing that the family would enjoy. But Barack would take Air Force One, while his family would follow only four hours later in a separate jet. That little Boeing 747 must just have been overweight with the additional passengers. And earlier that year, the annual Hawaii trip would also see the family travel early in an "office it the sky" jet which usually supports senior military commanders, but at a surprisingly affordable $63,000[8]. Never before had an Oval Office resident had such disregard for those who provide the funds that they indiscriminately waste. The integrity of our government system relies on the respect the elected officials maintain for those who they are supposed to represent. But throughout his first term it became apparent that was not a part of the Resident's character, and those who put him there seemed too weak or embarrassed to confront him; the media would look the other way again. At least the Nobel Peace Prize Committee Chairman has asked for the prize to be returned.

The excitement over the chosen one was so contagious the world would catch the disease. In a stunning example of either an absurd breakdown in vetting processes or just old-world official corruption, the Nobel Peace Prize would be awarded to a man for what he was going to do. The Resident was given the award for "extraordinary efforts to strengthen international diplomacy and cooperation between peoples."[9] That's rich. He would not be able to meet that ideal domestically, but they may be extraordinary in their powers to foresee the future, or maybe they just have a time machine secretly available. Not only was he the leader of a nation actively involved in two separate wars, but he had delivered no measurable change in his short time at the helm. And the region would deteriorate into chaos as a direct result of his involvement. It was a ridiculous display on the part of obvious international sycophants.

The committee claims the prize was "to deliver a boost to Obama"[10]; a clear statement of the European position of low expectations. It would take over 6 years, but the committee finally built up the courage to at least ask for its return, including the "really nice" case[11]. Another first for the Resident; it would be the first time in the 115 year history of the award that the committee asked for its return. But the absurdity of the award will prove to be a fatal wound to the once high esteem the committee once held. It's been said that the Resident was basically embarrassed by the award, claiming it was submitted without his involvement. That is very plausible, but it speaks volumes of the followers who submitted his name, as they actually had to be committed to their cause in order to even create a package for consideration. It's too bad the energy that went in to the product's support could be channeled to "do good" for the country. But then Obama has always had an 'inflated resume' anyway. His credibility would regularly be moored to a claim of expertise about the Constitution since he had been a professor of the subject.

Anyone who has attended college understands there is a wide spectrum of competency when it comes to professors and lecturers. Whether Obama taught classes at the University of Chicago or not is really beside the point. Americans find it hard to believe that he could claim expertise in a subject that he seems to fundamentally not understand. Written for the common citizen to read and understand, the Constitution seems to be alien to Obama's perspective of the country. What must be meant by the claim that he is a 'Constitutional Scholar' may be that he is well versed on the legal maneuverings available to implement anything you may like and claim it constitutional. The fact that he can find a willing participant in the judicial branch to validate his claim in no way eliminates the facts of the case.

It begins with something as simple as suggesting a law requiring "that all Americans vote,"[12] but the list seems endless and the avenues of unconstitutionality expand with every overreach attempted. Whether it is the regular, "If congress won't act, I will"[13], to the public attempt to intimidate the Supreme Court during his State of the Union speech[14], he either has disregarded the first several Articles of the Constitution, or he is blatantly challenging it. What Obama appears to be is a scholar of the constitutionally-claimed legal practices which have served to undermine the authority of the people themselves.

While the product was carefully managed through the campaign process, he could no longer be protected once in office. That's not to say he didn't clearly describe many of the core values incompatible with high office which he holds. It's just that the Praetorian Guard can no longer explain away what he 'meant to say' any longer. Now the issues are just not contextually reported, and everyone seems to just want to make it through the tunnel before the toll must be paid. It became clear the man who fought so hard to be elected President was in fact disinterested with the responsibilities of the office and the oath meant to bind him. The Resident despot would only increase his attacks on the American, and the traditions which we hold dear.

Preparations

> *Nearly all men can stand adversity. But if you want to test a man's character, give him power.*
> *- President Abraham Lincoln*
>
> *It is said that power corrupts, but actually power attracts the corruptible. The sane are usually attracted by other things than power.*
> *- David Brin*

The unbreakable chain of events which would lead to revolution was underway in and around the port city of Norfolk in early 1775. The Whigs were busy recruiting militia nearby, requiring increased supplies for the troops. Alarmed, the British Governor would remove gunpowder as well as evacuate his family to a Royal Navy ship in the harbor. The tensions would expand and escalate until the risks associated with the skirmishes caused the Governor to declare martial law; they threatened the safe passage along the only road in the region between Virginia and North Carolina. There would be a single bridge across the Elizabeth River, which the British ordered fortified in preparation for the expected engagement. In response, the Virginia assembly would order the Culpeper Minutemen to march on the Great Bridge[1]. By December 8, 1775, there would be near 900 in the camp, over 700 "fit for duty". The British had fortified a stockade on the opposite side of the bridge, which included cannon and other significant armament, but fewer troops. The unavoidable collision between the Whig forces and the British forces, now increased with Navy gunners, would explode that night, and provide a short but decisive victory over the Tories. However, the Whigs would again lose control of Norfolk about 3 weeks later. This Battle of the Great Bridge would become an important victory as the young nation would approach its birth.

The Culpeper Militia would soon be disbanded and many of the members would join the Virginia Continental Army as the American Revolution took shape. Many of these same revolutionaries would also find themselves wintered near Philadelphia at a camp named Valley Forge following the 1777 campaign season. But the encampment would be incapable of weathering the winter as over 2500 American troops would die of exposure, malnutrition, starvation and disease[2]. With the arrival of summer, the remaining force would leave Valley Forge and retake Philadelphia. The rest is history, our history. A Captain in the Eleventh Virginia Continental Regiment, a friend to George Washington, a young patriot who would weather the horrendous winter at Valley Forge, was also a Lieutenant in the Culpeper Militia at the Battle of Great Bridge, would later become a member of the Virginia House of Delegates, would lead the fight for ratification of the United States Constitution as a delegate to the Virginia convention, would win a seat in the House of Representatives with the help of Patrick Henry, and served as Secretary of State for John Adams[3].

But it would not be this long resume of service in the Executive, or the Legislative which would enshrine his name in the history of this great country. By 1835, John Marshall would be the longest serving Chief Justice of the Supreme Court. So effective was he at steering the court, he would find himself on the side of dissent only eight times in over those three and a half decades on the bench. But it would be the first important case of his tenure which would set the tone of his court, and start the slow, but inevitable, decline of the Judicial over the next two hundred years.

It was before he would put on his judges cloak when the table would be set. One of Marshall's final duties as Secretary of State would be to deliver the commissions to the hastily approved Federal judges and justices which John Adams had appointed on his last day in office and the Senate had approved en masse. Marshall would not complete the deliveries, and assumed his successor would. But the new President, Thomas Jefferson had other ideas. He ordered the remaining appointments to not be delivered, as one of the key objectives of the Jefferson administration was to be the removal and replacement of the Judiciary Act of 1801. William Marbury, one of those affected by this reversal, would fight for his commission in court. An American would rightly ask whether Marshall should have even been party to the review, given it was his oversight which led to the impasse. A recusal would not have been questioned. But he did not, and the case hinged upon a conflict of laws which each side would claim as their basis. In the opinion it would be Marshall who led the 4-0 decision upholding the right of Marbury to his commission, but decided that the court did not have the authority to force the new Secretary of State to deliver that commission. In effect, Marbury would find defeat, but his case would give the court a victory. In the decision, Marshall famously declared the doctrine of Judicial Review, claiming the right of the court to "say what the law is."[4] The result was the first time the Supreme Court would declare a law unconstitutional.

Jefferson would disagree with the outcome with an ominous and prescient declaration, "You seem to consider the judges as the ultimate arbiters of all constitutional questions; a very dangerous doctrine indeed, and one which would place us under the despotism of an oligarchy."[5] He understood this would result in instability injected into the carefully crafted constitutional balance. The opening for "corruptions of time and party"[6] would be entombed and the results would slowly eat away at the Republic until one day the court would claim authority over how the individual would choose to live. But along the way it would also provide the opportunity for some of the worst judgements which history cannot erase.

The Supreme Court had been a battleground for racial rights throughout our history, but the court has not proven a consistent champion for justice. It would be the Dred Scott which would be called the "Supreme Court's greatest self-inflicted wound,"[7] and "universally condemned as [it's] worst decision."[8] Scott would be declared to not have standing with the court on the basis that a slave, or descendent of a slave, could not be considered a citizen. And in addition, it found that the Missouri Compromise, which effectively made slavery illegal in the northern territories, to be unconstitutional on the basis that the law deprived the citizen from their own property. This would be only the second time for such a finding (first being Marbury.) While this case was an attempt by the court to manage the developing unrest in the country regarding slavery, it would also demonstrate the effect of inter-branch collusion as the event would unfold during a presidential transfer of power. The President-elect James Buchanan would attempt to manage the optics as best he could to have the 'issue' settled prior to inauguration. That would not be the case, as the ruling would be produced two days afterward, but it was a clear example of the increasingly inappropriate political pressure which was encroaching into the Judicial. Of course the issue would not be resolved, as the Civil War was just over the horizon.

Even though it would take a Civil War to finally end the institution of slavery in the United States, the rights of a black man as a citizen would not be resolved. The Civil War Amendments to the Constitution would create the legal authority for eliminating the impediments, but the society was still infiltrated by those who would not accept the black man as their equal. It would be 30 years later when the next 'landmark case' would strike another blow to human rights.

"Separate but equal" would describe the system of segregation which was in place in various parts of the country. Using a tactic of creating a conflict in order to generate standing for a court case, Homer Plessy purchased a first class ticket for a train ride in Louisiana, and proceeded to sit in the "whites only" car. Our legal system is based on the English system of Common Law, where the concept of precedent holds sway as what was once legal in years past would suddenly be overturned, or the opposite might occur. It's inconceivable that every possible conflict could be foreseen at the time a given law is enacted; there would need to be a method to adjust the law for the environment it is applied to. And this is why the Constitution provided the framework of the federal government and defined the strict limits to the extent of that authority. No clearer statement of that limitation can be made than the 10th Amendment itself.

The powers not delegated to the United States by the Constitution, nor prohibited by it to the States, are reserved to the States respectively, or to the people.

But it's along this path of precedence which the legal profession plays its game. By creating a series of minor movements through case precedent, a major shift in governance can be achieved. It appears Plessy was one such attempt, but it would not turn out favorably for the plaintiff. Plessy who did not 'appear black' needed to previously inform the railroad company of his intentions in order to precipitate the desired response. After the predicted and obviously prearranged confrontation, he was arrested by a detective, and removed from the train. The court's decision was to uphold the "separate but equal accommodations" position of the railroad company. Not only did this case prove a failure for Plessy, but the Plessy v. Ferguson decision would provide the legal foundation for decades of Jim Crow, as well as the re-segregation of Washington D.C. itself during the Wilson administration[9].

It was almost 60 years later before the court would correct this inexcusable mistake. Many people in the country are true believers in the unquestioned wisdom of the Supreme Court. This type of reverence should not be afforded to any group of people as they are only human themselves. But the unaware, uneducated or just ideological will continue to claim this panel holds the wisdom necessary to control the will of Man. While the court would regularly become the instrument of the popular throughout its brief history, often making horrendously bad decisions as those just reviewed, it would also find opportunities to correct the past evils.

The NAACP would create the events necessary to generate the appropriate legal foundations for the betterment of entire classes of unrepresented citizens. Oliver Brown was one of many original litigants in the class action case, and was the named plaintiff taking on the Board of Education of the city of Topeka, Kansas, chosen in order to put a man's name at the focus of the case in order to maximize impact. The outcome of the case was the overturning of Plessy v. Ferguson, stating "the doctrine of 'separate but equal' has no place [in this country]."[10] The NAACP's chief counsel would himself become an Associate Justice of the Supreme Court, Thurgood Marshall. But it wouldn't be only racial matters the court would find itself meddling in. The court would become a tool for the Administration during the Great Depression as well.

It would be FDR who would take on the federal system most aggressively by using the Judicial. But the Judicial wouldn't appear to be willing cohorts. During his first term, the Supreme Court would strike down several New Deal measures as unconstitutional. But as a true statist, FDR believed he held the keys to the solution for the country's woes. There would be only a government solution, and the Supreme Court was in his way. Understanding the court is a numbers game, needing more on your side than the other; FDR's not-so-sly approach would be to add enough sympathetic judges to the court to overwhelm his detractors. The Judicial Reform Act of 1937 was his attempt to allow him to add up to six additional justices for those who had reached the age of 70 years and 6 months, but refused to retire. He apparently thought old justices were a liability. The bill would never pass, but Supreme Court justice Van Devanter would finally retire, ushering in the first of 9 justices FDR would appoint. His first appointee would be Hugo Black, who once would represent the Ku Klux Klan[11], and who would become very influential in the more politically-friendly court.

It would be a stunning loss of American freedom, but FDR needed more power. The pesky Constitution continued to get in the way. The administration needed a test case to provide justification for the next round of big government solutions planned. Claiming authority over agricultural production with the 1938  Agriculture Adjustment Act, based on its constitutional authority over interstate commerce, the government limited the amount of wheat a farmer could sell. Roscoe Filburn, an Ohio farmer, would grow more than his allotted amount, keeping the excess for himself, only selling the legal limit allowed. But that didn't matter to the government, who fined him $117.11 in 1941. Filburn's position was that he didn't sell his wheat; therefore he had no effect on interstate commerce. But now with an administration-friendly court, the games of absurdity would begin to find their way into the lives of Americans. The court would find in the case of Wickard v. Filburn, the farmer in fact did violate the interstate commerce clause, not by selling goods across state lines, but by not needing to reduce his own legal sales in order to feed his own animals[12]. Not only could your activity be controlled by Big Brother, but now your inactivity as well. This precedent would now allow the attack of virtually any private enterprise imaginable, should they become the target of the leviathan.

In 2012, just in time for the upcoming election, the most aggressive attack on the liberty of the American would be on trial. Two years earlier, a cabal of progressives was able to pass the Affordable Care Act commonly called Obamacare, literally under the cover of darkness. This would be the crown jewel of the State, should it hold up in court. A virtual takeover of one sixth of the country's economy, it was a power grab like nothing in American history. The Legislature wouldn't even let anyone read this new law. The Resident became famous for the "If you like your doctor, you can keep your doctor" lie, as well as the "every family will save $2500" deceit. In the spirit of 'follow the money', it would be interesting for an investigative journalist to track the personal fortunes of the key players involved with the greatest heist in history. But an American knew that these scoundrels were part of society, and there was still some faith in the system to right the wrongs, even if they were by the Resident, and not accidental.

While the entire notion of the Federal government taking over the most personal of all enterprises in America turns an American's stomach, the entire plan, thousands of pages long, read by virtually no one, especially any of those who voted on it, would need to be challenged in the same suspect judicial system the State seemed to control. A key element in Obamacare is called the 'individual mandate', requiring every living soul to pay in to this new 'insurance' program. Now the radicals, malcontents, and all-around leaches on society would be firmly in the progressive camp since their objective is always to have someone cover more of their existence for them. But this amounted to a 'breath tax'. If you were breathing, you would be taxed for it. As with any Marxist program, only the productive in society would actually pay, this was just another method to further separate Americans from their income. The State of Florida would agree with the American view, and sue the U.S. Department of Health and Human Services. As an American would expect, a clear-minded judge found for the plaintiff. But of course, this legal game must be played, and payed. The Eleventh Court of Appeals would also find for the plaintiff. That's strike two against the leviathan. But it would go to the Supreme Court, where more and more political pressure has been found to affect the results.

The results would prove disappointing to freedom-loving Americans, to say the least. The Chief Justice of the Supreme Court clearly found his way into uncharted territory in order to justify this law. It required him to rewrite the law in order to provide justification, claiming where the law used the word
'penalty', it should really be considered a tax, much in the same way the Roosevelt administration argued the Constitutionality of the Social Security Program. But at least social security was based on income earned in a way that could find some arguable justification in the Constitution. The ACA however, could not be considered a tax since it was applied to those who didn't even have income. It's a legal dance on a head of a pin which will forever taint this jurist's credibility and legacy.

The Real Campaign

> "Pick the target, freeze it, personalize it, and polarize it."
> – Saul Alinsky, Rule 13[1]

When the Resident proclaimed that he would transform the United States of America, few appeared to take notice. Most just felt the Hope and Change promised would mean improvement. Much like Obama's blank canvas which allowed the masses to project on to him the candidate they thought he was, so too would be the objectives of his rhetoric. But he said what he meant; he planned to transform our country. In order to do that he needed to undermine the very foundation of our society, and it's quite possible he had accomplished just that in only his first term. His assaults would not be surgical strikes, but mass movements aimed at virtually every American institution.

Assault on Country

> "Show me how to get rid of the unlimited capacity of human beings to make themselves believe that they're somehow right and justified in stealing from somebody, or hurting somebody."
> - Sergeant Joe Friday (Jack Webb)[2]

> "Don't break things upon the name of progress or crack a placard stick over somebody's head to help him see the light. Be careful of his rights, because your property, and your person, and your rights aren't any better than his. And next time you might be the one to get it. We remember a man who killed six million people and called it social improvement."
> - Officer Bill Gannon (Harry Morgan)[3]

Radio host and author Michael Savage consistently identifies that a country is defined by its borders, language, and culture[4]. Language has been the target of the progressives for decades now, with the multicultural obsession justifying multilingual education. As a product of the Great Society era, the Bilingual Education Act of 1968 would institute federal requirements and funding support for multilingual education. The intent was claimed to be, as is many a progressive effort, noble. There is an emotional appeal to the development of children which garners support. But as with every effort to apply governmental support to a cultural issue, the results do not seem to meet the objectives. By the time No Child Left Behind was created in 2002, the system of educating many non-English speaking people would be insufficient to meet the now challenging standards implemented by the new program. However, the underlying problem is never addressed. An American becomes quizzical when confronted with a program which is aimed at educating children in their own language in an attempt to help them not fall behind their peers. What is missing is what is meant by 'peers'. If the child is advanced through the system never learning functional English language skills, they will be functionally crippled, and find themselves not only lagging these 'peers', but unable to even compete with them. It could be questioned whether the intent was actually to educate the children, or to successfully transition them from grade to grade, as that would be how the system's success would be measured. But there is a more sinister effect from this agenda, breathtakingly articulated by former Democratic Governor of Colorado, Richard Lamm.

At a Washington, D.C. overpopulation conference in October, 2003, Victor Davis Hanson had just finished a talk about his latest book, Mexifornia, where he exposed California's immigration problem, and how it would result in the destruction of the American Dream. But it would be Lamm, who followed and would leave the audience in silence. He set out an eight step plan to destroy America[5]:

1) *"Turn America into a bilingual or multi-lingual and bicultural county. History shows that no nation can survive the tension, conflict, and antagonism of two or more competing languages and cultures.*
2) *"Invent 'multiculturalism' and encourage immigrants to maintain their culture. Make it an article of belief that all cultures are equal; that there are 'no' cultural differences. Make it an article of faith that the black and Hispanic dropout rates are due solely to prejudice and discrimination by the majority.*
3) *"Make the United States a 'Hispanic Quebec'...celebrate diversity rather than unity.*

4) *"Make our fastest growing demographic group the least educated. [And] add a second underclass, unassimilated, undereducated, and antagonistic to our population. [And] have this underclass have a 50% dropout rate from high school.*
5) *"Get big foundations and businesses to give these efforts lots of money. I would invest in ethnic identity, and would establish the cult of 'Victimology'. I would get all minorities to think that their lack of success was/is the fault of the majority. I would start a grievance industry blaming all minority failure on the majority platform.*
6) *"Include dual citizenship and promote divided loyalties...Balkanize America...*
7) *"Make it taboo to talk about anything against the cult of 'diversity'.*
8) *Ban Victor Davis Hanson's book 'Mexifornia.' ... It exposes the plan to destroy America."*

When he finished, there was no applause. The crowd was stunned, for they realized they were witness to the plan.[6]

As Sowell describes, there is no merit to the racialist claims that the majority groups are responsible for the multicultural victim[7]. He provides chapter and verse toward a more rational perspective on how these issues are not unique to the United States, and that it is the United States which has developed the most effective civil society that enables the minorities to raise themselves into whatever majority they wish. But there is a large group reaping the financial benefits of maintaining this illusion.

While this had been in play for decades, it was not having the immediate effect needed by the Obama Administration; they needed to turn up the heat. It would be the sovereignty of the country which would be undermined. The approach would be to overwhelm the system, while at the same time restricting the country from defending itself until the problem had grown to such scale as to become effectively irreversible. Champions of socialism, Richard Cloward, and Francis Fox Piven were 1960's radicals who developed a strategy which was to wipe out poverty by providing a guaranteed income through "outright redistribution of income."[8] Regardless of "wrong-headed" academic nonsense, the effect would be to overwhelm the system and induce structural failure.

Cloward and Piven happened to both teach at Columbia during the same years Barack would attend. If he didn't know them, he seemed to absorb their principles, but this ideological methodology also aligns well with Alinsky approaches as well. In fact, it would be this same couple, married at this time, which would apply their community organizing skills to motor-voter programs, ultimately resulting in the Motor Voter Act of 1993. But even though automatic registration of all drivers' license recipients, citizen or not, would provide a framework for possible election fraud, its results appear to not have generated enough voters to tip the scales. What were needed would be more residents. The administration's outright assault on the border security of the United States would clearly be a suggestive approach to supply the needed population.

The Obama Administration's plan to reduce the immigration problem appeared to be eliminating the 'illegal' in alien. And that would be by legalizing them. Janet Napolitano would present the standard argument to the community of supporters which is echoed against virtually any challenge to the administration's plan for success. The justification for the administration's approach would be the fact that "we will never have fully effective law enforcement or national security as long as so many millions remain in the shadows…these immigrants [will] become full-paying taxpayers."[9] It continues to amaze Americans that if it's in their agenda, that even a hint of success justifies the sacrifice of national priorities, while an attempted strategy which doesn't support their agenda must provide 100% success. She would claim that providing legalized status of some sort to the 12 million illegal aliens in the country would somehow enhance national security, and protect American workers. The progressive mind is a dangerous thing; a wasteland to explore. But doubling down on the previous administration's look-the-other-way attitude would be the approach on the southern border.

Drawing support from the usual cast of characters, they would project an air of competency. It was of course a charade as is usually the case with progressive programs. By the end of 2012, if you can base effectiveness on the number of deportations from the interior, it had been showing significant reductions leading up to this point. "ICE is arresting and removing noticeably fewer illegal aliens from the interior than was the case five years ago," reported by Jessica Vaughan for the Center for Immigration Studies[10]. The most notable and consistent evidence for manipulation of numbers would be uncovered, as the administration would claim record breaking arrests, only to be caught in a statistical 'fabrication'. Over half of the arrests would be at the border by the border guards. Given the level of attention paid by the administration regarding their efforts in this area, an American could only assume this was part of a diligent effort to be ineffective in their responsibilities or it represents a lack of seriousness toward the security of the country that became a consistent theme within the administration.

Assault on Legislature

> *A government big enough to give you everything you want is a government big enough to take from you everything you have.*
> *- President Gerald Ford*

If there was to be hope that the government would move back toward its founding principles, or at least reduce the acceleration toward tyranny, the American would be disappointed. An early message sent to the Legislative would arrive on March 11, 2009, when the Resident would respond to the massive Omnibus Appropriations Act with a signing statement. Signing statements have been used since President James Monroe first applied this mechanism to voice the Executives concerns over conflicts produced over incongruent military rank issues created by Congress in 1822. They had been fairly rare, only 75 in total by 1980. But starting with the President Reagan, there would be hundreds produced.

As a candidate, and constitutional scholar of course, Obama would clearly identify the signing statement as an extra-constitutional process which he would not engage in. He would state, *"We aren't going to use signing statements as a way to end run around Congress."*[11] But now that he was no longer a candidate, he would no longer need to feign constitutional respect, and his 2009 Omnibus signing statement would clearly claim the superiority of his Executive over the Legislative.

The statement would declare that in the area of foreign affairs, he would not accept Congressional language "limiting [his] ability to negotiate and enter into agreements with foreign nations."[12] While negotiation would clearly be within the Executive's authority and responsibility, committing the country to agreements between foreign nations is also called a treaty, which is clearly not within the Executive's constitutional powers, but rather must be agreed to by the Senate. Because of the diminishment of the state's role in the federal government since the 17th amendment, this position had become less and less a point of contention between branches, but it would be the statement's challenge to the Legislative's "Power of the Purse" which would provide a more troubling position.

The Omnibus bill limited funds in support of "the use of the Armed Forces of the United Nations peacekeeping missions under the command or operational control of a foreign national unless my military advisors have recommended to me that such involvement is in the national interest of the United States."[13] The statement rejected legislative authority over anything he deemed interfering with his duties as Commander-In-Chief, which would be defined to his liking. Regardless of his petulant attitude regarding any constraints he would disagree with, the Supreme Court had consistently rejected the signing statement as having any weight relative to Legislative authority. But of course a constitutional scholar would understand this.

In addition to the U.N. support, constraints would be required through language requiring the coordination of expenditures with relevant congressional committees. Again, the Executive rejected this declaration of fiduciary responsibility, claiming congress has no role in the establishment of funding guidelines associated with implementing security improvements, declaring "that such requests [are] nonbinding."[14] This perspective that as long as we have checks in our checkbook, we will have money in the bank was a reflection of his own personal financial discipline and would result in unconstrained expenditures which would continue to grow and become a very heavy chain around the neck of the country.

Assault on International Credibility

> *We must adjust to changing times and still hold to unchanging principles.*
> *- President Jimmy Carter*

The Resident would proclaim that he would bring a "new dawn of American leadership."[15] And it was the worst fears of his detractors which would become reality. Never before had the country had its primary representative ignorant of statesmanship, if not rejecting of its core values. A relentless march toward destroying the hegemony of not only the United States, but of western civilization, would become a guiding principle of the new administration. Whether it was actually a surprise to the sycophants or not, results of calm reflection should easily separate those Americans who were swept up in the excitement of the mob and those who are themselves True Believers.

Operation Iraqi Freedom would become one of his core campaign issues, as he would be a consistent detractor. He would claim it "a misguided invasion of a Muslim country that sparks insurgencies, ties down our military, busts our budgets, increases the pool of terrorist recruits, alienates America, gives democracy a bad name, and prompts the American people to question our engagement in the world."[16] Americans aware of the events surrounding the region at the time would interpret this as typical political posturing, attempting to divide the voting public through carefully developed positions. But this was not a politician trying to energize his base and make others question their own positions. This was how he actually viewed the events. His lens would apparently shield him from the complexities and challenges of actual international engagements.

He would ignore the decade of hostilities which preceded it, the fact that the rules of engagement were part of the problem, which he would intentionally further incapacitate the military with, and that it was the Resident which would be the single most effective detractor of his own country. It would be a surprise to the country when they realized this 'intellectual' was really little more than a charlatan. But worse, he appeared incapable of self-evaluation or adjusting strategy, unless his objectives weren't for the improvement of the country which elected him. And it would be his own twisted values which he projected on to the American and the country.

Whether it was his deep belief that America was the cause of international conflict, his acceptance that international bodies should have authority over this sovereign country, his unmovable support for the baby killing enterprise, his perception that the individual is put on this Earth to serve the elites who found their way into power, he would claim to the world that these were our values and that he and he alone would decide our course of action. While apparently only providing moral support for other like-minded autocrats, he was also incapable of representing the light on the hill which the citizens of every other country look up to. His own belief that America does not deserve its position in the world would be reflected through his consistent diminishment of the country he fought to be elected leader.

Apology tours abounded. As a candidate, he would apologize to over three billion people for the country he disliked. But as Resident, he would begin with his purposefully damaging rhetoric so consistent most have stopped considering it. "My job to the Muslim world is to communicate that the Americans are not your enemy."[17] What? Only the left even thinks this way. This is equivalent to Americans saying during a discussion on drug trafficking across the border, "We are not at war with Mexicans." His natural tendency to make broad assignments to groups who happen to share the same identity he assigns them would be pathetic, if it didn't result in serious damage to progress. His foreign speeches were absurd in their context, but damaging to the country nonetheless. His complete disregard for his own country was on display one day in Trinidad, where he "sat through a fifty-minute anti-American harangue by Nicaraguan president Daniel Ortega, who condemned the United States for a century of what he described as imperialistic aggression."[18] Obama would only state that he was "grateful that President Ortega did not blame me."[19] He was incapable of filling the seat at 1600 Pennsylvania Avenue. It's unclear who seemed more embarrassed for their relationship, Obama or our country.

Assault on Energy

> *A decent and manly examination of the acts of the Government should be not only tolerated, but encourage.*
> *- President William Henry Harrison*

As is the case with most of his un-American positions, the Resident was clear about the future of energy for his country. The True Believer, unwavering to the laws of physics, decided he and his 'scientists' could produce a 'clean energy' solution through government regulation. As a candidate, he would proudly state, *"So if somebody wants to build a coal-powered plant, they can. It's just that it will bankrupt them because they're going to be charged a huge sum for all that greenhouse gas that's being emitted."*[20] How nice for those who have to pay their own electric bills. But this was more complicated as energy would be the focus of many objectives for this new administration. He would build a need based on his own circular reasoning resulting in vast amounts of 'wealth transfer' to those who helped him along the way. And it was justified based on the hocus pocus, nuevo-alchemist movement now masquerading as champions for the environment in battle with something they invented called 'Climate Change'.

While strangulation through regulation was a powerful tool to inflict damage on adversaries, it really was just part of the overall plan to increase the extortion from the richest country on the planet. His Secretary of State, Hillary Clinton and her husband had developed a fairly sophisticated money laundering scheme whereby international 'benefactors' would benefit from United States' funding sources which she could control. Dinesh D'Souza's book, *Stealing America,* outlines the troubling result of placing easily corruptible individuals in positons of power[21]. An American would find it laughable that his own Secretary of State, understanding he was keeping his enemies closer, would be able to keep the Resident unaware of these dealings. The only way that could occur is if she was not submitting required ethics documentation, which he would be responsible for reviewing. The position of ignorance being portrayed pegs the absurdity meter. That is unless he had an even bigger prize in his sights. And while his Secretary of State has become wealthy at the expense of her country, the Resident's plans would make hers insignificant. In addition, he wouldn't have to do it. He would have the government do it for him.

The scam of the century would be spear-headed by a program called Cap and Trade. Based on junk science claiming carbon dioxide poisoning of the planet by the evil first world countries, this effort primarily was a mechanism to steal more money from the producers in the country. In addition, it was to mandate 20% of energy had to come from 'renewable sources', which justified the need for additional billions in subsides and research necessary to buy off supporters. A review of the Constitution would uncover no authority for such a fleecing, but for the time-being it unsurprisingly found enough votes to pass the House. Even though the scam did not get its day in the Senate, the administration would be undeterred. The trail of wealth transfer would not be easy to cover as the EPA would implement a similar approach inside the United States with their Cap and Trade 'environmental policy', imposing arbitrary limits and unconstitutional rules through the virtually unbounded and no-less constitutionally-challenged 1990 Clean Air Act[22]. Should you violate these rules, penalties are automatically assessed. Conveniently, they even offer a 'Market-based Mechanism' of 'allowance' trading, providing an opportunity for one geographic area to pay another to reach some sort of balance. It is amazing that a group can decide for itself what to define as a legal limit, performs investigations, assesses alleged violators, represents America as Judge and Jury, imposes and collects fines, all without any public representation. How reminiscent of good old King George.

The EPA is an administration tool for intimidation and control over the productive power within this country. While it could've been an advisory group which could develop and justify legislation within the Federal Government's authority maintaining at least some appearance of

American values, it has instead turned into a very strong internal police force of enforcers masquerading as an environmental watchdog.

Assault on Military

> *National honor is a national property of the highest value.*
> *- President James Monroe*

The strength of the United States military is not guarded by these integrity-challenged elected officials. It's inside the hearts and minds of the American service member. To elected officials, it's believed to be measured relative to some budgetary expense level. As Gus Grissom proclaimed in The Right Stuff, it's true that with "no bucks, no Buck Rogers"[23], but the defense department struggles with the continuous evolution of imposing business practice changes in the hopes of correcting out-of-control expenditures. In effect, this is just the somewhat honest attempt to get the most out of a system designed to funnel money to the desired congressional districts.

It was during 1990's that the demise of the military would begin. The government, once responsible for the specifications of needed equipment, would relinquish its authority to the contractors who 'knew better' what was needed. It was a time where exorbitant costs such as a $700 hammer, or $600 toilet seat were plastered across the media. It was a clever media campaign which yielded *trillions* of dollars in contracts over the following decades. It also produced an additional untouchable budget line, as the large electoral base supported by this process would ensure the 'too big to fail' mentality would provide consistent support. If there is anything the Resident actually does understand, it's the power of the control of the money supply. While spending bills technically begin in the House of Representatives, he has also demonstrated that it is absolutely unnecessary for that to occur if he wants to spend it. He would attack the budget knowing that the military would pay the price before the Legislature would allow the major recipients of contracts to take the hit, who in turn would provide the financial support for reelection campaigns.

As the token American in the Cabinet, Bob Gates was a quintessential government executive. A career CIA employee, he would rise to be selected as George H.W. Bush's Director of that Agency. Called upon by the next Bush, he would be asked to direct the Department of Defense following Donald Rumsfeld. When the Resident moved in, he would take advantage of the patriot and ask him to remain as Secretary of Defense. In 2011, enormous pressure was applied to the Secretary to uncover real savings across the department's budget. Dutifully to the end, Gates would uncover $400 billion while the military was struggling to keep up with the administrations expenditure goals. It was a 'head-fake' as the Resident doubled down and announced that twice the amount would be required[24]. The result would be not only the crippling of complicated acquisition programs, but the expected attack on the service members themselves, eliminating over 100,000 members of the military, already stretched thin.

Assault on Citizens

> *The most terrifying words in the English language are: I'm from the government and I'm here to help.*
> *- President Ronald Reagan*

The tax code has long been a means to apply pressure directly to sectors of the economy and to provide indirect compensation or funds to those in favor or not. Covering thousands of pages, no one understands the entirety. Even a call to the IRS for support in clarifying a question leaves the caller responsible for the answer. While it has generated its own economy of sorts, producing entire professions to support public compliance, under the Resident it has been transformed into a de facto private enforcement arm of the State. He was going to go after the citizen for his own agenda.

True to form, the Resident's viewpoint was not hidden or even suppressed. He clearly was going to use the tax code to steal from one person in order to pay for another. Joe Wurzelbacher (Joe the Plumber) became a household name just before the 2008 election by confronting candidate Obama, "I'm getting ready to buy a company that makes

$250,000 to $280,000 a year. Your new tax plan's going to tax me more, isn't it?" Obama then responded unapologetically, "I think when you spread the wealth around, it's good for everybody."[25] But that wouldn't be enough. Clearly aware of the failure of the ideological approach to dealing with real problems, the administration would still refuse to deviate, and the tools of the Internal Revenue Service were applied to his detractors.

Exploding into existence during George W. Bush's last term due to his government-based solution to the financial scare of 2008, Americans had finally had enough and Taxed Enough Already (TEA) Party groups were formed. Where the deviation from fiscal responsibility and government restraint on the part of the Bush administration was partly the cause for the weakening of the base of the Republican Party, it would be the next administration that would claim the Tea Party actually represented the Republican Party as a means to detract and politicize the current Resident's un-American approach to all things. But with an upcoming election, that would not be enough. They must be silenced. And it would be more than just Tea Party related groups; the target list would be expanded to include anything that possibly represented American values. It wasn't the increased threat and follow-thru of audits of targeted conservative groups, but also the actual approvals of 501(C)(4) groups that would seem to be in opposition to the statist agenda. It would be another opportunity for Congress to demonstrate their impotence to the administration's playbook as well. They would draft very harshly worded letters to the IRS, 'We were really mad before, but now we're very, very mad.' The complete lack of accountability to the people would be on full-display as the IRS Commissioner, Douglas H. Shulman, decried that they "pride [themselves] on being a non-political, non-partisan organization."[26] That is unless you had criteria to single out organizations which are "Tea Party organizations applying for IRC § 501(c)(3) or IRC § 501(c)(4) status," expanded to include anything with "Tea Party," "Patriots," "9/12 Project," organizations concerned with "government spending, government debt or taxes," etc.[27]

If that wasn't enough, the IRS would violate the Hatch act, providing confidential information to liberal 'hit-squad' support groups, like providing an organization's donor list to the Human Rights Campaign as a tool to undermine the Republican Candidate, Mitt Romney, as he donated to the National Organization for Marriage[28]. While it is a dangerous sign that supporting something as traditional as marriage has been politicized to such a level where the donation to a supportive organizational is viewed more controversially than the fact that the state police had provided it, the continued demonstration of the impotence of the congressional leadership illustrated the disregard for the balance of power inherent in a constitutional republic.

Assault on Residents

> *Our most dangerous tendency is to expect too much from government, and at the same time do for it too little.*
> *- President Warren G. Harding*

It has been said that the fourth branch of the government is the administration, the leviathan with hundreds of departments and agencies, which for all intents and purposes is unanswerable to the citizens of the country. The ever-encroaching arm of government intervention has found its way into every corner of the individual's life through the power of federal rules and regulations. In 2011, there would be an astounding 169,301 pages of federal regulations, growing over 11,000 pages in just three years [29]. In 2010, it would cost the federal government over $55 billion to fund and enforce these regulations[30]. But it would be the cost to the people that is the most outrageous. It was estimated in 2008 that the compliance cost was 'astronomical' at $1.75 *trillion*, or about 12% of the GDP[31]. That was more than the total of all pre-tax profits of almost $1.5 trillion. By 2013 this compliance cost had risen to over $2 trillion[32]. That is roughly half of the total federal budget. The cost of government is now almost $6 trillion ($4 trillion direct appropriations + $2 trillion regulation.)

In 2011, Congress passed a total of 81 bills into law, but the leviathan had released over 3800 regulations[33]. Along with the regulations would be the enforcement posse which each department would now decide they must maintain. It seems absolutely constitutional for the law enforcement agency, the Department of Justice, to have law enforcement capabilities. But as identified by D'Souza, it seems extra-constitutional to have SWAT teams within the Department of Agriculture, the Office of Personnel Management, the State Department, the Department of Education, the Department of Energy, the U.S. Fish and Wildlife Service, and more[34]. The police state is already here.

In 2012, this 'straightjacket' of regulation was at the cost of an estimated 2 million jobs in the energy sector alone. Overall the number of Americans "not in the civilian labor force" would rise to a record 88,921,000[35]. It would continue to climb, as the administration would continue to claim reductions in unemployment, but the media would carefully obfuscate for the State. While the Chamber of Commerce is clearly in the tank with the State, it would provide an estimate of the household share of the burden in 2008. It's estimated that while the cost in jobs was significant, the actual cost to American households was $15,586[36]. And to reemphasize, that is for each household. That had obviously risen in the three years since, as the regulatory cost had risen over 12%. And in a 2013 paper by John W. Dawson and John J. Seater, "*Federal Regulation and Aggregate Economic Growth*", they found if the level of regulation had remained at the 1949 level, the average household income in 2005 would have risen to an astounding $27,500 per month, and the current GDP of approximately $17 trillion, would in fact be almost $55 trillion[37]. The State is strangling the golden goose.

By 2012, it appeared the Obama Administration had accomplished virtually nothing in regards to the reforms promised in 2008. In fact, it was worse than business-as-usual, as the Orwellian Cass Sunstein was brought in as the 'Regulation Czar', famous for his 'Nudge' theory which basically calls for the State to make better personal decisions for the individuals as they seem to make poor ones themselves. What could be more personal than the choice of organ donations, where he advocated the concept of "presumed consent"[38], which would require an individual to explicitly claim their desire NOT to donate? But the State's public relations apparatus would be a willing participant to the ruse by avoiding these subjects all-together.

The Judicial was also under assault through out-of-control regulations. As described in Blackwell and Klukowski's *The Blueprint*, the result is needed expansion of the court system[39]. Expansion is needed in order to handle the steadily increasing caseloads. At the same time, Chief Justice John Roberts agrees, but doesn't lobby for increased funding needed to support the expansion. It's like trying to understand a Federal Reserve chairman statement to congress at times. But the reality is that most noted authors on the subject are lawyers themselves. They fall into the old 'to a hammer, every problem is a nail' solution. They view solutions through the use of more court cases. It should be considered that this is a result of the out-of-control government and it this government which needs to be reduced (as well as the number of lawyers.)

Assault on the Economy

> *Whoever controls the volume of money in any country is absolute master of all industry and commerce.*
> *- President James Garfield*

Usually a top issue of every presidential campaign, the economy would not be an exception during the 2012 election season. The country was still looking for improvement, and there was a global recession as well. While the administration would continue to dissemble the state of the union to distract from their performance, it would be the actual pocketbook affects which should appeal to the voter at large. But things weren't getting better; they had been steadily getting worse. Over the previous 4 years, the ratio between the Census Bureau's determination of the poverty line for a family of four with 2 kids, and the Social Security Administration record of median income for each year continued to decrease, indicating the regression of the wage earner in America. In addition to personal income, the government was sliding further and further into debt.

The Progressive is infatuated with Keynesian Economics, but that is hardly a surprise as it most closely aligns with the socialistic approach to society's problems. Fundamentally Keynes believed that a combination of low interest rates and government investment would drive an expansionary economy in times of financial crisis by inducing additional investment. While it really has never worked, the false claim would be that this was the approach that pulled the country, and the world, out of the Great Depression. Americans find unending entertainment in the revisionist approach ideologues attempt to apply in order to justify their thievery. That is until it has real effects. Accepting that the New Deal was successful at one thing, and that was instituting the State as the provider for the country, the continual manufacturing of demand in order to justify supply served only to extend the damaging effects of the depression. It's said that during the 1930's, FDR would take great care with the expenditures which he was directing, even though he more than doubled the previous decade's spending during that decade. As a result the national debt was approximately 40% of the gross national product, and the country was still in trouble. It would be World War II which finally kicked out the aimless spend-thrift nature of the government and created some needed course correction. The country would emerge without the would-be king and return the economy to the people. And it flourished. But it would only be a matter of time before Progressives would find their way back into the Executive.

A review of the spending habits of the federal government would highlight that until recently, the government growth would not change substantially except as a result of some national emergency. It's true that the spending levels would usually decrease appreciably post-crisis, but it would never retreat to its former level. And the biggest crises a nation would endure would be war (see Figure 2).

Scanning the spending charts over the life of this country would lead an American to realize that the growth of government might be directly correlated to wars. Our first war, the War of 1812, resulted in a spending level over twice that of predecessor years.

The next, the Mexican American War would see no decrease as it would approximately triple. The spending after the Civil War would quadruple to support reconstruction activities. Even the short-lived Spanish American War would see a modest post-war increase in the budget. It would triple after World War I, as well as after World War II. But what

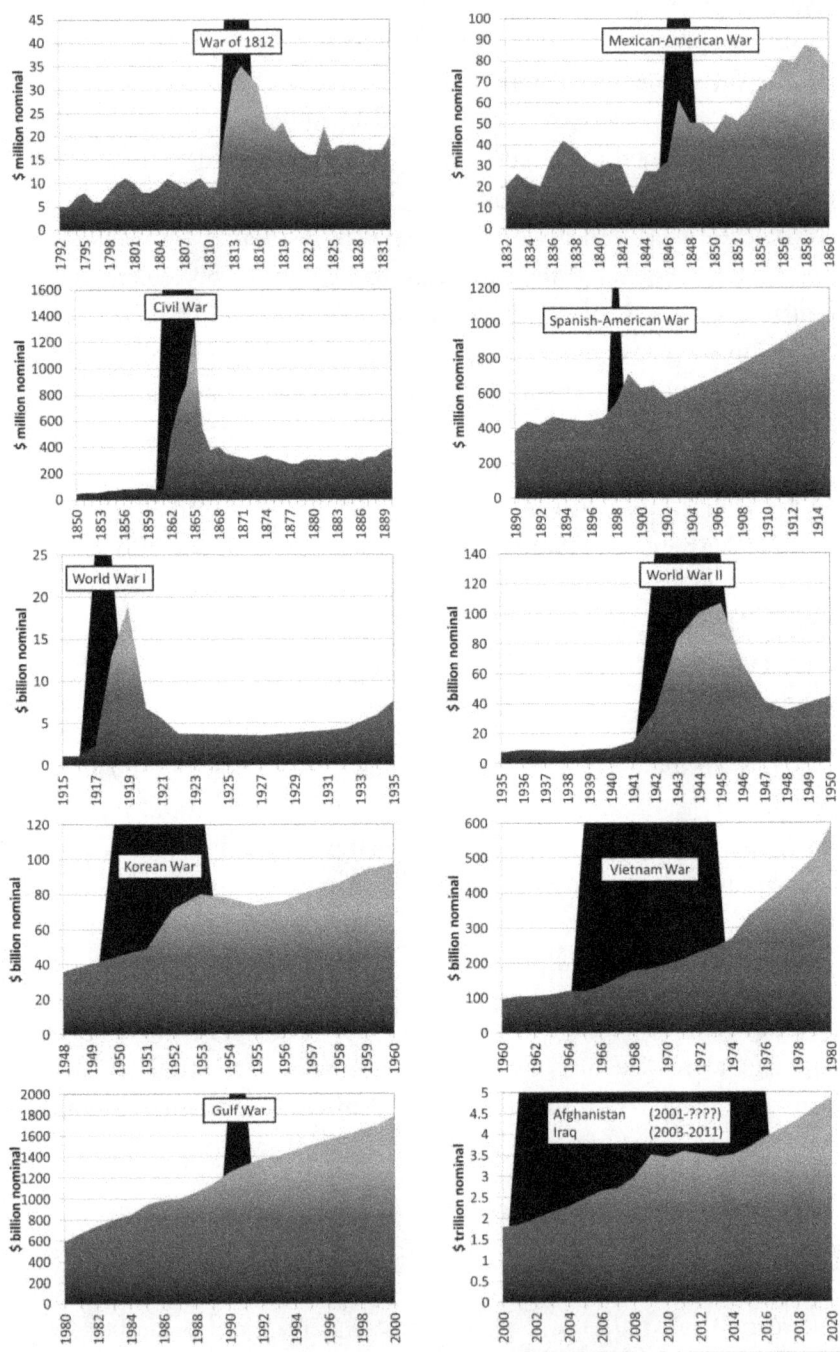

Figure 2: Total Federal Spending[40]

is clear from the figure is that the government wouldn't even make an effort to return to pre-war spending levels for every war after World War II. The recipe was unambiguous: increasing crisis begets increasing budgets. And an actual declared war would not even be required from this point on, or even a shooting war!

While Kennedy may have laid the foundation for the U.S. involvement in Southeast Asia, LBJ would clumsily attempt to wage a limited effort while his legacy dreams would lie inside the country. He would grab the baton from movements begun decades prior to press forward with his Great Society. And to  emphasize the crisis-attitude to be projected, it would be called the War on Poverty. Only LBJ knew the war would not be winnable in the field of battle, but in the voting booths of the future. The country would not see another year where spending was less than the year prior until Barack Obama's Residency, which turned out to be more a result of the previous year's profligate spending than any actual responsible restraint in the administration.

In fact, the previous administration had been chided as unpatriotic because of its irresponsible financial practices when it had added almost $4 trillion to the national debt over its eight years. At the end of the Bush administration, the public debt would be almost $10 trillion, and 67% of the gross national product. The concern weakened Republican support and helped this Democratic nominee win the election. But in just 4 years, the Obama legacy would include over $6 trillion in additional debt, rising to 99% of the GDP. It would be a result of the same Keynesian approach which had failed before. But these were much smarter people, and they could turn lead into gold. Americans would watch wrong-headed elites bring about damage that enemies could hardly achieve. But somehow blame would be directed elsewhere.

In a much more entertaining presentation of the absurdity revolving around the budgetary irresponsibility plaguing the American, Mark Steyn would chronical the ridiculous positions supported by the media challengers in his book, *After America*. A celebrated part of the administration's strategy would be labeled the "Buffet Rule," which was projected to raise less that what the government spends in a single day. The successful return on that investment would provide a balanced budget in a short 514 years[41]. And the Praetorian Guard continued to sit on their hands.

Assault on Healthcare

> "If you tell a lie big enough and keep repeating it, people will eventually come to believe it. The lie can be maintained only for such time as the State can shield the people from the political, economic and/or military consequences of the lie. It thus becomes vitally important for the State to use all of its powers to repress dissent, for the truth is the mortal enemy of the lie, and thus by extension, the truth is the greatest enemy of the State."
> - *Joseph Goebbels*

No greater example (to date) of the un-American agenda of the State is Obamacare. The program which steals from contributing members of society in order to control distribution and opportunity for the people it feigns support, effectively transferred one sixth of the economic production of the country, shrouded in a façade of health care. The fact that it's now an entitlement based only on your existence in the country, but must be provided through the forced labor of others, is a sad testament. The myth of some magical system which will provide for all will remain a myth. It's more alchemy by those in command of the levers of power. The public would be wise to remember the promises which generated its support, if it isn't too late.

The lies were repeated ad nauseam and people eventually came to believe it. Much like the megaphones claiming Man-Made Global Warming would produce irreparable damage by now, the State had obviously paid off enough critical supporters to claim credibility. In the end, the hucksters were to become wealthy, and the believers, fools. And it was already coming to light before the 2012 election. The reality would be much different, as the cost of a family did not go down, but in fact was projected to rise. The doctors would no longer even be available because you would no longer be allowed to go to your doctor unless he happened to be on your specific plan.

As described in Sean Hannity's *Conservative Victory*, the entire premise for the program had been based on lies[42]. The greatest country on Earth did not have 47 million people without health care. What the country had may have been 47 million people who didn't pay for personal insurance policies. This country already had a fantastic system of health care providers which would supply emergency care for those who would find themselves in need, as well as a Medicaid system which provided support for those who couldn't afford it. The dirty little secret was that most of the people who could afford insurance simply decided not to buy it. It wasn't because they couldn't afford it. It turns out the facts did not matter, as the Progressive objective had nothing to do with the well-being of the citizen, unless that citizen was a contributor.

These assaults were but a portion of the actual battles instigated by the Resident and his administrative Generals on the American People. The assault on the financial system through the Dodd-Frank legislation expanding iron-fisted control over the banking industry, the war on the oil industry specifically through the gamesmanship surrounding leasing and permits, and more is presented in great detail by David Limbaugh in *The Great Destroyer*[43]. The expanse of the offensive operations by the administration had been thorough and effective, but not complete.

Failure Again

> "In the civil society, the individual is recognized and accepted as more than an abstract statistic or faceless member of some group; rather, he is a unique, spiritual being with a soul and a conscience. He is free to discover his own potential and pursue his own legitimate interests, tempered, however, by a moral order that has its foundation in faith and guides his life and all human life through the prudent exercise of judgment."
> - Mark Levin[1]

The American on-looker couldn't help but notice that even though the Resident was far from the savior predicted, he was in fact quite the opposite, unable to create even modest improvements toward those promised. The Resident's failures not only included an attempt to stand by his oath of office, but even the list of 'accomplishments' over his 4 years would be dominated by failure. That is unless his goal was to lay waste to as much of America as would previously had been thought impossible.

Should he be judged relative to his success as an adherent to the duties of the President of the United States, his bust might fall somewhere near Andrew Johnson and Bill Clinton. Those two being the only Presidents who have received a certain specific level of recognition: impeachment. But that seems unfair; unfair to Johnson and Clinton. The unraveling of the United States over just his first 4 years will not treat the ideologue well. But after his unwavering doctrinal march away from the ideals which had made this country great, an American may need to consider that this wasn't a product of amateurish incompetence, but rather the objective. The goal was to "fundamentally transform the United States of America," and that may very well have happened already. There is a word for the removal and replacement of an existing government establishment, seizing power illegally. It's called a coup d'état.

His contempt for the American may have never been as exposed as it was in Roanoke, Virginia on July 13, 2012 during a campaign stop. The hyper-partisan confluence of his disrespect for the American and his need to energize his base would explode onto the headlines as he decried that, "If you've got a business – you didn't build that." The justifiable uproar was only enflamed by the Praetorian Guard media who went to great lengths to diminish the negative effect on the Resident and to again explain what he meant to say until they could claim it was old news and would provide the audiences another 'shiny object' story to keep them moving along.

But this was no slip of the tongue, taken out of context, or exaggerated by the opponents in order to gain some leverage. This was the Resident, now campaigning for his reelection, telling America what he thinks of the American Dream. His un-American core just couldn't understand America. He was clearly trying to deliver a message of connectedness, in that we are all participants in this society. Each one of us is a critical part of the community, and in our own way provides a contribution which, in turn, supports another in their endeavors. It is this civil society which has built a great country, and improved many others. What he produced in just a few sentences that day was the essence of his un-Americanism. The United States was created by Americans with a government which was to secure the liberty of its citizens, as well as others willing to accept the responsibilities that come with it. It was a government which was to serve the people, not lord over it. What the Resident affirmed was his belief that the people's right to existence was as a result of the government's benevolence. He believes in the almighty power of the State and actually believes that the greatness of this country is a result of that State, which may provide some insight into why he feels justified in attacking the various activities within the civil society which he sees as contradictory to orderly compliance.

The assaults appear to have been a carpet bombing campaign against everything American. Domestically, the savior and his team of anti-American radicals had doubled down on past efforts and done everything in their power to dilute the population of language and culture. They had led an unrepentant attack on the traditions of the country and its republican system of government defined in the Constitution. They were decimating the military, and turning citizen against citizen through the implementation of the police state. And finally, they had created precedent of the State over the very lives of its inhabitants.

Internationally, the country had lost much of the good will gained over the last century as the United States of America was the defender of freedom across the globe. The leader of the country was more interested in becoming friends to those who wish us harm, than to provide support to struggling countries demonstrating their steadfast commitment to the ideals which Americans hold dear. But it was eight weeks before the election, and the manipulation in other country's affairs was 'coming home to roost.' The Resident's Secretary of State had decided she would implement a little 'Democracy Project' of her own.

It would be 2011 when Colonel Muammar Gaddafi decided the support of the American administration's fantasy called the *Arab Spring* was not in his country's best interest. Hardly an American ally, as Ronald Reagan had ordered bombings himself decades before, but he was no longer a threat to American security. At this time however, he had become a target of Secretary Clinton. Could it be because he didn't support the upcoming Clinton Global Initiative summit? Who's to say? But for some reason, that same year, Secretary Clinton decided the United States had to participate in a United Nations effort to bring Gaddafi to his knees[2].

As is usually the case when amateurs and ideologues are provided the decision authority over serious activities, the results can be devastating. Ghaddafi was overthrown and killed in 2011, producing a failed state which exploded onto the screens of the American viewer on Sept 11, 2012, when the embassy in Benghazi was overrun and four great American's were brutally killed, one the Ambassador, the direct representative of the President. The administration's response was un-American and cowardly, and the resulting cover-up, aided by media shielding, has brought discredit on all those involved at the highest levels. The unapologetic lies and deceit which followed demonstrate the absolutely unethical and irresponsible characters involved. While it's clear the Secretary was intimately involved in the deaths of those fine Americans, other Americans can only wonder if the reason no accountability has been made for these events is because unnamed participants exist at an even higher level. But this event would have no effect on the election. The voters decided those in power were less important than what they were providing. It wasn't just scandal in the State Department causing unwanted queries into the incompetence of the administration. The border patrol had also been used as sacrificial pawns to further their cause.

On December 14, 2010, Brian Terry would be allowed to defend himself against heavily armed Mexican criminals with bean bags. Only in the mind of the insane could authorities rationalize the protection of our country's border, and the agents charged with the mission, with bean bags. Naturally, Brian Terry never saw the sun rise the next morning. He will be another sacrificed to the utopian objectives of those afflicted with the illness called Progressivism. Of course the incompetent and irresponsible would establish a cover-up, with media support. But as it turned out, the United States border guard was killed by a weapon provided by his own government. The resulting congressional investigation provided a conga line of bureaucrats which would describe an intricate web of obfuscation and rationalizations incomprehensible to the sane mind.

The lies were apparent to even the most unaware American willing to listen, but somehow this greatest administration in the history of administrations couldn't find information, seemed oblivious to their own actions, and were amazingly calloused to the damage they were perpetrating on the American southern border. Operation Fast and Furious appears to have been a lame-brained concept from the beginning, even though claimed similar to a program attempted by the previous evil administration which was cancelled due to its ineffectiveness. It was an effort to track the cartels by tracking their use of these weapons. It's hard to imagine responsible Americans being so detached from the human carnage resulting from such participation; but such is the result of a life insulated from the citizenry. Katie Pavlich documented the details of the program and much of the cover-up in her book, *Fast and Furious*[3]. What some Americans seem to be missing is the uproar by Mexico. While there are many killed on our side of the border each year, it is but a shadow of the massacre occurring across the border, and our country was providing the weaponry. It's quite possible the Mexican government was partnering with our State and Justice departments to perpetrate this crime against citizens on both sides of the border. But through all the destruction, the Resident was still standing. And so were the problems which he believed that he and he alone could correct.

It's difficult to ascertain whether the savior intended on the outcome, but the activities witnessed over the first 4 years of his residency leaves little room to distinguish otherwise. While past administrations have replaced the key functionaries throughout the government with those supportive of the new regime, the shadow government created since 2009 is without peer. An independent power structure had been implemented, out of reach of the Legislature, unanswerable to the people. Authorities far beyond even that of FDR, our last imperial President, had been seized. The lack of Legislative resistance would be seen as impotence, or it could be accepted as concurrence. The abdication of judicial authority and public mockery it endured also indicates the courts will not intercede. The State has finally assumed control of the arms of the government. Without a dramatic resurgence of the 'several states', the country Americans learned about in civics class (in schools that would still at least teach it) may now be a subject taught only in history class. The choice now is who is in control of the State.

OCTAVIAN

Purpose

> *To the frustrated a mass movement offers substitutes either for the whole self or for the elements which make life bearable and which they cannot evoke out of their individual resources.*
> *- Eric Hoffer[1]*

It would seem a surprising victory to an American. Not only had the incumbent performed with reckless incompetence, but the damage inflicted across virtually all sectors of the civil society was breathtaking in scope. And by the time the election would arrive there would be few who would still listen to the conga line of excuse merchants blaming the previous administration for their folly. The American was finally getting wise to the deception.

The lead up to the 2010 election would be an epic transfer of political power in Washington D.C., and throughout the state governments as well, the pendulum was to swing back to the Republicans. It would not be because the Republicans inspired support, but rather the Democrats had been a disaster. In Washington, the Democrat hegemony would last but one Congress, as additional grass root American patriot organizations would join in the fight to free the government of its statist control. The losses in the House of Representatives were the largest since the Great Depression, as the Republicans gained 63 seats and took over majority control. They would also gain 6 seats in the Senate, but would fall short of the amount needed to claim a majority. The message was clear; Americans had awakened to the corruption at Foggy Bottom. But it wasn't just felt in the Federal Government; it was a tectonic shift of control across the states as well.

Where the populace had slowly grown weary of the Bush administration and began to relinquish the state legislatures and Governorships to the Democrats in increasing numbers over his presidency, it would only take the first term of the Resident to cause a loss of all gains, and then some. Going into the midterm election season, the Democrats controlled roughly 2/3 of the state legislatures, and held the majority of Governorships. The 2010 election results would show a complete flip of power, leaving 2/3 of the states in Republican control, as well as regaining the same number of Governorships as was held during the first term of the Bush administration (See Figure 3).

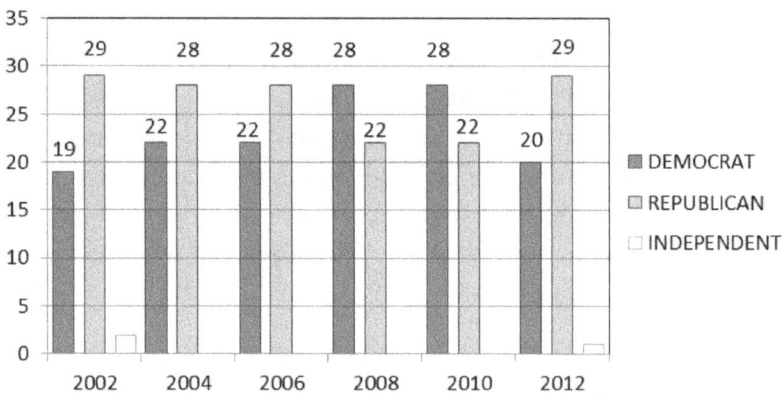

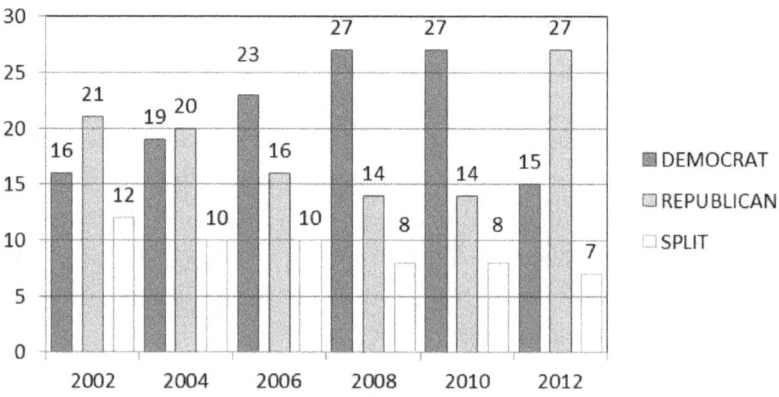

Figure 3: State Political Makeup (measures in Jan)[2]

The message was clear, the un-American Democratic agenda was not acceptable, and it was time to clean house: the House of Representatives first, then the Senate, and ultimately the White House. All the Republican Party needed to do was to pick up the ball.

In days of elections past, a sitting president was only safe from party challengers if the party believed he couldn't be beat. It was curious to many Americans that the Democrats didn't even have a challenger willing to stand up to the failed administration. The Republicans naturally had a large field of competitors battling for the chance to face the Resident in the general election, representing the wide spectrum of the political party's base, but the presumptive winner would be the former Massachusetts Governor, Mitt Romney. The single most divisive issue in the country was to be the Affordable Care Act and the illegitimate method used to ram it down the American's throat. The fact that the Republican establishment selected the only other person in the race that had implemented a similarly progressive program while he was Governor would be unexplainable. During the primary debates he would never admit it a mistake, only that he wouldn't have brought socialized medicine to the country the way the Resident had. This was not a bold color choice, but the insignificant contrast of pastel.

The choices for Republicans included additional capable candidates, a former Senator who clearly had the internal character traits which the country had sorely missed over the past four years; a libertarian who may have never been successful at building a majority coalition to accomplish anything, but whose steady resolve and commitment to the country could not be questioned; and a former Speaker of the House, brilliant and experienced, the last man to battle the beast and win, bringing the country the only surplus budget years in memory. But the establishment had the competition well in hand, and Governor Romney sailed through to the nomination. The Republicans were cautiously optimistic for their chances. The American observers were hopeful.

Even the Resident appeared to be feeling the heat. By the end of the second presidential debate, he was on the ropes having been severely trounced. The wind was out of his sails, he appeared tired and a bit lethargic, a far cry from his normal youthful persona. And he was going to have to endure the third and final debate only two weeks before the election. He was defenseless. His policies were disastrous; his solutions had proven futile. But as the challenger entered the ring that night, the country was watching, waiting for the knock-out blow. What was witnessed was the opposite. The strong and articulate competitor of the second debate that was expected gave way to a meek and constrained challenger in the third debate. His passive tenor and weak demeanor contrasted to the surprisingly regenerated Obama. In that small moment, all gains had been lost, and the Republican that had built a perception of superiority and made many Americans believe he could improve the country's predicament had vanished and the election with it.

Americans would wonder why someone who had fought to get to this position, finding himself in the lead only a couple weeks before the election, would all of a sudden take a fall. This was what he had worked for his whole life; politics was a family tradition. Americans would wonder whether there was something else at play, something more sinister. There had to be. Little else could explain the flaccid performance. Could he have unknowingly given the public a clue without intending to?

He would be recorded by President Carter's grandson at a private fund-raising event where he stated that "47 percent of the people will vote for the president no matter what." Released by Mother Jones less than two months before the election, it provided the necessary ammunition to turn the race into class warfare. It was almost comical to watch the Resident claim that the challenger was for the rich while he was for the little people, especially in between golfing junkets in his personal Boeing 747. But the subject of the comment was worth considering.

For the previous four tax years, the percentage of people who ended up paying no taxes, or who actually received more in return than they paid in through supplements like the earned income credit, was between 43% and 50%, depending on the year[3]. That is just the people filing taxes. Figure 4 presents IRS data from 1950 through 2010 illustrating that less than 50% of the public actually even files a tax return, and of those the number of people who have either been refunded all the taxes withheld or received more in return than they paid during the year has risen dramatically to over 40% of the filers in the first 2 years of the administration. The data is from the IRS, and an American would also

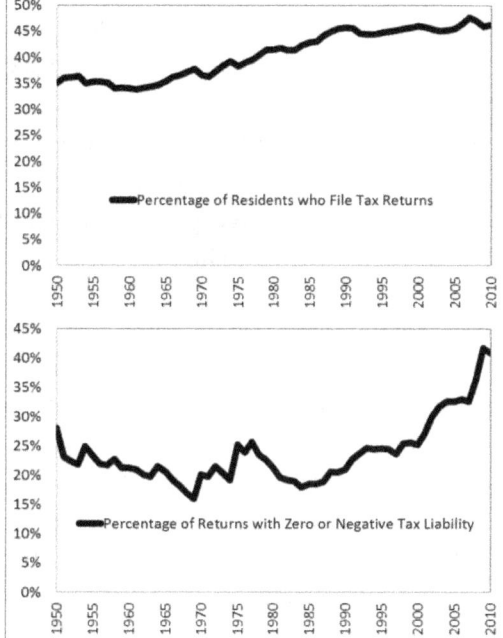

Figure 4: Income Tax Participation (1950-2010)[4]

find it interesting that the data after 2010 is conveniently not readily available.

If you add to that the others who may not even file tax returns, but ultimately find themselves dependent on the government in some way, such as the senior citizens reliant on Social Security and Medicare, the educational institutions beholden to the government on grants and student loans, the contractors with livelihoods tied to the lucrative defense machine, the construction industry supported by infrastructure revitalization, and now the health care industry, it's apparent that far more than 47% of the country is somewhat dependent on the health and well-being of the National Government.

The effect on the election was the elimination of an issues-based campaign relative to actual federal government responsibilities. The election has been transformed; it's now but an illusion. If one candidate can effectively threaten the livelihood of the public through scaremongering by claiming the other will  push granny off the cliff, they will secure the dependent class vote, which is now the majority of the voting public. The failure of the Republican nominee wasn't because he was a poor candidate, although he did make some mistakes. It would be the result of dichotomy between the core values of the old parties. One seemed hell bent on the destruction of the constitutional foundation of our government through redistribution mechanisms primarily as a tool to maintain their own power and its lucrative benefits, and the other attempting to be a less irresponsible alternative. But with the asserted dominance of the State over the Republic during the previous 4 years, the establishment had effectively removed the chains of constitutional restraints. As a result, the party structure, controlled by the establishment, had transitioned from a seemingly cooperative arrangement into a collusive partnership over the term. The Democratic and Republican wings of The Party had now begun to effectively cooperate.

Romney understood the precipice the country was looking over, but he assumed he still had a chance. However, the power of the State now lies in the dependence of those it rules over. The Resident, the Democrat, the leader of the State realized this earlier. The transition was a fait accompli. He had transformed the United States of America, once the beacon of light, into something different. No longer beholden to 'We the People', the State had seemed to have broken free of its constitutional restraints and was now set adrift.

The Resident may have a single event on the other side of the world which he would ride through victory, as SEAL Team 6 eliminated Osama Bin Laden from the living. It was apparently enough. During his victory speech, as is the case with most, would be the words of promise, "You elected us to focus on your jobs, not ours. And in the coming weeks and months, I am looking forward to reaching out and working with leaders of both parties to meet the challenges we can only solve together: reducing our deficit, reforming our tax code, fixing our immigration system, [and] freeing ourselves from foreign oil." Over the past four years the actions behind these words had been absent. Now with no elections to worry about, only legacy would become his administration's interest. As a President he will not be remembered for greatness. He really never tried to be the President, it wasn't in his DNA. His singlemindedness and laser focus on his objectives had been somewhat constrained by the drudgery of the legislative process. With that charade no longer needed, he could now direct his efforts to something bigger.

No More Distractions

> "This is my last election. After my election I have more flexibility."
> -Barack Obama[1]
>
> "I understand. I will transmit this information to Vladimir."
> - Dmitry Medvedev[2]

With his final presidential campaign left for the history books, Barack now would be unleashed from those inhibiting pressures which accompany the need to maintain the façade for future elections. He was now free from the chains of maintaining the appearance of meeting constitutional responsibilities, as well. The need to cooperate with opposing forces within the governmental structure had been eviscerated over the past four years, and his command of the State was now validated by the illusion of an election.

While the Resident was still protected by the Senate, the Republicans maintained their control of the House of Representatives which would limit the effectiveness of his maneuvers. Remembering that the most aggressive campaigns against the Constitution were during FDR's New Deal era, and the period after implementation of LBJs massive Great Society, if we look back at Figure 1, we can see this also coincided with absolute dominance over the legislative levers of control by the Democratic Party. Figure 5 illustrates the hegemonic periods of each party since the creation of the Republican Party. It's clear that through the 19th century, the Democratic Party was a relatively minor player in the real decision processes within the legislature. Even though they resided in the Oval office over 40% of the time, the period of time the Republicans had control of both houses of the legislative branch dominated.

It's also remarkable to notice the other two periods of massive shift away from constitutional governmental constraints discussed earlier would be during Woodrow Wilson's first term and the Resident's first term. The Progressives before Wilson prepared the battlefield for him and would usher in the 16th and 17th amendments implementing the income tax, and removing the state's role in selection of senators, respectively. And the Resident, of course, seized control of the health care system.

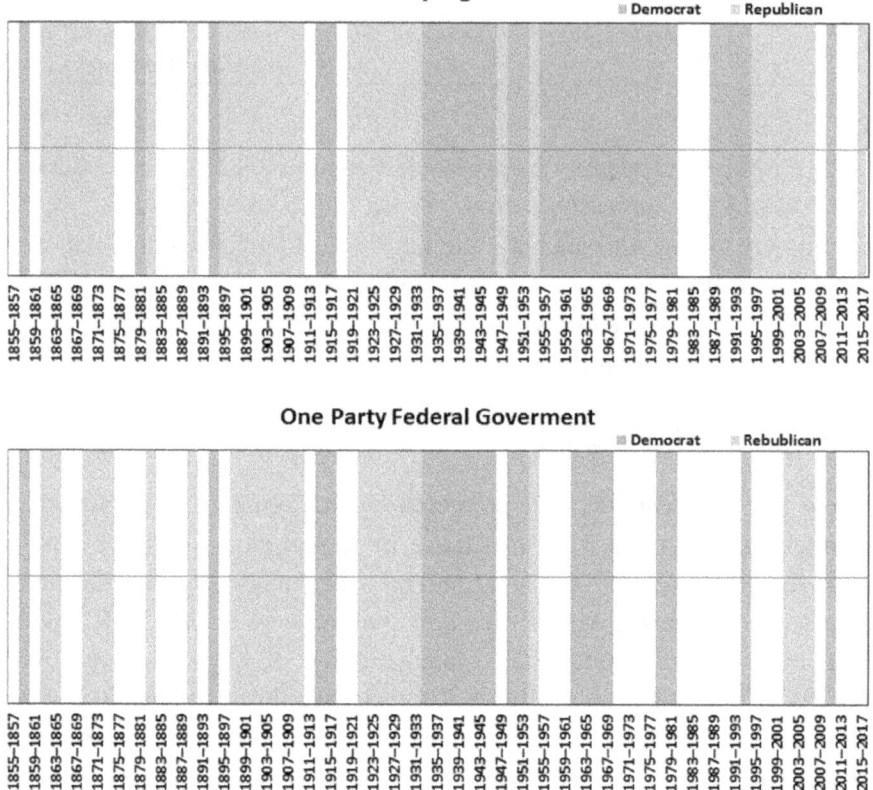

Figure 5: Electoral Hegemony

Other than a single congress during Eisenhower's presidency, the Republicans haven't been able to achieve the dominance necessary to drive the agenda since the beginning of the Great Depression. That is until the scandalous Clinton Presidency motivated the voters to shift political party control. It would be the last Republican administration, while demonstrating the finest of American values abroad during the country's time of crisis following 9/11, which would succumb to the statists domestically, and doom their legacy to the enabling of the financial collapse quickly approaching. This historical perspective again brings to mind the exceptional tenure of the greatest president of the 20th century, and how the country was improved in spite of the lack of control over all the levers of power. Ronald Reagan demonstrated that the levers of power were necessary only if the objective was to be unconstitutional actions. The presidency alone can move the legislature if the agenda is good for the country. Which brings us back to the Resident, who demonstrated the presidency is powerful enough to move the country in spite of the limits imposed by his oath of office. All he needed was compliant leadership in the other branches of government. And those parts unwilling to just go-along could always be nudged. Redistribution makes those who dole out the favors rich and powerful.

The Resident's obsession with tax increases may actually be because he believes in the words that come out of his mouth. He might actually believe that providing someone a fish is better that teaching them to fish. Or it could be a smokescreen he knows tugs at the heartstring of his base, while pulls along those who actually benefit. His obsession is a true believer's perspective of the Keynesian economic assumption that you can inspire economic growth through artificial demand. By stealing the property of one to provide to another only generates animosity in the victim, and a sense of entitlement in the receiver. But the real winner in this game is the middleman, for the receiver provides support for the middleman. The house always wins. The producer in a Marxist society always loses. Such is the utopian objective of the Resident.

The agenda of the second term is a doubling down on the redistribution theme which had demonstrated such a superb success during the first four years. As is the case with any government program, the program is never the problem, it's the limited resources provided. The goal is to increase the flow from the producer to the consumer, at the benefit of the State. Let's run down those items for 2013[3].

- Individual Tax Reform: Return upper income voters to the higher Clinton tax rates.
- A new Alternative Minimum Tax at 30% for those earning over $1 million (the Buffett Rule).
- Corporate Tax Reform: Reduce the top corporate rate to 28%. (Which of course never happened)

- Employment: $60 billion in Infrastructure Investment as part of a larger $447 billion jobs program (half the amount saved by winding down our wars?)
- Health Care: Implement Obama Care in 2014.
- How about a Carbon Tax?! Great idea.

Add to that the 66% increase in capital gains taxes for 2013, and he's well on his way. 'Obamacare' was on its way and it looked to be the biggest tax hit to every American, not just those evil rich people. But there are other areas still ripe for destruction; they include announcing the end the war in Afghanistan in 2014. How neighborly it is of us to tell the enemy how long they need to wait until we give back everything gained in return. They also claim to support "all forms of energy" production. That is of course as long as it isn't fossil fuel based, coal based, or pretty much anything else that is economically viable. If you are a campaign donor and want to get rich with a scheme to produce energy from algae, come on up! But the administration will not give up on its support for the Dream Act either. In addition, there would be increased Social Security deductions and death taxes. They are hammers, and every problem is a nail. And the solution is always the same, theft. Combine these with the assaults on gun owners, law enforcement, border security, immigration, free speech, religious liberty, and even the internet itself; it looked like he might not even have time for golf.

The golf would not only continue, but fill even more of the Resident's activity schedule. Now that the last election was behind him, he would naturally feel less restraint, fewer distractions. This would translate into almost doubling the rate of his golf game, playing over 140 games during the first 3 years of his second term. An average of almost once a week would be stressful for anyone, but combine this with the challenge of having to travel on Air Force One to most is a testament to the importance he places on his leisure activities, while the country decays. Even more than the abundance of his leisure activity, would be the apparent priority it would have over the duties he had sworn to uphold. His callousness may have best been on display one day in 2014, when he took time out of his busy schedule to deliver a statement about the recent beheading of a U.S. journalist named James Foley. With all the warmth he could muster he would deliver a nice message of condolence. And then he would immediately leave for his planned golf game. Admitting "bad optics", he enshrined his complete lack of attachment to the office he had been resident in for the previous 5 years. But it would be the travel which would hit absurdities even the media seemed ill-equipped to challenge.

Legacy

> *I do solemnly swear that I will faithfully execute the Office of President of the United States, and will to the best of my Ability, preserve, protect and defend the Constitution of the United States.*
> *- President Barack Hussein Obama*

It was before he even took the oath of office for the second term that the direction of the administration changed to 'legacy'[1]. Little regard would be provided to the duties of the office which had so badly been neglected during the first term. In fact, the powerful influence that the office of the presidency, and the country as a whole, has over world affairs would be used as a tool to support others who are aligned with the True Believers and bludgeon those who would cry out that the king had no clothes[2].

International Devastation

> *Above all, we must realize that no arsenal, and no weapon in the arsenals of the world, is so formidable as the will and moral courage of free men and women. It is a weapon our adversaries in today's world do not have.*
> *- President Ronald Reagan*

While an administration's hesitance toward unwavering support of the state of Israel may be considered within the bounds of justifiability given that past unyielding support appears to have had little effect on eliminating the regional conflict, Americans were perplexed by the unveiled visceral hatred the Resident has toward that little country struggling for survival. The American cannot deny that it appears the Resident projects fault on the part of the victim. In the twisted logic of the anti-Semite, it is much like some would place fault on the victim of rape, due to what they may have been wearing.

The Resident appeared to be so obsessed with legacy that he was willing to have the United States "sacrifice [Israel] to demonstrate…total surrender to the holy cause"[3]. His belief that the removal of that small democratic state in the sea of anti-Christian ideologues would somehow provide historic greatness demonstrates the smallness of the man, for it is greatness which is demonstrated by those who stand with the oppressed. But it was not only the historically steadfast support by the United States which he singlehandedly attempted to eviscerate. It would be magnified by the overturning of decades of righteous challenge to those murderous regimes in the region which had publically committed to the annihilation of Israel. Beyond their objective to eliminate the State of Israel, these regimes support and defend the killing of Americans and attacks on the United States. Iran, for example, had spent the past decade providing most of the materiel for improvised explosive devices (IED) to those in Iraq, which would be the cause of most American casualties[4]. Did that affect the Resident's calculations? It doesn't appear so. It was 'Bush's War' anyway, right? But for all the love the administration had been sending Iran's way, it didn't seem to change the progress of the game. So he decided to forfeit.

The Iranian nuclear program was apparently an open secret for decades. Begun with the support of the United States before the fall of the Shah, reactors for power generation had been approved prior to the overthrow. After the revolution placed the theocratic oligarchy in command of the country and those imprisoned within, steady progress toward a military nuclear capability began. It was early in the current century when the International Atomic Energy Agency (IAEA) could no longer claim ignorance, and was forced to investigate. The years of absurd cat and mouse games created increased international sanctions as an attempt to somehow impose human decency on a regime hell bent on the destruction of western civilization, publically announcing objectives of "Death to Israel...Death to America"[5]. Many Americans could not help but see the reemergence of the anti-US and anti-Israel United Nations once again playing their part in the 'community organizing' campaign against western civilization, which primarily yields funding, but also plays to the America hating countries and cultures around the globe.

Truly the most striking example of the ineptness of the United Nations and the disregard the Resident has for the country he claims to represent would be the Iranian nuclear deal of 2015. Imitating a devastatingly suicidal posture reminiscent of the pre-World War II England, the hapless U.S. State Department, in cahoots with the America-hating U.N., would create a one-sided deal in Iran's favor which even Iran stated they wouldn't support. "No notice" inspection teams would be required to provide a warning up to 24 day in advance before they could visit a site, and in return the U.S. would provide $150 billion in 'sanctions relief'[6]. For those Americans paying attention, there is no evidence this money will make it into the Clinton Global Initiative accounts. It is however relieving the financial pressure of the sanctions which was mounting as Iran struggled to maintain its internal mechanisms while it also providing millions to external terrorist groups killing Americans and Israelis like Hezbollah and Hamas[7]. They can now find the additional resources to further their intercontinental ballistic missile (ICBM) program, prohibited under the agreement, and not challenged by the Resident. As is typical of the True Believer, he would sacrifice those around him for his cause, but an American would never risk the lives of his own family for their ideology. It turned out the Ayatollah wasn't the only tyrant appealing to the Resident. There were plenty in our own hemisphere as well.

As we remember, Cuba was a Spanish conquest until the Treaty of Paris, a result of the Spanish-American War, when independence was once again claimed. A key cooperative agreement between the U.S. and the newly independent Cuba would solidify the relationship between neighbors. The Platt Amendment at the turn of the 20th century provided support for an agreement for the lease of land to support a "coaling and naval station at Guantanamo Bay" (GITMO). At the turn of this century it would serve as a refugee camp, but famously transformed into the prison after the beginning of the 'War on Terror' in 2002. The Resident, unwaveringly obsessed with the closure of the facility, continues to claim it is GITMO which inspires those who wish Americans harm. That's ludicrous as it didn't even exist prior to the attacks on 9/11. Could it be related to the fact that the representatives of the U.S. government provide validation for their murderous assaults on not only western civilization, but their own people as well? It's those who live under the 7th century ideology of inhumanity which have been at war with the United States since its inception, and we can no longer ignore its threat to western civilization as a whole. Maybe they just had the ability to see into a future where the country would have the gall to imprison and interrogate enemy combatants rather than just summarily execute them, which incidentally all began as a result of 9/11. The Resident's revisionist projections are 'aid and comfort' and each release of these combatants, allowing them to continue to carry out their murderous ideology, is an embarrassment to patriotic Americans.

While the Resident continues to be frustrated by Americans not interested in his gimmickry related the promise of a GITMO closure, it wouldn't be his only foray into the activities on that island 90 miles south of Florida. He decided he would wash away decades of righteous rejection of the murderous totalitarian Cuban government by reopening official diplomatic relations with the Castro regime. Apparently never having met a murderous regime that he didn't find more appealing than the America he was supposed to be the President for, he declared "The Cuban Thaw" was under way. But then again, borne of radical counter-cultural roots, 'birds of [an ideological] feather [would] flock together'. No longer would the anti-American sentiment inherent in his soul need to be shielded. And the regime would not have to account for the seizure of property by Fidel Castro or the thousands of deaths at the hands of his second in command, the brutal Ernesto 'Che' Guevara, that were an integral part of their revolutionary coup.

These international agreements, almost cynically superficial in relation to the realities of the situations, are both planned to become part of the exaggerated, if not fictional, legacy of the Resident. But even greater than international achievements between countries would be something encompassing the entire globe, not just those distractions between countries which will ultimately be transformed themselves one day.

An agreement claiming progress toward the battle against Climate Change must now be included in the Resident's list of achievements. Created from a group of self-validating enthusiasts, the concept of man-made global destruction is ridiculous; purveyors of these theories channeling ancient alchemist dreams. Products of 'science' degrees, possibly unaware of their own internal compromises developed through a sort of group-think as a result of a need for acceptance; it's interesting that science is claimed in order to support this world-wide attempted thievery masquerading as a religiously propagandized environmental movement, but is also a testament to the failure of the current education system. It's not that the relatively controlled avenues for educational materials appear to have been infiltrated by True Believers, but it seems many of the educators themselves have fallen victim to the ruse. Any subject that is completely fabricated and substantiated not through observation and experience, but by manipulation and motivated by State-sponsored financial support burgeoning from within academia should at least be questioned. The fact the State is attempting to eliminate blasphemous challenges to the 'undeniable' scripture of climate change is alone substantial evidence of the fraud.

> It was the 1970s when a limited academic study by 'scientists' claimed a looming ice-age was on the horizon and threatened humanity, a result of carbon dioxide and other particulate matter created by the evil industrialized nations of the world. Something had to be done! The sky was going to fall! What fell like rain would not be the global temperature, but the support of grant providing institutions like the National Science Foundation, and even the United States Department of Agriculture (USDA)[8].
>
> But wait! The temperatures weren't going down, they may be going up. We'll call it Global Warming, find an easily corruptible spokes-person, a former Vice President would be perfect, and take another run at the fund providers. In the 1970's it seemed to be simple generation of hysteria to motivate grants for their own benefit. The Global Warming movement of the 2000s however was hijacked by the community organizers and became not only a heated academic battle, but had also expanded into the global political sphere, a necessary ingredient for world class wealth transfer.
>
> But wait! The temperatures aren't rising like predicted. Was it because we elected the Resident? What enemy of the State had eliminated the looming disaster before the spoils could be retrieved? Something had to be done before the population got wise to the miscreant behavior of their preachers, as the ideologues had become firmly entrenched. There were

major plans for things like 'Cap and Trade', ingeniously designed to make others fantastically wealthy, already in play. The name would now become Climate Change. This supposedly world-wide movement, based on a collection of anecdotal pieces of evidence, consistently refuted, and predictions, consistently incorrect, would not be stopped, especially with the Resident now as a key propagandist.

It's interesting to a quizzical American that if something is 'undeniable', how could people find fault with it? If it was such an inevitability, why couldn't this particular Resident find cooperation with the compliant legislature for the support for whatever deal he had planned for the United Nations Framework Convention on Climate Change (UNFCCC) in Paris? They had already sold out their own country in order to support his government health care scam. Is this even less believable to those who are not True Believers[9]? But if there is one thing the legacy relies upon, it will be Obamacare.

Domestic Devastation

> "One of the traditional methods of imposing statism or socialism on a people has been by way of medicine. It's very easy to disguise a medical program as a humanitarian project; most people are a little reluctant to oppose anything that suggests medical care for people who possibly can't afford it."
>
> -Ronald Reagan (1961)[10]

Passed in 2010, and carefully calculated not to take effect until 2014 in order to avoid an impact to the 2012 election, Obamacare has already turned out to be exactly what the opponents feared it would be. As is the case with all State-sponsored solutions, the Praetorian Guard media was at the ready to manage the fallout. They had been very effective at defusing discontent over the botched rollout of the website needed to allow those to sign up for the program; the web site requiring 'investment' unmatched in the history of web site development would not only be dripping with cronyism, but wouldn't even be created by an American company[11]. There has been little attention paid to the effect on the industry. While the Resident continued to expand the office's authority by applying extra-constitutional powers ceded by the weak Legislative, he would affect dozens of changes to the law in order to support those in favor and punish those who would challenge. There will be no review of the program by the media until they can identify a replacement to attach blame. But what is undeniable is that the transition from a somewhat capitalist system of customer and provider which existed in America until the Resident's administration to the government controlled access to services the government will find accepting is already entrenched as an entitlement program. Many people have had to find new doctors, because they weren't allowed to keep theirs, and the costs have exploded. The promise was that you could "keep your doctor", and that it would "save each family $2500". Both undeniable lies at the outset, but the American family will now have to pay the cost. Not only are they not saving money, but with the exorbitant deductibles now attached, they effectively are paying several times more than that.

As far as the government program itself, it would now cost about $2 *trillion* over a decade. That amounts to about *$50,000 per person*. This is also with the expectation that the number of enrollees will double by 2025. That's $50,000 to not get what you pay for[12]. To the observing American, it will be interesting when the real beneficiaries of this massive transfer of wealth are uncovered, and how history will treat them. These are those inside the crony circle who collected the windfall of government supported thievery. But guaranteed control of the State and its media component will ensure the story is muted and the guilty are never brought to justice.

The sycophants are also counting on a claim of successful immigration reform to be part of the Resident's legacy. The push is on to find a way to not only provide a legal avenue for Democratic Party election support, but also maintain indirect support through demagoguery as a result of the progressive community organizing approach to problem solving. Should a responsible American identify that persons in this country, in violation of the law, are by-definition illegal aliens, he or she is vilified as a heartless person who lusts for family tragedy. It's not acceptable to the establishment to identify the irresponsible seduction of the families, inducing them to migrate here illegally with the promise of support from the welfare state, is at the heart of the problem.

Obscured from the discussion is the fact that the educated observer realizes almost half of those here illegally are here because they had violated their own agreement necessary to be granted temporary visas. They are here beyond the agreed to term of the visa they were granted. How can that be the American's fault? It is theirs and theirs alone. They traveled here as a citizen of another country, under the agreement made to both their country and ours that they would return when the time was over. This was the predicament that the Resident's step-father was in when he was recalled to Indonesia. Was that America's fault? Was it not unexpected ramifications of visiting another location, only to find that new location beneficial, resulting in a desire never to leave?

The current argument over the highly publicized H-1B visa program brings the subject to irrational levels. The program is designed to allow American companies to look outside the country for needed skills unavailable inside the country. That's it. For example, it's actually against the law for a company to import a group of workers at a lower wage to supplant higher paid employees, which was recently witnessed at Disney[13]. The American clearly recognizes the societal dangers of having your Justice Department look the other way when violators are your financial supporters. It must only be against the law if you get caught. Would any rational observer think a similar occurrence by a fast food chain like *Chick-fil-a* would go unnoticed? It would be against the law if it was, say, an enterprise antagonistic toward the establishment, like a Tea Party group. What is really horrible about the position the administration is taking, and the media is insulating them from, is what the H-1B program actually does.

You are allowed to come to the United States to work for the company who sponsors you. You are not allowed to change employers unless you pay a "fixed sum for liquidated damages" which is determined when you request to leave, not when the contract is signed[14]. Didn't we have a civil war over such an established form of indentured servitude? Is this not the heaven-sent administration which was to bring to a close the results of those scars of centuries past? And the H-1B program is only the tip of the iceberg. A comprehensive review of the hypocrisy has been covered in great detail in *Sold Out* by Michelle Malkin and John Miano. But this is a country of immigrants, right? Wrong. This is a country of citizens, who were obviously once immigrants, or descendants of immigrants. No country can survive the importation and non-assimilation of incongruent cultures. Whether or not our corrupted immigration program is a symptom of our slowly sinking ship, it is the economic iceberg ahead which our Titanic is approaching that may seal our doom.

The game of numbers played by masters of misdirection and obfuscation leaves most Americans confused about what the actual state of the economy may be. Those that have work have seen wages continue to be outpaced by the cost of living, but at least they are still employed. The publicized unemployment numbers appear to have improved, but the number of workers out of the workforce is at an all-time high of almost 50 *million* people. That's almost a third the number of those that file income taxes. How can unemployment be an honest value in single digits while 25% are without work? It could be the same scientists who calculated that the car you drive is going to cause the seas to rise. But the single most effective measure of the economic impact as a result of his time in office may be the result of the irresponsible and uncontrollable spending which he so famously chided his predecessor about.

As is clear in Figure 6, if the Bush administration had increased the debt about 15% over eight years relative to the gross domestic product (GDP), and justifiably characterized as "irresponsible", what can be said for the Resident as he has more than doubled that irresponsible and unpatriotic performance, leaving the country owing over 100%, with no reversal in sight. For those who purchase a home, you may owe the mortgage

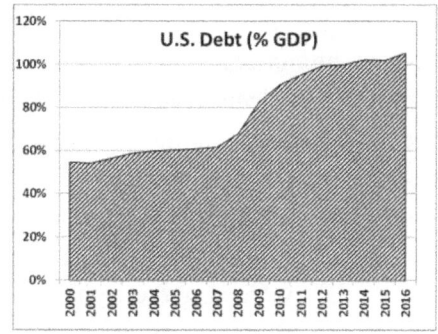

Figure 6: U.S. Debt 2000-2016 (%GDP)[15]

amount on that home, but over the life of the loan, you will pay several times that amount. This is the case of the national debt as well. The other dirty little secret is the IOUs taken out on your behalf. Not just yours, but your kids, and grandkids as well. These are the 'unfunded liabilities' which include the social security slush fund your government has been using for their own purposes, the promised Medicare benefit, and more estimated at over $200 *trillion*[16]. The apple may have been bitten years ago by others, but the Resident has made no effort to reduce the looming crash. In fact, the accelerated pace of 'transfer', or stealing could be a bad sign.

The level of thievery has risen to such a level that Alinsky himself, master of the game, would stand in awe. The Clintons may have made themselves wealthy through the Clinton Global Initiative coupled with her access to the highest offices in the country where the decisions were made, if not making them herself, but the staggering amount that has been bled from the country at this point may leave the United States beyond recovery. Will the coming economic collapse result in social collapse as well? In high density areas, how could it not?

Survival in areas where complex logistics structures are relied upon in order to support the community will be stressed beyond ability. The country is witness to the effect of organized thuggery at the hand of the community organization process right now as the puppet masters are manipulating useful idiots like those covering for the various 'occupy' movements, the 'Black Lives Matter' movement, and others to fuel discontent and create social instability. There are not only un-American, but anti-American masterminds who now see the end game nearing and are using others to nudge events to their ends. What the founders realized was a population without the means to stand up against the tyranny would soon be conquered. The Second Amendment was not so you could go hunt for your meal. It was to never let those who would decide they were above the citizenry become unaware that those who try to impose despotic governments on an armed citizenry will meet effective resistance. This is why gun control is under constant threat by the Progressive, and why this year it became a centerpiece for the

Resident's administration's agenda. Beware the labels of 'common sense gun control'.

If we look over the list of agenda items as he entered office listed in the Residency chapter, the American will notice that list had little to do with what his real agenda was. Little effect on the improvement of government can even be claimed by even their most supportive drones. One thing is for certain, the Resident will most definitely have a legacy like none other.

The ridicule which should have mounted as a result of the botched Obamacare website roll-out alone would be muted by the Praetorian Guard media, and even the scandal of just the creation of the website should've been enough to warrant investigation. But by this point, the media may have actually become immune to the daily troubles in our nation's capital.

The media would even downplay the fact that most of the people signing up for coverage were actually being placed on Medicaid, as they did not qualify for the real plans available. The entire system was of smoke and mirrors, and this was supposed to be the single most important achievement of the entire first term.

The Campaign Continues

> *The major premise for tactics is the development of operations that will maintain a constant pressure upon the opposition.*
> *- Saul Alinsky, Rule 10[1]*

The Campaign chapter collected several of the Resident's focus areas as he attempted to inflict a scorched Earth strategy on the civil society. After reflection, an American may realize the ever-increasing battlespace of agenda items had remained, but the fury of upheaval had been reduced during the second term. Was this reduction in manufactured crises due to a more seasoned administration or actually a realization that the tactical detonation of conflicts was not as effective as other, less overt approaches? Time will tell, but the Resident no longer had to worry about self-control as preparation for future campaigns. The reduction in constraint, along with the time no longer needed to prepare and execute a reelection campaign, allowed the fronts to be expanded.

During the 1960s, researcher Martin Segilman and his team developed a series of somewhat sadistic experiments to evaluate the effects of painful stimuli on dogs. Placing a dog in a cell with a barrier between two sections, one section's floor connected to an electrical source, he would apply painful shocks to the dogs, causing them to jump around randomly until they were able to relocate to the other section where the electrical shock was not felt. Over time the dogs would learn to jump to the insulated section quickly as the shock was applied. The resultant demonstration of negative reinforcement would be defined as *escape learning*.

The experiment was expanded to add a light in the cell, which would be turned on a few seconds before the electricity would be applied. After dozens of trials, the dogs would be exhibiting signs of escape learning. But the dogs also started to jump before the electricity was applied. In fact, dogs began to sit near the barrier and simply walk over to the insulated side immediately once the light came on, without electrical shock being applied, demonstrating *avoidance learning*. This was all expected outcome, as escape learning and avoidance learning had long been in the tomes of psychology. But this is the point that the Segilman experiments began to expand on this previously understood research.

In the next series of tests, dogs would be constrained while the painful shocks were applied. The inability to escape conditioned the poor animals so that by the time they were introduced into that original cell with only a small barrier between the electrically connected and insulated sections, the dogs would no longer jump around as in previous experiments in an effort to separate themselves from the painful stimuli and move to find the safe area. They would just "stop moving, lie down, and begin to whine."[2] Their conditioning was so powerful that they didn't even try to escape the situation they had found themselves in. This behavior was defined as *learned helplessness*[3]. This psychological manifestation is a common result of prolonged incarceration, and an expected outcome in prisoners of war.

It appears the United States has traveled through the phases described above. The American would exhibit escape learning by relocating to areas more in tune with their own social needs. The New World was conquered and developed as a mechanism to escape the oppression felt an ocean away. The country was created under a system of well understood laws, which allowed an informed citizen to demonstrate avoidance learning by predetermining negative outcomes from political movements incompatible with their values and traditions, and motivate themselves to relocate among the states to find their most supportive lifestyle. But after the Progressive century, there is nowhere left to move which is out of reach by the controlling hand of the State. The result is a condition of learned helplessness, as the country appears to have succumbed to some sort of sensed inevitability. The continued assaults on America appear to have increased in nature, but resistance is diminishing.

Assault on Free Speech

> *Absolute freedom of the press to discuss public questions is a foundation stone of American liberty.*
> *- President Herbert Hoover*

It's called the Fairness Doctrine, and as with most applied government labels, it's in fact quite different when the true goals see the light of day and the illusion is discovered. It's a police state thought control mechanism resurrected from a 1949 policy imposed by the Federal Communications Commission (FCC) which required the holders of network broadcast licenses to provide "honest, equitable, and balanced" programming, as judged by the commission itself[4].

While fundamentally un-American in the imposition of communications standards, the Fairness Doctrine applied to the only three television sources of the day, as well as limited radio station coverage which fell within the FCC jurisdiction. In reality this was an establishment tool to control the media either directly or indirectly through threats of application. The days of limited information sources are a distant memory with the almost uncountable television channels, terrestrial and satellite radio channels, as well as internet resources available. The idea that the message from a single source can have a significant effect on the population is ludicrous. An American wonders why it seems the subject only comes up as a tool for use by Democrats. Americans understand Progressive policies are 'so good they must be mandatory', but must their positions be protected from illumination? While it was finally officially revoked from the FCC bag of tricks until 2011[5], it continues to be placed into the arena for discussion. These threats have been squarely aimed at conservative talk radio, and the popular hosts such as Mark Levin, Rush Limbaugh, and Sean Hannity, but the charge has been the ridiculous claim that their programs are not 'equitable', while there are ample alternatives available in virtually any locale. The general attack on those who dare to challenge the establishment has recently been elevated to specific topic areas, critical to the State's need to control the messaging and thoughts of the population.

The Attorney General has just announced interest in targeting 'Climate Deniers', claiming that evil "fossil fuel industry" has built a "climate denial apparatus."[6] She has gone so far as to refer the subject to the FBI for them "to consider". The twisted minds of those in positions of authority beyond the ability to manage the responsibility that comes with it will once again bring forward the police state all too common during the 20th century.

Assault on Law Enforcement/Justice

> *A president's hardest task is not to do what is right, but to know what is right.*
> *- President Lyndon B. Johnson*

If in fact there is an actual institutional racial component precipitating the high profile alleged police brutality cases recently, the Resident had all but eliminated its honest appraisal by injecting hyper-racialism into the conversation. We can take his Vice President's word that he has a big stick, but to an American, he is just acting like one. And it's costing American lives.

It was four years ago, February 26, 2012, when a 17 year old was killed when an overzealous community watch volunteer confronted him, was accosted by him, and shot him in self-defense. The facts that the election season was in full swing and the victim was black were all that the Resident needed to enflame the discourse. He would jump into the discussion ignorant of the facts in order to take advantage of the mayhem decrying, "If I had a son, he would look like Trayvon." Trayvon Martin was a suspended student wandering through a neighborhood which had recently experienced a string of robberies. There was nothing to imply Trayvon had been a part of these earlier crimes, but George Zimmerman decided to confront the young man just the same. The racialist-in-chief could not restrain himself, "Trayvon Martin could have been me 35 years ago,"[7] and he would go on to imply his doubts about the integrity of the justice system. His Alinsky roots couldn't help but stir the pot. The resulting social media storm would be this century's mob, uninterested in the truth, but swept up in the emotion of the group. Poor Sanford,

Florida would be under attack. But the furor did produce the desired effect for the incumbent as the Trayvon Martin case had effectively overwhelmed election coverage[8]. Did an American consider this a coincidence? Hardly. The objective was to create as much distraction as possible in order to obscure the Resident's dismal failures. But the flame was lit, and the radicals ignited. The next election season would need a distracting fire as well, and a small suburb of St. Louis would provide him the fuel.

The administration would find the events great timing for a crisis as another black man would attack a uniformed officer, who returned the gesture by fatally shooting him. The 18 year old Michael Brown was killed after trying to wrestle the gun from Officer Darren Wilson. It was a sad day in Ferguson, Missouri, just outside of St. Louis, when the Resident decided this was just the controversy he needed to distract the public once again from the destruction being brought on this country. He did everything he could to exact maximum benefit from the situation, even sending his racialist Attorney General into the mayhem while eluding to the white vs. black war he wanted to exacerbate. As the truth of the story would be revealed, the officer's account would be verified, but the officer's future and the city would be in ruins as the importation of the radical support arm was used to inflict maximum benefit, at the cost of law enforcement, and the police themselves.

As a direct result of the Resident's irresponsible response providing validation to the rioters and malcontents, on December 19, 2014, Police Officers Wenjian Liu and Rafael Ramos would be assassinated as they sat in the patrol car in Brooklyn, New York. The low-life perpetrator and coward, Ismaaiyl Brinsley, would turn the gun on himself immediately afterwards but had telegraphed his intentions through social media stating "The Take 1 Of Ours ... Let's take 2 of Theirs", and finally "This may Be My Last Post." Another post would say "I Rather Die a Gangster Then [sic] Go To Sleep A Coward," under #ShootThePolice[9]. He would die a coward, and will not be missed, but the murder of two police officers by a miscreant like this was brought on by the desire for the Resident to earn his place in the community. The True Believer however is incapable of realizing the blood on his hands.

This disconnected antagonism is applied throughout the spectrum of his interactions, but it may be the effect on critical international relationships which may ultimately become the most damaging.

Assault on Israel

> *Israel was not created in order to disappear—Israel will endure and flourish. It is the child of hope and home of the brave. It can neither be broken by adversity nor demoralized by success. It carries the shield of democracy and it honors the sword of freedom.*
> *- President John F. Kennedy*

While it's hard to identify what is in one's heart, it is possible to convict one on circumstantial evidence. As an American can no longer question the Resident's disdain, if not outright hatred, for the traditions and values which is America; among those traditions are the international relationships which have supported the dominance of the civil society of western civilization. The Middle East has but a single democratic state, little Israel, which is in a day-to-day struggle for its very existence. The bond between the American and Israeli peoples, government, and states are one of the longest, healthiest relationships our country has ever maintained. But their society is in many ways similar to ours, which may be one reason the Resident has sought to diminish our relationship, and demean their country's leadership.

It would begin immediately after he entered office, where he and his Secretary of State, Hillary Clinton, decided to throw in with the anti-Semitic U.N. so-called Human Rights Council, which had a history of ignoring genocidal activities in Africa while they manufactured so-called abuses by the state of Israel. This would send the message that the administration would no longer provide support for the little nation on the eastern shores of the Mediterranean. But that would not be enough.

The Resident decided to apply his own special ability to "lead from behind" to avoid getting involved where he could do some good, and apply the all-too recognizable undermining commentary in an effort to bring about the change he would really be interested in. In an all too consistent approach of forecasting the mandatory outcome with less than an elementary knowledge of the facts, he decided to go all-in for the Palestinian leadership. He would begin preaching to Prime Minister Benjamin Netanyahu about Israel's responsibility to create an acceptable arrangement for the Palestinians. He would conveniently ignore the facts that the Palestinians have been, and continue to be, dedicated to the eradication of the Israeli state.

It wouldn't be enough to just suggest alternate routes to a goal we all wish could be found, but it would be his own sense of superiority over others that gave him the self-appointed authority to dictate that Israel stop building homes for their people in their own country. He went so far as to proclaim that Israel should cede back territories claimed during previous wars of survival.

While leaders of countries understand there are changes as peers move in and out of office, the fundamental relationships are between the states, and not the individuals, and could be relied upon. This is not the case with the Resident, for as is painfully obvious, he doesn't represent the American. He is too big for such constraints. The Oval Office is not big enough to satisfy him. He wants more. He would demonstrate his contempt of the trusted relationship in early 2012 when he sent out his card-carrying member of the Party and compliant Secretary of Defense to undermine what must've been a planned attack on Iran, as reported by David Ignatius of the Washington Post, "Panetta believes there is a strong likelihood that Israel will strike Iran in April, May or June [before Iran commences with building] a nuclear bomb."[10] Stunning to those who have watched Iran publically state that they will wipe Israel of the map, our country just shot at Israel first. But the administration's media wing is also all-in.

When a suicide bomber kills innocent Jewish settlers, it is rationalized as a result of the oppression inflicted by the Jewish people. When the Resident found out Israel had requested a shipment of Hellfire missiles for their military defenses, he stepped in and blocked them. The Resident demands that the challengers commit to a knife fight, and them provides his personally chosen victor a gun. The Resident also provided his own campaign team in support of Netanyahu's challenger in an effort to sway the Israeli election. The willingness of a leader to sacrifice other people, in fact another society, in order to meet his own warped view of what the world should be has been witnessed several times during the past century. And only devastation is left in the wake.

Assault on Civility

> *There is nothing wrong with America that the faith, love of freedom, intelligence, and energy of her citizens cannot cure.*
> *- President Dwight D. Eisenhower*

It seems whenever the Resident inserts himself into a conflict, the conflict expands. He was to be the one who could bring us together, reduce the friction in society, and make us all want to get along. Even after six years of mining the societal battlefield, he claimed, "One of my core principles is that I will never engage in a politics which I'm trying to divide people." There wasn't the Obama smirk. There wasn't a 'but'. He might actually believe that, which may indicate his truly amazing separation from reality. Some claim he would have a form of serial mendacity defined as "Gaslighting: A form of mental abuse in which false information is presented with the intent of making a victim doubt his or her own memory, perception and sanity."[11] An American may wonder if his intention is to gaslight others, or it has become such second nature that he is effectively becoming his own victim. He does appear to have been drinking his own bath water.

While we have seen that he particularly loves to fan the flames of conflict when it comes to racial issues, he is not immune to other areas where some sort of un-American fire can be set, although he seems to try to insert a racial element whenever possible in an attempt to dissuade others from confrontation. He would jump on the gay-marriage train, fight for illegal immigration, and even push forward for replacing men with women in combat.

The Resident will never go down in history as an individual with strong principles. As a candidate for Senate in 2004, he would state, "I am not a supporter of gay marriage."[12] It was eight years earlier in 1996 when he would claim, "I favor legalizing same-sex marriages, and would fight efforts to prohibit such marriages,"[13] which would again be his position once he was comfortably in the White House. But the educated American would ask himself (or herself,) what business does the Federal Government even have in the discussion? Much like the always available abortion industry hysteria which can be called upon when needed, there is nothing in the Constitution that implies a group of bureaucrats were ever supposed to participate in the lives of the individual. But applying similar worn out strategies of division to the gay community that played so well with the racialist community proved to be successful. Where the government does have responsibility would be in the legal 'migration and importation of peoples,' as outlined in Section I. For those who've been paying attention, this would imply the Legislature controls the immigration policy of the country, not one guy with a pen and a phone.

In fact there is a long history of immigration processes that would flummox a national chess champion. Whether the immigration laws are reasonable or even executable is not what's in question with this administration; it's whether the administration even needs the law. The Resident is using the subject to further increase friction and division within the country[14]. The immigration problem is a direct result of the welfare state, which has developed a large dependent class which makes for a very profitable business resource for those who contribute to campaigns. The continuous broken-record claim that parents will be sent home, and the kids left here orphaned, seems to generate the kindling needed for the racialist's spark when needed. With the unwavering support of the Praetorian Guard media, there is no room for adults in the room who may be interested in the large numbers of 'Other Than Mexicans (OTM)' crossing the southern border, or the increase in internal terror-related attacks. We'll never see those elected officials offering their neighborhoods to unvetted immigrants. But they are more than willing to offer our daughters up to combat.

Whether or not there is a small segment of our society that wants to be allowed to become a special operations soldier is immaterial to the national security of the United States. On one hand it's unexplainable how a father of young daughters could so callously direct the policy, but on the other, it may not be about the military at all. It's really just another assault on the traditions and values of the American. Over the past couple decades the military had transitioned from the war winning branch of the Federal Government to the social science experimentation laboratory for the counter-cultural champions finding their way into position of power. While the Resident doesn't appear to actually be an adherent to the 7th century anti-Christian ideology of murder and hate, he clearly admires that culture. It may be that society's absolute disrespect for the female which provides the indifference necessary to create such a miserable statement of the value we hold for women in this society.

A couple decades ago there would be a wave of expansion within the military, the opening of many non-combat related positions to women. Because even True Believers must adapt their planning to reality from time to time, many personal requirements would need to be altered. For example, certain positions which previously required certain physical characteristics, such as the ability to lift 100 pounds, would have to be adjusted. If you were a female, you just didn't need that capability any more. The American may ask; if the positon required a person to be able to lift 100 pounds, and we assign another that can't, what happens? Good question, because the military would now have to provide a helper to accomplish those tasks. But the American asks again; wouldn't that develop an environment of contempt as the positions now became symbols of entitlement, no longer representing service to the country? Right again.

As is the case with many of the Progressive industry's objectives, the agenda requires the supporters to become their own sacrificial lambs. By creating some sort of 'right' to a self-selected military position, requiring a separate set of standards, the individual is used as a pawn in a bigger game. Those who are actually called to the service of their country are being sacrificed to those whose objective is to undermine that very service itself. So the American asks again, is this actually for the good of the military, or even the new 'employee', or is it really an attempt to undermine and diminish the military capability of the United States? Another great question, left to the observer who can answer this: If non-combat positions were effectively compromised in order to support the elite's social experimentation policies, how will the division within combat roles affect this country's military capability?

Assault on America

> *But I contend that the strongest of all governments is that which is most free.*
> *- President William H. Harrison*

The current immigration crisis of Middle Eastern refugees flooding into Europe and the United States has been created by the cabal of European leaders who found themselves blessed with our administration's desire for acceptance. No longer would the undeniable superiority of American values provide the guiding light for improving the human condition around the world. It would be the weak elected officials which would be seduced by the Euro-think which evolved through millennia of strife. While it's possible what the world is witnessing is a result of years of incompetence on the part of the international community, manifesting itself into the largest global crisis in memory, the introduction of large numbers of refugees from a culture whose ideological goals have been dominated with the eradication of western civilization is irresponsible. Allowing the immigrant groups to avoid assimilation into the host country's culture and not demanding respect for the borders, language, and culture of their host is not only a recipe for disaster, but is criminal negligence on the part of the political leadership who claim justification.

European culture continues to languish in a caste-like system, where the leadership believes they have God-given rights to their aristocratic behavior. Millennia of experience has not dissuaded the repeated cycle of falling for a just master, rising to revolution against the despotic ruling class, only to slowly fall back into the search for the next just master. The American rejected this nature of dependence centuries ago, created the greatest country on the Earth, and had secured liberty, which is now decreasing at an alarming rate.

Enamored with being accepted by the international ruling class, the Resident and key officials appear more intent on solidifying their future prospects abroad than at home. An American would initially be confused by this behavior of those entrusted to manage the country. The results continue to bring more and more danger to the doorsteps of our homes. The complex and incoherent activities undermining the country and risking its future seem to be the result of incompetence colliding with obliviousness. How can so many things be going wrong at the same time? Those hopeful successors to the Resident will have an enormous task ahead, should they have a chance to right the ship. But the American will finally remember the principle of Ockham's Razor, in choosing among the competing hypotheses, the one with the fewest assumptions should be the one selected. So is it that all these events are a result of incompetence, resulting in an unending array of calamities for someone else to correct? Or could it be that these are not independent or a result of incompetence at all? Could this disastrous frontier we are looking over be exactly what was planned all along?

Although believed to be alien to the United States of America, the past century has seen many nations disintegrate into the abyss of socialism. The model is consistent; a self-proclaimed savior promises to unchain the dependent, and deliver a better future. The dependent bites of the apple of hope, only to find darkness in the result. But it's always too late to claim alarm once the seduction had occurred, for the world once known has vanished, along with the hopes once hoped and the dreams once dreamt. For some reason the un-American masses would hear seductive lure in Marxist philosophy. It's astonishing today to continue to witness the celebration of socialistic ideals among the allegedly educated intellectual, given history's damning evidence identifying the dehumanizing impact which only brings misery and destruction. While the American has yet to live through the unavoidable carnage which travels with true socialism, it's even more amazing to see the European communities' embrace.

Whether it is Lenin's Russian revolution bringing about Stalin's extermination of his countrymen, Mao's land reform requiring that "one tenth of the peasants would have to be destroyed" in order to bring about the needed change, or the Killing Fields of Cambodia, the cost for the saved is the death of those not among the selected class[15]. Recent examples of the unavoidable results of the mental affliction would be the collapse of Venezuela, the latest portrait of success for the radical.

> *"Pretty soon your son won't decide when he's in school, where he will go or what he will do for a living. He will wait for the government to tell him."*
> *- Ronald Reagan (1961)*

AUGUSTUS

Matriculation

> *Few men deserve liberty; most men wish only for a just master.*
> *-Sallust*

The United States of America has transformed into the massive State which has metastasized and consumed virtually all aspects of the once great republican government. It did not happen overnight, nor will retreat be willingly offered. The pathway of precedent may have begun with small incursions and rationalizations, but we have found our way to this point nonetheless. The Executive has diminished the states in the union to little more than administrative appendages after generations of incorporation. The Judicial and Executive have seized extra-constitutional lawmaking powers, insulated from the reach of the citizen, with rarely even a protest from the Legislative. The leviathan's expanse has become far too large for the government of the people, by the people, and for the people to manage. The State developed under the myth of servitude to the masses now serves itself.

Americans are stunned when considering the wanton corruption on display, and the apparent lack of accountability present in today's bureaucracy. It should be noted that the Article II, Section 2 of the Constitution provides the President with the "Power to grant reprieves and Pardons for Offenses against the United States, except in the Cases of Impeachment." It is quite possible the various investigative bodies can clearly predict the result should they actually charge and convict those who are providing their support for the highest offices.

It has been the "peaceful transfer of power" which has provided periodic shifts in direction which had supplied the citizen with the illusion of hope. With each passing election cycle, the promises made would be kept at a diminished rate. But the country would continue election after election, with the belief that it would be the coming election which would result in a better course, only to be denied satisfaction once again. The American citizen would continue to play the Charlie Brown to the political elite's Lucy van Pelt; with each election, the football would be placed, and each time, it would be removed just when the kick was to be made. Charlie even knew it was going to happen, but was nevertheless irresistibly pulled into the charade anyway[1]. The State has now transitioned from the growing pre-adolescent form which began to realize its own power into the young adult who is no longer willing to sit second chair. The elections have been a carefully planned and coordinated media event for decades, where the once competitive sparring partners have been reduced to cooperative agents for the State, each taking their turn at the helm to the benefit of both.

But the helm is no longer within reach of the American. What is now witnessed is that the un-American radical, which has taken control of the State, was not part of the political establishment. Those currently in power have been able to maintain some effective power over the system, but see decades of control beginning to dissipate with the next election. They have wrestled away control of the Democratic Party for the time being, solely due to their 'temporary' position in the Executive, but not the Democratic Wing of the Party. It appears the Republican Wing of the Party is in no better position itself. The State establishment appears to be cornered as a result of dramatic rejections of their candidates. Their two-sides-of-the-same-coin methodology doesn't look like it is going to work out as planned this time.

The primary establishment candidate, awaiting indictment, and probable conviction of the most damaging criminal acts against our country in at least our lifetime, is the presumptive nominee for the Party. Her competitor was to be from the other 'dynasty', presumptive and assured to be "the only one that can win." Even the Praetorian Guard media appears to no longer be as successful at delivering the State's messaging, needed to provide the illusion of credibility.

In order to control the challenge to their candidate's weakness, the Democratic Wing of the Party had effectively reduced all internal competition prior to the campaign, only to find a challenger who was so far left of even the Democratic Party that he would register Independent until April, 2015, converting to Democrat just in time to qualify for the primaries. The party welcomed him as a competitor, probably as a way to help their progressive champion candidate appear to be more centered, resulting in a more receptive attitude amongst the ignorant. But this may have backfired, as the establishment is realizing the years of increasingly progressive activity may have resulted in the slow, but inevitable, emigration of Americans from the increasingly radicalized positions the Democratic Wing of the Party had developed. The proud socialist would appeal to the Democratic wing's voting base consisting of the vast collection of identity-based self-interest and counter-culture groups. Although the momentum and pre-determined super delegate process in the not-so Democratic Wing of the Party appears behind the future inmate, the State can only support her as long as they are assured of her viability. It may turn out the establishment will not have their candidate on the ballot in 2016, as they had planned. But the other wing of the Party is in no better shape.

In early 2016, the establishment has found itself a minority in the Republican Wing of the Party as well. Apparently applying the old formula of providing a challenger in the general election who would put up a noble, but predictably failed, attempt to beat the State's preferred candidate was thought to be the same recipe of choice. But selecting the once-Governor, and brother of the last Republican President, was not to be in the cards. The lack of enthusiasm for a candidate has never dissuaded the Party in the past, but the tides have turned. The public is no longer as compliant as before. Is it the American is finally getting wise to the ruse? The establishment candidate could not even get on the leader board, as top vote-getters would be 'outsiders'. The establishment is scrambling to find someone who can win the party nomination, for the future leadership of the State is now in question. It would not be their second string candidate, the young Senator from Florida, either. Did anyone notice the fact that the minute establishment began to support him, he became less viable? It looks like all hope now rests with the Ohio Governor, who has been the little engine that could. He has certainly demonstrated his consistency as spokesman for the establishment cause. While it appears the State will not have a representative from the Republican Wing this election which wins the necessary delegate count prior to the convention, a wise American would not count them out just yet.

Still in the primary season, it appears possible there may be no establishment candidate which can rise to the top and represent the State in the general election. But the risk to the State is limited should the Democratic ticket be victorious. Even if the non-establishment Democratic nominee would be elected, the State should be able to maintain control of the apparatus through the vast entrenched politically appointed base. It's fairly clear the socialist from Vermont doesn't have the army of bureaucrats at the ready which would be required to man the battle stations of the State ship. It's the other side which is in question, and seen as the real threat.

The two leading non-establishment candidates for the nomination for the presidency from the Republican Wing of the Party are 'outsiders'. The business Icon is in many ways similar to the outsider in the Democrat race. He may begrudgingly be accepted by the establishment, but is clearly uncontrollable respective of State activities. And in many ways he is the opposite. He has spent a lifetime of making 'deals' with whoever can further his cause. It's also becoming clear he may be master shape-shifter, and protected by the media himself. The fact that he had been a major donor and supporter of all-things liberal-Democrat until a couple years ago should set off warning sirens amongst Republicans, but it isn't. It's unclear what his principles may be, but at least his love for the country which has provided him such success appears unquestionable. And he clearly has the ability to infuse the State with an army of effective followers. Much more than the current administration, the direction may not be to the liking of the establishment. His message boils down to the establishment message, which is that the government just needs a competent driver at the helm, and everything will be 'great again'. But haven't we seen this before? It's starting to feel like Groundhog Day in American.

The most damaging item in the 'presumptive' Democratic candidate's background, assuming she can avoid indictment, will be Benghazi and the actions leading up to it. An aware American will notice the Republican Wing is about to nominate the person who himself had historically aligned himself with her destructive decision to go into Libya in the first place. This is eerily similar to the 2012 election as the challenger to the Resident had himself implemented a similar government controlled healthcare plan, rendering him impotent to the challenge.

> *I can't believe what our country is doing. Gadhafi, in Libya, is killing thousands of people. Nobody knows how bad it is and we're sitting around. We have soliders all over the Middle East and we're not bringing them in to stop this horrible carnage. And that's what it is, a carnage. ... Now we should go in. We should stop this guy which would be very easy and very quick. We could do it surgically, stop him from doing it and save these lives. This is absolute nuts. We don't want to get involved and you're going to end up with something like you've never seen before. Now, ultimately the people will appreciate it and they're going to end up taking over the country eventually. But the people will appreciate it and they should pay us back. But we have to go in to save these lives. These people are being slaughtered like animals. ... We should do it on a humanitarian basis. Immediately go into Libya, knock this guy out very quickly, very surgically, very effectively and save the lives.*
>
> *Donald Trump, 2011*[2]

Will his answer be the same as Romney's? "I wouldn't have done it the same way." Is it possible the State has already been manipulating the contestants and their campaigns in an attempt to control every possible outcome? Of course it's possible. And with what's hanging in the balance, it should be expected. But he Icon's primary competitor would be the State's least favorite selection, to put it mildly.

It appears possible that the Texas Senator, fearless guardian of the Constitution, could win the Republican Party nomination. His positions are unapologetically counter to the State's authority and dominance. His track record is consistent and he has been brilliantly successful at it. While the State will see the 'deal' maker as a less-than-perfect, yet possibly an acceptable alternative, the State knows it's fundamentally incompatible with a President who promised to diminish its span of control and authority over the lives of the people. The State must destroy this candidacy before the nomination. But even the State has only so many arrows in its quiver.

The Democratic Wing of the Party executes a nomination process which is reminiscent of totalitarian regime practices where an election is held, but the outcome is never in question. The super-delegate system appears to effectively require the competitor to win virtually all statewide contests to have a chance at winning the nomination, ensuring the establishment candidate will be selected. Early in the race, this may still be possible with the looming criminal investigations into the activities of their nominee, as well as her dynastic family as well. The Republican nomination process is not quite as controllable.

While the establishment is trying to compose the correct combination of issues which could create support for an establishment representative, the task has become monumental at this stage, probably insurmountable. The momentum has completely shifted toward outsiders. The State will have to choose the outsider whom they feel can best serve their interest. Whoever it may be, it is a surety that this will not be the Texas Senator. But the Texas Senator has an impressive campaign already, and it may be too late for the establishment as the front-runner is consistently showing signs of independence. As has previously been observed, the election system may have already run its course, first demonstrated in the 2012 election cycle. The establishment has created a dependency class which all but assures control of election outcomes, as long as the candidates do not stir the enthusiasm of the American. The American, feeling unable to affect the outcome, is lulled to sleep, turnout is low, and the establishment maintains control. But there is danger on the horizon.

Should the independent socialist and the constitutional 'purist' become the only options; the State will see that the absurdity of the Democratic candidacy will not appeal to the mainstream of the country. At the time this book was going to print, a predictable landslide for the American candidate has put the State and its establishment control into a corner; and beware a cornered animal. The movements are already being made, and it's the American citizen's increasing infatuation with presentism which is laying the foundation for the real change the State has prepared for.

Contested Conventions

> Rule 1: Power is not only what you have, but what your enemy thinks you have.
> Rule 9: The Threat is usually more terrifying that the thing itself.
> Rule 11: If you push a negative hard enough, it will push through and become a positive.
> -Saul Alinksy[3]

It would be the election of Woodrow Wilson that marked the beginning of the end of the republican government put to paper 125 years prior. The infusion of European intellectualism into the conscience of the country's elite would forever alter the course of our government as the State started to come to life. The caucus system had been in place since the election of 1796, as a method to coordinate the nominees from the political parties. The 1912 election would be the first to see the use of the new presidential primary as a hopeful mechanism to better represent the public desires for the party nominee.

Twelve states would select their candidate using primaries during that election. But these primaries were considered "non-binding", resulting in convention defeat for the more popular candidate, Theodore Roosevelt. The establishment would back their sitting-President, Roosevelt's successor, William Howard Taft, as the nominee. The result was Teddy's third party candidacy, and ultimately Wilson's victory. But it would be the Democratic national convention in 1968 which would provide insight into the ability of the establishment to control the party's nominee.

While initial expansion of states' participation using primaries grew to twenty in 1920, only twelve states remained which chose their delegates in this fashion from 1932 through 1968. The infamously riotous Chicago convention to nominate the Democratic Party nominee would provide insight into the establishment's ultimate authority over who would be allowed to represent the party, as well as the strategy to incite violent uprisings as mechanism to affect the outcome.

Robert Kennedy and Eugene McCarthy would challenge President Johnson for the nomination, but the convention would see a very different competition. Shortly after realizing the challenge to a sitting President was to be successful, the President made his famous announcement that he "would not seek, and would not accept" the nomination of his party for the presidency, and the establishment's candidate selection would be transferred to Johnson's Vice-President, Hubert Humphrey. But Humphrey chose to not even compete in any primaries, as they weren't controlled by the party leaders the way they were in the caucus system. It would be an assassin's bullet which removed the challenger, Robert Kennedy, from contention and rocked the country that season. Even though Humphrey had held a sizable lead prior to the shooting, he didn't have a majority. It was estimated Humphrey would've been the nominee anyway, but it's reasoned that Kennedy's death helped to avoid a 'Brokered Convention'.

A convention is 'brokered' when there isn't a clear winner at the beginning of the convention, the convention becomes 'open' and a 'contested convention' may ensue, ushering in the selection results from back-room dealings. The party rules change from time to time, but to avoid a brokered convention there is currently a requirement for a clear majority of delegates to be in support of a single candidate. In 1968, at the time of Kennedy's death, Humphrey held a solid lead, but with only 46% of the delegates, to Kennedy's 32%. The 'brokered' threat would dissipate, but in the end Humphrey would lose to Nixon in the general election. The threat of a brokered convention has recently come with an ominous foreboding of treachery. Even though brokered conventions were the standard for more than the first hundred years of the country's electoral processes, Americans can sense the sea-change that has occurred. The country's government of the 19th century bears little resemblance to the current State. While not allowed into the inner sanctums of the controlling party structures, Americans rightly sense the masterminds' intentions may not be in line with the country's wishes. The stakes seem much higher now.

Because the Democratic Party required two-thirds majority to avoid a brokered convention until 1936, a brokered convention was a standard occurrence. But this was before the State had taken control of the 'several states', as well. For most of the country, while not immune from the effects of bad governance as in the case of the Smoot-Hawley Act, the public was by and large relatively unaffected by the federal government's activities before this time. While the most recent brokered convention nominees were Thomas Dewey in 1948 for the Republicans and Adlai Stevenson in 1952 for the Democrats, the last President selected by a brokered convention would be Franklin Delano Roosevelt in 1932. Like the 1968 election, there have been several other conventions which narrowly avoided being brokered as well, as recent as the Republican convention in 1976 with Ronald Reagan's unsuccessful bid against sitting-President Gerald Ford, and Democratic conventions of 1980, 1984, 1988, and 2008.

But like the 1968 election, the 2016 election season promises to include the 'Largest Civil Disobedience Action of the Century'[4]. Many groups with ideological foundations similar to the Resident, like the George Soros-funded MoveOn.org, are beginning to organize. The AFL-CIO is "all in behind the Democracy Spring" as the groups are demanding that they listen to the people[5]. As usual it's not 'the people', but their people, meaning 'them'. The un-American groups masquerading as anarchist movements are gaining momentum. The controllers are Marxist ideologues, but their armies are people in search of a just master. They don't realize it is this great country that provides them the venue for their outrage. Other countries provide you but a single opportunity; you rarely would get a second.

The 2016 candidate pool appears to be managed in an attempt to dilute the popular sentiment against an out-of-control federal government. The establishment, whose power and control lies within the boundary of the government authority it has seized, has no incentive to allow an outsider to take control of the reigns. The last time a President would be elected as an establishment challenger would be 1980, and it was Ronald Reagan. He would become widely recognized as a great President. The true legacy of a President is not what is spun by sycophants, but a result of perspective based on actual accomplishments. The American is now witnessing the result of the State's fan-boy marketing. Now that history has turned a more balanced perspective toward the Gipper's administration, many realize he was the greatest President since Abraham Lincoln. Those who are part of the establishment realize the State's loss of control at this time in history would forever reduce their power as the ability to manipulate events through the election system may have all but evaporated. One way to invalidate the public may be not through the specific outcome of a brokered convention, but the opportunity to simply bring into question the validity of the result.

The Constitution provides specific dates for elections and the following transfer of power. An American might consider what would happen should the result of a convention be contested. With non-establishment candidates leading the charge for one major party's nomination, and still a threat in the other, it's in the best interest of the establishment to inject competition sufficient to reduce the leader's delegate count to less than the required majority. Should this happen, the back room could then drive the decision. In the case of the Republican field, at the time of this book's publishing, the establishment appears to support a fight where the competition remains a three-way affair, ensuring no winner can be claimed during the first convention ballot vote.

In the case of the Democratic field, things may actually be much worse. Even though the State is firmly controlled by the Democratic Wing of the Party at the current time, the establishment's presumptive nominee will find it difficult to resurrect her image, even with the sycophantic media complex managing her personal relations. She will do well to find herself not incarcerated as her corruption continues to publicly unfold. As such, she is literally in a fight for her life, as she finds herself in a position where her only opportunity to live out her years a free woman may be through the successful election. As the details continue to trickle out, even this is beginning to appear fantasy. As soon as the State realizes their only candidate remaining is the avowed socialist, with little demonstrated affinity for the goals and aspirations of the State, we may see the entrance of an 'emergency' candidate. This also allows the insertion of a candidate held in the wings which needed to avoid public scrutiny. The fact that both parties are appearing immensely incompetent with regards to fielding a reasonable leader for the country should be setting off alarms throughout the population. An aware American may consider this evidence of the fact that the country realizes elections may not actually exist anymore; they are but theater of distraction. And brokered convention results could lay the foundation of further systemic manipulation as the battle if for control of the State.

Should the State find the candidate who ultimately claims victory through the national convention to be incompatible, it's very possible there will be a flood of legal challenges, claiming the candidate is in some way ineligible for the ballot. As witnessed during the 2000 Bush-Gore campaign, there is no lack of willing judicial participation in the political chicanery of an election campaign. Even after there was no chance the declaration of the winner could be overturned, the Florida Supreme Court continued to demand recounts. The media faithfully obscured the critical evidence in their own public trial of the case leading the public to think there was something that should be done, or even could be done. They were even able to drag the United States Supreme Court into the middle of the manufactured controversy, in which they had no jurisdiction, all in the hopes of creating the myth of impropriety. Even if Florida had not already certified the outcome of the election, or it was to be invalidated somehow, the U.S. Congress would have found for George W. Bush. The State relies on the ignorance or compliance of the populace for its own ends, and the populace eagerly provided itself as support during that charade. After witnessing the Legislative time and again compromising principle for purpose, it's not surprising the American public is skeptical of its intentions. By now, Americans are no longer convinced their representatives have their best interest at heart.

With all the shenanigans which have plagued the government over recent years, it's not inconceivable that the State political parties may withhold a nominee's name from the ballot based on a legal challenge, claiming it would be far worse to have the name on the ballot, only later to be told to remove it. Or worse, that the election would be invalidated through a 'mistake' which would allow an ineligible candidate to impact the election, let alone win critical electoral votes. Should the establishment realize it's beneficial to not have a name on the ballot, is it inconceivable that might happen? The objective of the State and the establishment that benefits from it is not to select the best person available for the Oval Office, but to make sure the power base is unaffected. Should a candidate threaten their power, the candidate will have to be made ineligible in some way. But with the well-defined objective in sight much the same as a great general would, the masterminds will make sure there are other roadblocks, should someone make it past this hurdle. One would be the rise of a credible third party candidate in order to divert enough Electoral College votes in the national election to send the election to Congress for decision.

Third Party Candidates

> *A good leader can't get too far ahead of his followers.*
> *- President Franklin D Roosevelt*

A credible third-party candidacy had already been floated. The wealthy, ex-New York Mayor could fund his own nomination process and change the outcome of the election in much the same way the Teddy Roosevelt's candidacy resulted in the disastrous Woodrow Wilson presidency, or more recently, where Ross Perot would be the reason the Democratic party candidate would win the election in 1992. But even with all the hype generated by the media, a third-party candidate has not had a credible chance of actually winning in modern times. Although each election could provide that first example of a third party victory, it's astronomically improbable. The party loyalists easily outnumber the observant. However, the goal for the State is not to win with a third party candidate, but to remove the opportunity for the electorate to choose their President. Although the State operates unmoored from the Constitution, it will make use of it when it serves their purpose.

Should an election result in no candidate receiving the majority of the Electoral College votes, the constitutional process would send the decision to the Legislature. The 12th Amendment, slightly modified by the 20th Amendment describes the particulars of the decision process. In the case of the presidential decision, each state will cast a single vote based on the state's representative's selection for president, from a list "not exceeding" the top three electoral vote winners from the general election. The winner must then get a majority of the states' votes to be declared the winner. An examination of the legislature would indicate a clearly Republican advantage, as the Republicans are currently enjoying a majority for 33 of the 50 states (see Figure 7). Advantage Republicans! Not so fast. Let's examine this further.

State	Legislators		Dominance		State	Legislators		Dominance	
	Republican	Democrat	Rep	Dem		Republican	Democrat	Rep	Dem
Alabama	6	1	+5		Montana	1	0	+1	
Alaska	1	0	+1		Nebraska	2	1	+1	
Arizona	5	4	+1		Nevada	3	1	+2	
Arkansas	4	0	+4		New Hampshire	1	1		
California	14	39		+25	New Jersey	6	6		
Colorado	4	3	+1		New Mexico	1	2		+1
Connecticut	0	5		+5	New York	9	18		+9
Delaware	0	1		+1	North Carolina	10	3	+7	
Florida	17	10	+7		North Dakota	1	0	+1	
Georgia	10	4	+6		Ohio	11	4	+7	
Hawaii	0	2		+2	Oklahoma	5	0	+5	
Idaho	2	0	+2		Oregon	1	4		+3
Illinois	8	10		+2	Pennsylvania	13	5	+8	
Indiana	7	2	+5		Rhode Island	0	2		+2
Iowa	3	1	+2		South Carolina	6	1	+5	
Kansas	4	0	+4		South Dakota	1	0	+1	
Kentucky	5	1	+4		Tennessee	7	2	+5	
Lousiana	5	1	+4		Texas	25	11	+14	
Maine	1	1			Utah	4	0	+4	
Maryland	1	7		+6	Vermont	0	1		+1
Massachusetts	0	9		+9	Virginia	8	3	+5	
Michigan	9	5	+4		Washington	4	6		+2
Minnesota	3	5		+2	West Virginia	3	0	+3	
Mississippi	3	1	+2		Wisconsin	5	3	+2	
Missouri	6	2	+4		Wyoming	1	0	+1	

Figure 7: U.S. House of Representatives Party Affiliation (2016)

Of the 33 States which republicans hold a majority in congress, eight are by a single seat (AK, AZ, CO, MT, NE, ND, SD, and WY,) and five more are by only two votes (ID, IA, MS, NV, and WI.) A state with a single member advantage could be removed with a single 'present' vote, resulting in a split vote, which would be as effective as one for a secondary candidate. A single vote for the other candidate would have the same effect on a state's representation with a two vote advantage as it would effectively invalidate another voter and again place the state in a position where it couldn't vote 'for' the Republican candidate as well.

Any combination of 'present' votes from the single vote advantage states and single votes contrary to party unity in states with a dual vote advantage, which can reduce the vote to less than 26, can result in a President not being selected. To reemphasize this last point, if the establishment can affect a single legislator in 8 of the 13 states in play, there will be no President selected in 2016 if the decision is sent to the Legislature. Do not forget the media will be insulating the public from the activities, and the State will be calling on its ideological armies to inflame dissent: dissent toward Americans clamoring for representation.

After all that has been observed over the Resident's time in office, is it far-fetched? Consider the passage of Obamacare, as chronicled by Jay Sekulow in *Undemocratic*[6]. A colluding Department of Justice convicted Senator Ted Stevens of Alaska only two weeks before the 2008 election on charges they knew he was innocent of, resulting in the Democrat Mark Begich being the deciding vote. Stevens' innocence would come to light, but not in time to reverse the damage caused by the fraudulent election. This was only to protect a single legislative action, albeit the most draconian seizure of an American's rights in the country's history, but a single move just the same. But the idea of overturning the entire election in such a brazen manner may seem a bit overt. An American may wonder how else the election could be won without the consent of the people. It's possible they could enlist the support of the blind lady of justice. The courts could be called upon in support of invalidating key local and state elections caused by voter fraud.

Invalidating Results

> *Rule 2: Never go outside the expertise of your people.*
> *Rule 3: Whenever possible, go outside the expertise of the enemy.*
> *Rule 4: Make the enemy live up to its own book of rules.*
> *Rule 12: The price of a successful attack is a constructive alternative.*
> -Saul Alinksy[7]

Remembering that the Resident made a name for himself by organizing the Chicago Project Vote campaign for Bill Clinton with the objective to deliver the vote in 1992, the same approach can be made to not deliver a winner, but rather to deliver a crisis. Should there come to light substantial voter fraud in a key voting area where a challenge could flip, or at least invalidate the result in the favor of the State, there is little doubt legal challenges will be made. The reporting of illegal voting over the years has been largely ignored. The un-American efforts of late to import large numbers of low-skilled refugees and immigrants, as well as the State's inability to recognize and confront the illegal alien problem, combined with the militant rejection of state efforts to verify voters, has prepared the battlefield for a crisis. The country witnessed the prelude to this insanity which exploded over 'hanging chads' in 2000. Where the voting fraud had been used in an attempt to usher in an otherwise unelectable politician, it can now cause the opposite. The courts could be brought into the election to invalidate key voting areas. The legal groundwork could already be underway as open primaries provide a superb opportunity for fraud. Reports of candidate's names not found on ballots, people being turned away from polls, and more will provide evidence of wrong-doing and the need to intercede. The case will be brought to a compliant court, where predetermined justice will be the objective, and truth may not have a say. What is in play now is the opportunity for checkmate.

One thing that has been consistent in the recent past, and especially during the past administration, is that party affiliation has really not provided a bulwark to the statist agenda. And there will undoubtedly be many lame ducks as well, more interested in their personal future than one might hope for. An American can rightly question the assumption that a Republican representative would be expected to vote for any nominee from the Republican party, especially if the nominee promises to challenge the State to which most officials have been compromised. It may seem inconceivable that the overt undermining of the intentions in the Constitution would take place, but that exact situation has become more common place with each passing year.

The Legislative however, would understand the implications of such activity. It may be an opportunity for checkmate, but it is also the Rubicon, for once crossed, there can be no retreat. The reality is that the event will end the Constitutional Republic for which they at least pay lip-service to at the present time. This will for all intents and purposes eliminate the legitimacy of the President-elect, should they even continue to masquerade as such. But once the State has shown itself and taken position on the battlefield, there is no longer a need for a new President. Until the move has been made, it may still be advantageous to maintain the charade as to validate a national crisis of some sort and use the Constitution against the country.

Should the current Congress not choose a president, through whatever chicanery can be summoned, it could be passed to the next congress, required to be in place a couple weeks before the end of the presidential term, on January 3, 2017, as defined in the 20th Amendment. Although the lame ducks would have departed, the new members would be in no better position as their future will depend on their own positions. There would have been many weeks of media bombardment, providing justification for the current situation and support for the State's desired outcome. The stalemate could continue. And keep in mind, the date which the Electoral College is not set in the Constitution, but rather at their "Time of chusing". Should this continue to January 20, 2017, the Vice President would be sworn in as President "until a President shall have qualified." Should the shenanigans described earlier occur, it would not be unreasonable to expect there might be an issue with the Vice President as well.

Although not quite as complicated, the Senate would choose the Vice President from the top two electoral vote-getters. This immediately provides the opportunity for a split-party administration: technically possible, but unlikely, unless the purpose would be to generate further systemic fractures. The observant American would also consider that the Senate, which has evolved into a redundant legislative body at best, or at worst a tool for the State to impose its will, has not proven itself recently to be the upper chamber defined by the founders. Consistent in their role as blocking back to the State runner, they can be relied upon to not represent the will of the people. The American aware of the practices of this body would not find it outrageous that they may claim justification to not even have a vote simply because of the claimed catastrophe which would ensue should the President-elect be chosen from a different party, or some such nonsense. For those countrymen who have watched unending melodrama from the Senate as a method to obscure their true intentions, the availability of tools which they could bring to bear seems endless. An American may be skeptical that these events could occur, but there is a countless supply of options for the State. And they are adept at generating crises, real or imagined, which are used to move their ball down the field. Should the Vice President not have been "qualified," the legislature would then select someone to "act accordingly until a President or Vice President shall have been qualified." Who might that be?

Should the State understand the risks involved with such an overt attack on the Constitution and traditions of this country, it may realize the play could be made much earlier, allowing the elected officials to claim impotence over activities. Should a crisis, real or manufactured, cause the election not to occur on the "Tuesday after the first Monday in November," it could create chaos in the system deflecting attention from the establishment's true objective. The resultant furor over the 'unprecedented' events would develop into a 'constitutional crisis,' providing a barrage of claims and counter-claims providing cover for the State's actors, whose objective is not to elect the next president, but to maintain control.

As we have seen during the 2000 election season, the state certification of election results could be called into question raising early confusion. While the Judicial has no direct role in elections, they could be used to generate sufficient controversy as to confuse the ignorant regardless of actuality. The eligibility of the candidate can also be questioned, resulting in a complex game of chess between the individuals and the State apparatus. The battle will take place on that ground somewhere between fact and fiction which we call journalism, controlled by the highest bidder. The cases will be made, the excuses provided, and apologies transmitted, but far too late to save the country from its fate.

The United States' first and greatest President, General George Washington, posed to himself this question, "What is most important of this grand experiment, the United States?" to which he answered himself, "Not the election of the first President, but the election of the second President. The peaceful transfer of power is what will separate our country from every other country in the world." If the transition does not occur on January 20, 2017, what will be the path ahead? It is undefined, except that the Legislature can decide on whether a President and Vice President will even be put forth. It does not define this as an 'elected' President.

Even the Constitution states a President can only be elected twice. It says nothing about how long he can serve, other than the term length would be four years. A crisis erupts! And which group thrives on crisis? Should there not be an eligible President-elect on January 20, 2017, there will be no opportunity to transfer power. The alligator tears will flow for the current Resident had been looking forward to spending more time with the family, exhausted from driving the country into the ground, as he would also be provided as the only one who would be in a position to guide us through this uncertain period: uncertain for the American, but not the State. But as described in Eric Hoffer's *The True Believer*, "A mass movement is pioneered by men of words, materialized by fanatics, and consolidated by men of action." It seems clear the Resident is but a fanatic who fancies himself a man of words. Beware the men of action.

Rewind

> *Whatever is done well enough is done quickly enough.*
> *- Augustus*

The establishment realizes it's looking at a possible shift in power and prestige, comfortably maintained over the past 25 years through the tidal ebb and flow secured by cooperative control of the Executive between the Republican and Democratic Wings of the Party. The current competition for the Resident's seat appears to be producing someone who will prove not to be friendly to the status quo, and could bring a halt to (or at least weaken) the oligarchy. If the Party can contrive enough confusion and conflict to cause a President to not take the oath of office on January 20th, 2017, there will no longer be concern for such threats.

For a President-elect to not have been "qualified", the legislature would need to fail at its duty to select the winner, either through the regular

Electoral College process, or through the backroom dealings they are most noted for. The Legislative has demonstrated their ability to rationalize the most notorious legislation in order to meet the needs of their contributors, but this relatively nonviolent coup would be hard to complete; hard to achieve unless there arose a substantial concern over the legitimacy of the election results, manufactured or not. The outgoing lame-duck congress would be weary of their personal future outside the government, whereas the incoming would be weary for their professional (and personal) future inside. It's quite possible the decision process will become carefully crafted as to not provide "qualified" selections due to unsettled issues created through the campaigns and election processes.

To create a credible level of concern over the legalities of the voting system, the Judicial would be called upon. The goal isn't a permanent decision, only the few that can generate delays sufficient to miss the January 20, 2017 deadline. There will be opportunity to call into question valid results based on illegal voting activities, polling location demonstrations and intimidation, or there could even be 'irregularities' resulting from support system failures such as power outages or cyber-attacks. The election is big business, and the stakes have never been higher.

And of course, last but not least, the Praetorian Guard media will be in the foreground to provide maximum obfuscation of events, misdirecting concern, and feigning corruption not by the establishment, but by the American. The precipice America now looks over was not brought about by a single person, but by a century of un-American manipulation and compromise. The confluence of the country's looming national crises may have been exacerbated by the current Resident, but was supported by those others elected as well. The office of the Presidency relies on a person who believes in the traditions and values of those who make this country great, but sadly the Resident does not. And because of this, his desire to diminish, and ultimately to destroy, the constitutional republic may come to a successful end should this election season be allowed to play out as the State has planned.

Corrective Actions

> *The truth is that all men having power ought to be mistrusted.*
> *- President James Madison*

Many Americans find themselves feeling helpless to the activities hundreds or thousands of miles away in Washington, D.C., previously unaware of the leviathan that had encroached into every orifice of their lives, having realized their "unalienable Rights [of] Life, Liberty, and the pursuit of Happiness"[1] have dissipated into the government minefield of regulation each must carefully navigate to avoid reprisal. The State has grown so large as to consume the entire value of the economy, but still remains insatiable. The government, once of representatives, now of masterminds, has seized the rights of the citizenry and claimed authority over those lives. So, we can revisit the questions from the Introduction:

Three hundred years ago, this grand experiment we call the United States was not even a thought in young Benjamin Franklin's head. Do you think this country will exist three hundred years from now? That would be longer than the Roman Republic existed. No other system of government had lasted for that long. It's hard to imagine ours would not see a similar fate. Isn't it?

About a hundred years ago, the Progressive movement found their way into the White House, and brought with it the fondness for European socialism and affected the removal of state participation in governmental decisions. Do you think this country will exist in one hundred years? The country's government is already in the early stages of bankruptcy, with no intention of reducing its consumption. It can't continue along its current path for long. Can it?

About fifty years ago, the government had transformed from the protector of the citizen's liberty to the provider of the citizen's needs, resulting in the justification for out-of-control spending, while it nurtured a learned helplessness among many sectors of society. Do you think this country will exist in fifty years? The current rate of increase for core entitlement programs alone is projected to eclipse total revenues before then. In fact, the annual interest payment on the national debt alone will eclipse the entire budget of the Defense Department should interest rates rise to a more historically responsible level. There appears no serious effort to curb spending in Washington D.C. It seems like the train is heading to the cliff and no one is willing to stop it. Doesn't it?

Seven years ago the country witnessed what George Washington identified as that element that separated "this country from every other country in the world," which was the peaceful transition of power. We are anxiously waiting to see one occur again next year. Or will we?

Does the citizen believe that the future of the United States is assured, that tomorrow will be just like today? Or is it possible the transformation is complete and tomorrow will bring the change they had planned all along? The American will not throw in the towel. The constitutional republic created by Americans, but currently under the control of a radical, may not yet be uncorrectable. There are many problems with the government which has helped us arrive at this station, and they must be confronted.

Domestic Correction

> *Few men have the virtue to withstand the highest bidder.*
> *- President George Washington*

A pessimist may think it may be too late already, but the 'several states' can and must reassert their authority over the State. There can be no easy way out of the morass which has enveloped this once great civil society, and there are none but our youngest that had not, in some way, taken part. But for one thing we can be certain: the State is not the answer. The current Article V Convention of the States movement must quickly take root and apply overwhelming pressure on the State through the Constitutional amendment process to realign and reassert the 'several states' participation in federal government decisions through the repeal of the 17th Amendment. This will allow the States to once again select the Senators, and will bring them back into the decision processes. For the following corrections will never be supported by the State, nor their Legislative arm.

Some may say the federal government spends money like a drunken Marxist. But Marx couldn't comprehend the scope of this thievery. The level of fiscal operating debt and even annual deficit are staggering and beyond comprehension of the American. The government expenses must be limited to its revenues. And to not be caught unaware, the government must be limited to how much revenue it can collect. An Amendment must be imposed to cap revenue, and require a balanced budget. Both are critical, as one without the other is only more of the same. The revenue cap alone will drive more debt, and a balanced budget requirement will effectively usher in requirements for even more taxes to cover planned expenditures.

Eliminate Omnibus! Each program must stand on its own. Begin with the constitutional departments and prioritize the rest. Pass one budget before legislation is begun for the next. After the money runs out, so do the approved budgets. This might effectively provide a mechanism to prioritize, and ultimately remove less important departments and offices.

Limit appropriations requests to a total of 90% of the previous year's revenue, plus remaining funds from previous year. Much like our home budgets, when the money runs out, so does our spending, and continually writing checks based on the next paycheck is the recipe for disaster.

In 2011, Congress passed only 81 laws. It seems that with so few, they can take their time; require that all bills (and references) be read allowed on the floor of the house before votes are allowed. That should slow them down. The days of the 2000 page products used to cover the tracks of questionable activities should then be numbered.

Abolish the Internal Revenue Service. The source of all State power rests within the ability to pick winners and losers. Even winners know the State can quickly turn on them, and it has created a fearful, but malleable and compliant serfdom. The tax code is their mechanism to apply pressure, as well as benefits, to those they wish to punish, or reward. The Constitution provides justification for an income tax, but by specifying a particular tax it virtually removes authority from others. A simple flat tax of some sort should be put in place. The byproduct will not only be the elimination of a virtual internal police force, but also the massive Executive and Legislative army in place to manipulate and control it, as well as reducing much of the mass of the legislative bills produced which are used to affect the tax code. Removing these excessive items would allow the representatives to read the bills they are voting on as well. Americans would call that a "win-win".

The hidden cost of government is the regulation burden. While an entire industry exists only to support the tax system in this country, the elephant in the room is the regulation costs which are imposed, much like the tax system, to effectively select winners and losers. Estimated at around $2 *trillion* annually, this is a result of the abdication of legislative responsibility. For example, the EPA may have a budget on the order of $10 billion, but the indirect cost to the country is many times that amount, estimated to be $353 billion per year in 2012[2]. The regulations are held as law in the court systems, yet they were never passed by the only body authorized to create laws. When the State controls judge, jury, and provides the executioner, the American is without recourse. All regulation must be approved by the people, through positive and active legislative concurrence.

But it is the size of the leviathan that must be targeted as well. The depth and breadth of the hundreds of departments and agencies which are not even constitutionally justified must be dealt with. Call on the immediate divesting of the majority of responsibilities in the Departments of Commerce, Education, Energy, HUD, Health and Human Services, Interior, and Labor, by transferring back to the states those things states are responsible for. The federal level may have justification for some cooperative facilitation, but the states must once again become sovereign. The Progressive century is over, and that experiment has proven a colossal failure. For those few who still think the State functions are there for some inherent good and not the source of power and enrichment for those in control, the American in you will at least admit the demonstrated futility in the current exercise. The further support of these entities will result in the destruction of the country they purport to support.

The State will attempt to counter with their most powerful auxiliary weapon, the bench. The court cases will mount, claiming need for due process, or other hogwash. The Article V Convention of the States must put in place sufficient judicial controls to remove the long standing precedent of judicial overrides, as well as corrupted judges. Should wise "little-r" republicans identify methods to put the 'legislation from the bench' Jeanie back in the bottle, reapplication of constitutional constraint may prove enough. But an American realizes that among Man will not an angel be found, and there needs to be clear limitations on these individuals. An ability for a super-majority of the both chambers to remove a Supreme Court Justice would be a welcome improvement; better yet, an annual confirmation requirement for continued service.

These are but a few ideas and most are discussed in much greater detail in Mark Levin's book, *The Liberty Amendments*[3]. To date, 5 states have passed resolutions to support the Article V Convention of States process (AK, AL, FL, GA, and TN,) and about 30 others have applications in progress. The time is now, but that time is also short; let perfect not be the enemy of good. A clear reassertion of the 'several states' authority over the federal government by the immediate repeal of the 17th Amendment would send shock waves through Foggy Bottom. That alone could be the "single flap of a sea gull's wings [which] would be enough to alter the course of the weather altogether."[4]

International Correction

> *That government is best which governs the least, because its people discipline themselves.*
> *- President Thomas Jefferson*

The State is bank-rolling the international socialist movement through the international money laundering service called the United Nations. Or to be clear, you the American are. The U.N. has proven itself as impotent as its predecessor, the League of Nations, with regards asserting effective control of rogue state actors. But it is the U.N., in general, that has evolved to absurd heights. In 2012, the United States government provided roughly a quarter of the $41.5 billion budget. The U.S. dues are more than the bottom 178 countries *combined*.[5] And what does the American get for their generosity? Contemptable hatred at times, but mainly it's a program built around the shake-down methodology that only a community organizer would find appealing. Oh, and he does.

The scandalous Iraq Oil-for-Food program is a great example of the good the US gets from our involvement. The approximately $10 billion 'investment' was provided under "UN financial oversight", which proved "unequal to the task of preventing a rogue regime from stealing." And this program was hailed as "the most successful use of international sanctions on record."[6] Amazing how easy it is to discard other people's money. And to top that off, the US effectively pays the dues of bad actors such as North Korea and Iran due to the Marxist funding scheme loosely tied to the "from each according to his abilities, to each according to his needs" philosophy un-Americans find attractive. The result is an international welfare program no more successful than our domestic attempts.

Much of the billions provided to the UN come from another international program which could bear scrutiny as well. The US Agency for International Development (USAID) has become a nice little slush fund for foreign 'investment'. It is fundamentally a state-based quid pro quo system, allowing the US to apply pressure the old fashioned way: threatening to cut funding they have become reliant on. No clearer example would be the elimination of Yemeni funding in 1990 for their refusal to support the Iraq coalition as US Ambassador Thomas Pickering declared, "That was the most expensive No vote you ever cast."[7] The question is, if you have to buy friends, are they your friends? Because much like welfare, friends it will not purchase, but enemies it will generate when it's removed. For their 2016 presidential budget, here are some of their top objective areas.

- $5.3 billion to counter ISIS and support humanitarian needs in the Middle East, of with $1.1 billion is to support 'diplomatic engagement'.
- $1 billion to address the root cause of migration from Central America, which includes $142 million to pay Mexico to enforce its *southern* border.
- Investing in the Global Climate Change scam, including the Green Climate Fund. Enough said.

These few areas are questionable at best. Regardless of good intentions, the 'democracy projects' this program supports should be reviewed, and at least audited. A cynical American may wonder if that might uncover connections to certain famous global initiatives, and how they might be found to be collecting their own government's foreign aid 'investments'. That American may wonder if this money even finds its way back into political campaigns. Our support for these endeavors are said to be critical, there must surely be some good that can be done, especially in the war-torn Middle East.

But this sort of support is being demonstrated to be folly, should the practitioners be willing to observe. After 70 years of international support to the Middle East, there is virtually no positive result, as a whole. Much of the culture is mired in the 7th century anti-Christian ideology and looks on western civilization with contempt. The Syrian crisis however was a chance to kill two birds with one stone, and import our own destruction, should the Resident's crowd prove unworthy of the task. The importation of international cultures incompatible to your own is like drinking salt water while stranded at sea. You may have a momentary sense of relief, but you have effectively brought on your own demise. It's heartbreaking to see many of those in need that may be willing to assimilate, risk being judged apostate, and give America a try; many are high risk and there is no way to provide a reasonable level of security to the American at risk. We notice the elites aren't clamoring to have these groups move into their neighborhood, but the Resident continues to ridicule others who are concerned for themselves. The assertion of sovereignty by the states must include sovereignty over their citizenry as well.

Patriotic Opportunity

It would seem that all hope is lost for the individual American. Even if the country is granted a reprieve through a transition of power on January 20, 2017, it will only delay the inevitable as the Progressive-infested infrastructure of our government is still in place, and growing. The solution, as mentioned previously, lies within the Constitution itself. Article V provides the ability for the States to reassert their superiority over the federal government and realign our badly deformed national government. But that will require the participation of at least 34 states in a convention. In today's digital age, this should not require a single physical location; it could be a virtual convention, avoiding the expected public spectacle of predictable manufactured disturbances designed to upset progress. Ratification requires passage in 38 states.

But this will require public participation. As previously mentioned, 5 states have already passed resolutions in support of the convention. Contact the Representatives in your particular state's legislative bodies, and demand your state's participation. But you must also demand their support for ratification. Do not let the media shield the activities from the light of day. And do not let the hysteria over possible 'runaway' convention distract you from your mission. It's more nonsense. Those rational, clear thinking Americans which are still out there will recognize the arguments against the amendment process as ridiculous subterfuge. On one hand, the idea that an agreement with 38 somewhat independent legislative bodies will somehow turn out worse than what is going on now seems pure fantasy. And on the other, the American recognizes that the State has been operating as an unaccountable body rewriting the Constitution at will already. It becomes clear the only one threatened by an Article V convention is the State itself. The individual still hold enormous power as long as the Constitution still exists, but calling your representative is only part of what the individual can do.

The individual's power is within our common American core values. Recognize our own need for mutual support, and find the patriotic organizations which are supporting the United States of America. One example is the *Convention of the States* project[8]. But always stay vigilant to the infiltration of un-American detractors with the ranks, as there will be a great number who believe the State is their answer. Much like the struggles the TEA Party groups had experienced, so too will these.

Conclusion

> We are a nation that has a government—not the other way around.
> And that makes us special among the nations of the earth.
> - President Ronald Reagan

The Resident, product of new world and old, promised a change for the good. The hope of a frustrated country projected American values onto this un-American soul. A product of formation outside of American values, educated into radicalism, unconcerned with the precedent of absolute failure of socialistic endeavors, he is a "True Believer"[1]. Buttressed with like-minded administrators, provided cover by the Praetorian Guard media sycophants, he would find his moment in history aligned with the structural failing of the country he decided needed transformation.

From the earliest days of the United States, there had been a consistent effort to overturn the Constitution. As reasonable men would rationalize small deviations along the way, the disturbance from the flap of a sea gull wing has given way to the divergent response now seemingly uncontainable. From the moment the Supreme Court claimed legislative authority challenging President Madison, through their unwillingness to stand for human dignity when opportunity arose to support abolition, right up to today when the court decided the government has a right to the life of a person in order to support the Resident's Affordable Care Act, the Judicial system has demonstrated the effect of allowing untouchable men make law. This was supposed to be the society based on the rule of law, not the rule of lawyers.

The Legislative Branch, originally striking a balance between the populace and the states, provided a friction-filled environment producing a resistance to reactionary change. This was not a mistake in the design, but a key feature to inhibit overreach and rationalization. It was that control mechanism would be forever changed with a constitutional amendment removing the states from the decision process, ushering in the opportunity to apply federal government solutions to the crises searched for at home. The clever separation from decision and responsibility has devolved into a compliant source of revenue support for unbridled spending by the administration.

The Executive Branch, originally chartered with responsibilities for international relationships and to provide for a stable currency and the common defense of the states, had effectively been able to incorporate the states themselves into the federal government as a result of the Civil War. The Great Depression would provide the opportunity to transition states' authority for internal matters to the federal government, and it would be a result of the civil rights movement that the executive would claim authority over the livelihood of the residents within the states. The confluence of a compromised Judicial, the compliant Legislative, and the authoritative Executive has given birth to the all-consuming State.

Borne of designing men, the uncontainable and unanswerable administration has assumed authority over the original three branches of government. As the Judicial demonstrates their reluctance to challenge, and the Legislative impotent to demands, recent decades had witnessed the State absorbing the last vestiges of federalism. But until recently, the person selected to oversee the leviathan had brought with them a certain reverence for the values and traditions inherent in the civil society. While there have been both constructive and destructive administrations, the American inside the person in the Oval Office was never in question. That was until 2009. They say "elections have consequences," in order to deflect what has occurred since.

The American would be dumbfounded as they watched the selection of a person who was devoid of American values, unappreciative for the gift he had been given, unaware of the civil society which provided him his opportunities. But it is the good-natured American heart that is often gullible and could believe another's claims. However, the American would be stymied as the Resident was elected again, with virtually no successful American accomplishment, and a consistent display of anti-American activities. Was it that the American was unable to see the Resident's superior vision, or was it that the American no longer needed to in order for someone to get elected? As the attention continued to be focused on the possibility of unscrupulous masterminds stealing *an* election, it appears that Americans were caught unaware as the magicians have stolen *the* election from the United States. The transformation may already be a fait accompli, as the elections are but a ruse to keep the masses distracted as the State selects the successors. But the State realizes the façade of the electoral process must be discarded should the result threaten its own livelihood. It very well may be that the Resident was the key to our own survival, as it was he who caused the American to stir and awaken to a country almost lost.

Many others have been calling for a return to responsible governance for many years, but to no avail. A recent call to the young people in the country to rise up and claim their heritage was provided by Mark Levin in *Plunder and Deceit*, which supplies an extremely thorough evaluation of the amoral threat to the their futures at the hand of the State[2]. He calls for a change in approach, the demand for a new civil rights movement, this time for the American. It will be from the youth which the future has been stolen, it may be they who are left the duty to reestablish the land of liberty. But it appears it is the youth now who again find the socialist most attractive.

After all has been said and done, it seems like the end may be inevitable. But before it is, we need to ask ourselves what makes this great country great? Is it the State that attempts to provide as much as possible to the people in order to keep them docile and compliant? If that's the case, the end is already in sight as other people's money is running out. Is it the State that creates innovation and jobs? The past seven years is proof-positive that unfathomable amounts of tax-payer money creates virtually no jobs as the money had to be stolen from job creating enterprises in the first place. Only the reduction of government constraints can let loose the power of the market, and create jobs. Is it the State which has made the United States the envy of the world? The State can't even pay countries to like it. Is it the State which has created the country? Or is it the American, which created the government and which is the source of our revolutionary triumph? If you are an American, you know this answer. If you are not, it's not too late to unleash the chains of the State and claim yourself as an American. For should the State collapse, as they all do, the American will still be here and will rebuild that shining light on the hill which is the hope of the world.

It should be remembered that at the time of our Revolution only about a third favored it. A third maintained support for the crown, and the remaining third, neutral. It appears our divisions of interest may be similar today. The time is now, as there may not be a Constitution to amend next year. And without the Constitution, there can be no United States of America.

> *Freedom is never more than one generation away from extinction. We didn't pass it to our children in the bloodstream. It must be fought for, protected, and handed on for them to do the same, or one day we will spend our sunset years telling our children and our children's children what it was once like in the United States where men were free.*
> *- Ronald Reagan[3]*

Acknowledgements

This book was only possible with the love and support of those around me, not just of today, but along my path as well. As I expect this to be like many of my explorations, a short-lived attempt to satisfy my own curiosity about whether I could do it, this is a great opportunity to put down in perpetuity many of those who are responsible for the good things this life has produced. The responsibility for the 'not-so-good' portions rests solely with the author.

As an engineer, I often consider English my second language. Even just the thought of writing a journal article, much less a book such as this, was always a fearful gambit. These pages were immensely improved with help from my better half and partner-in-crime, Marina, along with my brother-from-a-different-mother, Mike. Thank you both very much as it was difficult to perceive the many possible misinterpretations of subject matter that a reader could find very sensitive. There is no avoiding certain topics as these are precisely the defensive minefield used in order to control discourse by the forces now laying siege to the country. There is plenty of ammunition amongst these pages to allow those threatened to bamboozle the unaware, but the unregulated mind will see through this misdirection and understand this isn't about a single person, or even a small group of masterminds. It's the result of a cancerous ideology which has infiltrated the very foundation of our civil society, and the players on stage are more a result of circumstance than strategy.

It all starts with family in America, and mine is a normal American family. I love them all very much. My parent's families travelled from Europe in the second half of the 19th century. The first generations worked very hard to build a foundation for the next, and each made sure the next started better than the last. Each generation is demonstrably better educated, on paper anyway, and rewarded with the privileges fought for by the previous generation's sacrifices. We are the American dream. One of my childhood memories was watching the Democratic convention in a small mountain cabin during the summer of 1972. I was mesmerized by the spectacle, but even now I can't explain why. It's interesting how far the Democratic Party has shifted, demonstrating even then their 'far-left' positions with the nomination of Governor George McGovern. But at the age of nine, their message already seemed alien to my American soul.

My parents provided an all-American upbringing to a brood of siblings, which was understood to be the tradition for our own. But there is another family for which I will always be indebted to as well. While my childhood years would provide the solid foundation for my future, it would be a friend's family which would help me understand how my place in this world would not be measured by what I would become in as much as it would be how I participated in the lives of others and what they might become. I will forever be thankful for the lessons I learned from Tre and his mother, Janice.

My own internal spark which caused the course correction for a successful life can be traced to a single event, and reinforced with another 3 years later. The birth of a child, my child, awakened me from the aimless, happy-go-lucky slumber of my youth. I will always be thankful for the gift of two fantastic kids, Adriane and John, with his beautiful family, who amaze me with their good and independent souls. As only a parent can really appreciate, the child teaches much to the parent as well. I was hopefully able to be a calming and supportive agent for good in the lives of several others along the way as well. To Alison, I'm proud of who you've become. To James and Laurel, thank you for letting me into your family. Watching you each bloom into adulthood has been a fantastic gift. And to Jamie, I hope whatever path you found has made all the difference.

To my guide star, my staunchest supporter and my inspiration for this book, Marina, you make each day better than the one before and drive me to want to be better with each of those passing days. Any strength I appear to have is really a reflection of the belief you have in me.

APPENDIX

The Constitution of the United States of America

We the People of the United States, in Order to form a more perfect Union, establish Justice, insure domestic Tranquility, provide for the common defence, promote the general Welfare, and secure the Blessings of Liberty to ourselves and our Posterity, do ordain and establish this Constitution for the United States of America.

Article I.

Section. 1. All legislative Powers herein granted shall be vested in a Congress of the United States, which shall consist of a Senate and House of Representatives.

Section. 2. The House of Representatives shall be composed of Members chosen every second Year by the People of the several States, and the Electors in each State shall have the Qualifications requisite for Electors of the most numerous Branch of the State Legislature.

No Person shall be a Representative who shall not have attained to the Age of twenty five Years, and been seven Years a Citizen of the United States, and who shall not, when elected, be an Inhabitant of that State in which he shall be chosen.

[Representatives and direct Taxes shall be apportioned among the several States which may be included within this Union, according to their respective Numbers, which shall be determined by adding to the whole Number of free Persons, including those bound to Service for a Term of Years, and excluding Indians not taxed, three fifths of all other Persons.][1] The actual Enumeration shall be made within three Years after the first Meeting of the Congress of the United States, and within every subsequent Term of ten Years, in such Manner as they shall by Law direct. The Number of Representatives shall not exceed one for every thirty Thousand, but each State shall have at Least one Representative; and until such enumeration shall be made, the State of

---

[1] Changed by Section 2 of the Fourteenth Amendment

New Hampshire shall be entitled to chuse three, Massachusetts eight, Rhode-Island and Providence Plantations one, Connecticut five, New-York six, New Jersey four, Pennsylvania eight, Delaware one, Maryland six, Virginia ten, North Carolina five, South Carolina five, and Georgia three.

When vacancies happen in the Representation from any State, the Executive Authority thereof shall issue Writs of Election to fill such Vacancies.

The House of Representatives shall chuse their Speaker and other Officers; and shall have the sole Power of Impeachment.

Section. 3. The Senate of the United States shall be composed of two Senators from each State, [chosen by the Legislature thereof,][2] for six Years; and each Senator shall have one Vote.

Immediately after they shall be assembled in Consequence of the first Election, they shall be divided as equally as may be into three Classes. The Seats of the Senators of the first Class shall be vacated at the Expiration of the second Year, of the second Class at the Expiration of the fourth Year, and of the third Class at the Expiration of the sixth Year, so that one third may be chosen every second Year; [and if Vacancies happen by Resignation, or otherwise, during the Recess of the Legislature of any State, the Executive thereof may make temporary Appointments until the next Meeting of the Legislature, which shall then fill such Vacancies.][3]

No Person shall be a Senator who shall not have attained to the Age of thirty Years, and been nine Years a Citizen of the United States, and who shall not, when elected, be an Inhabitant of that State for which he shall be chosen.

The Vice President of the United States shall be President of the Senate, but shall have no Vote, unless they be equally divided.

The Senate shall chuse their other Officers, and also a President pro tempore, in the Absence of the Vice President, or when he shall exercise the Office of President of the United States.

---

[2] Changed by the Seventeenth Amendment
[3] Changed by the Seventeenth Amendment

The Senate shall have the sole Power to try all Impeachments. When sitting for that Purpose, they shall be on Oath or Affirmation. When the President of the United States is tried, the Chief Justice shall preside: And no Person shall be convicted without the Concurrence of two thirds of the Members present.

Judgment in Cases of impeachment shall not extend further than to removal from Office, and disqualification to hold and enjoy any Office of honor, Trust or Profit under the United States: but the Party convicted shall nevertheless be liable and subject to Indictment, Trial, Judgment and Punishment, according to Law.

Section. 4. The Times, Places and Manner of holding Elections for Senators and Representatives, shall be prescribed in each State by the Legislature thereof; but the Congress may at any time by Law make or alter such Regulations, except as to the Places of chusing Senators.

The Congress shall assemble at least once in every Year, and such Meeting shall be [on the first Monday in December,][4] unless they shall by Law appoint a different Day.

Section. 5. Each House shall be the Judge of the Elections, Returns and Qualifications of its own Members, and a Majority of each shall constitute a Quorum to do Business; but a smaller Number may adjourn from day to day, and may be authorized to compel the Attendance of absent Members, in such Manner, and under such Penalties as each House may provide.

Each House may determine the Rules of its Proceedings, punish its Members for disorderly Behaviour, and, with the Concurrence of two thirds, expel a Member.

Each House shall keep a Journal of its Proceedings, and from time to time publish the same, excepting such Parts as may in their Judgment require Secrecy; and the Yeas and Nays of the Members of either House on any question shall, at the Desire of one fifth of those Present, be entered on the Journal.

---

[4] Changed by Section 2 of the Twentieth Amendment

Neither House, during the Session of Congress, shall, without the Consent of the other, adjourn for more than three days, nor to any other Place than that in which the two Houses shall be sitting.

Section. 6. The Senators and Representatives shall receive a Compensation for their Services, to be ascertained by Law, and paid out of the Treasury of the United States. They shall in all Cases, except Treason, Felony and Breach of the Peace, be privileged from Arrest during their Attendance at the Session of their respective Houses, and in going to and returning from the same; and for any Speech or Debate in either House, they shall not be questioned in any other Place.

No Senator or Representative shall, during the Time for which he was elected, be appointed to any civil Office under the Authority of the United States, which shall have been created, or the Emoluments whereof shall have been encreased during such time; and no Person holding any Office under the United States, shall be a Member of either House during his Continuance in Office.

Section. 7. All Bills for raising Revenue shall originate in the House of Representatives; but the Senate may propose or concur with Amendments as on other Bills.

Every Bill which shall have passed the House of Representatives and the Senate, shall, before it become a Law, be presented to the President of the United States; If he approve he shall sign it, but if not he shall return it, with his Objections to that House in which it shall have originated, who shall enter the Objections at large on their Journal, and proceed to reconsider it. If after such Reconsideration two thirds of that House shall agree to pass the Bill, it shall be sent, together with the Objections, to the other House, by which it shall likewise be reconsidered, and if approved by two thirds of that House, it shall become a Law. But in all such Cases the Votes of both Houses shall be determined by yeas and Nays, and the Names of the Persons voting for and against the Bill shall be entered on the Journal of each House respectively. If any Bill shall not be returned by the President within ten Days (Sundays excepted) after it shall have been presented to him, the Same shall be a Law, in like Manner as if he had signed it, unless the

Congress by their Adjournment prevent its Return, in which Case it shall not be a Law.

Every Order, Resolution, or Vote to which the Concurrence of the Senate and House of Representatives may be necessary (except on a question of Adjournment) shall be presented to the President of the United States; and before the Same shall take Effect, shall be approved by him, or being disapproved by him, shall be repassed by two thirds of the Senate and House of Representatives, according to the Rules and Limitations prescribed in the Case of a Bill.

Section. 8. The Congress shall have Power To lay and collect Taxes, Duties, Imposts and Excises, to pay the Debts and provide for the common Defence and general Welfare of the United States; but all Duties, Imposts and Excises shall be uniform throughout the United States;

To borrow Money on the credit of the United States;

To regulate Commerce with foreign Nations, and among the several States, and with the Indian Tribes;

To establish an uniform Rule of Naturalization, and uniform Laws on the subject of Bankruptcies throughout the United States;

To coin Money, regulate the Value thereof, and of foreign Coin, and fix the Standard of Weights and Measures;

To provide for the Punishment of counterfeiting the Securities and current Coin of the United States;

To establish Post Offices and post Roads;

To promote the Progress of Science and useful Arts, by securing for limited Times to Authors and Inventors the exclusive Right to their respective Writings and Discoveries;

To constitute Tribunals inferior to the supreme Court;

To define and punish Piracies and Felonies committed on the high Seas, and Offences against the Law of Nations;

To declare War, grant Letters of Marque and Reprisal, and make Rules concerning Captures on Land and Water;

To raise and support Armies, but no Appropriation of Money to that Use shall be for a longer Term than two Years;

To provide and maintain a Navy;

To make Rules for the Government and Regulation of the land and naval Forces;

To provide for calling forth the Militia to execute the Laws of the Union, suppress Insurrections and repel Invasions;

To provide for organizing, arming, and disciplining, the Militia, and for governing such Part of them as may be employed in the Service of the United States, reserving to the States respectively, the Appointment of the Officers, and the Authority of training the Militia according to the discipline prescribed by Congress;

To exercise exclusive Legislation in all Cases whatsoever, over such District (not exceeding ten Miles square) as may, by Cession of particular States, and the Acceptance of Congress, become the Seat of the Government of the United States, and to exercise like Authority over all Places purchased by the Consent of the Legislature of the State in which the Same shall be, for the Erection of Forts, Magazines, Arsenals, dock-Yards, and other needful Buildings;—And

To make all Laws which shall be necessary and proper for carrying into Execution the foregoing Powers, and all other Powers vested by this Constitution in the Government of the United States, or in any Department or Officer thereof.

Section. 9. The Migration or Importation of such Persons as any of the States now existing shall think proper to admit, shall not be prohibited by the Congress prior to the Year one thousand eight hundred and eight, but a Tax or duty may be imposed on such Importation, not exceeding ten dollars for each Person.

The Privilege of the Writ of Habeas Corpus shall not be suspended, unless when in Cases of Rebellion or Invasion the public Safety may require it.

No Bill of Attainder or ex post facto Law shall be passed.

No Capitation, or other direct, Tax shall be laid, unless in Proportion to the Census or Enumeration herein before directed to be taken.[5]

No Tax or Duty shall be laid on Articles exported from any State.

---

[5] See Sixteenth Amendment

No Preference shall be given by any Regulation of Commerce or Revenue to the Ports of one State over those of another: nor shall Vessels bound to, or from, one State, be obliged to enter, clear, or pay Duties in another.

No Money shall be drawn from the Treasury, but in Consequence of Appropriations made by Law; and a regular Statement and Account of the Receipts and Expenditures of all public Money shall be published from time to time.

No Title of Nobility shall be granted by the United States: And no Person holding any Office of Profit or Trust under them, shall, without the Consent of the Congress, accept of any present, Emolument, Office, or Title, of any kind whatever, from any King, Prince, or foreign State.

Section. 10. No State shall enter into any Treaty, Alliance, or Confederation; grant Letters of Marque and Reprisal; coin Money; emit Bills of Credit; make any Thing but gold and silver Coin a Tender in Payment of Debts; pass any Bill of Attainder, ex post facto Law, or Law impairing the Obligation of Contracts, or grant any Title of Nobility.

No State shall, without the Consent of the Congress, lay any Imposts or Duties on Imports or Exports, except what may be absolutely necessary for executing it's inspection Laws: and the net Produce of all Duties and Imposts, laid by any State on Imports or Exports, shall be for the Use of the Treasury of the United States; and all such Laws shall be subject to the Revision and Controul of the Congress.

No State shall, without the Consent of Congress, lay any Duty of Tonnage, keep Troops, or Ships of War in time of Peace, enter into any Agreement or Compact with another State, or with a foreign Power, or engage in War, unless actually invaded, or in such imminent Danger as will not admit of delay.

Article II

Section. 1. The executive Power shall be vested in a President of the United States of America. He shall hold his Office during the Term of four Years, and, together with the Vice President, chosen for the same Term, be elected, as follows

Each State shall appoint, in such Manner as the Legislature thereof may direct, a Number of Electors, equal to the whole Number of Senators and Representatives to which the State may be entitled in the Congress: but no Senator or Representative, or Person holding an Office of Trust or Profit under the United States, shall be appointed an Elector.

[The Electors shall meet in their respective States, and vote by Ballot for two Persons, of whom one at least shall not be an Inhabitant of the same State with themselves. And they shall make a List of all the Persons voted for, and of the Number of Votes for each; which List they shall sign and certify, and transmit sealed to the Seat of the Government of the United States, directed to the President of the Senate. The President of the Senate shall, in the Presence of the Senate and House of Representatives, open all the Certificates, and the Votes shall then be counted. The Person having the greatest Number of Votes shall be the President, if such Number be a Majority of the whole Number of Electors appointed; and if there be more than one who have such Majority, and have an equal Number of Votes, then the House of Representatives shall immediately chuse by Ballot one of them for President; and if no Person have a Majority, then from the five highest on the List the said House shall in like Manner chuse the President. But in chusing the President, the Votes shall be taken by States, the Representation from each State having one Vote; A quorum for this Purpose shall consist of a Member or Members from two thirds of the States, and a Majority of all the States shall be necessary to a Choice. In every Case, after the Choice of the President, the Person having the greatest Number of Votes of the Electors shall be the Vice President. But if there should remain two or more who have equal Votes, the Senate shall chuse from them by Ballot the Vice President.][6]

The Congress may determine the Time of chusing the Electors, and the Day on which they shall give their Votes; which Day shall be the same throughout the United States.

No Person except a natural born Citizen, or a Citizen of the United States, at the time of the Adoption of this Constitution, shall be eligible to the Office of President; neither shall any Person be eligible to that

---

[6] Changed by the Twelfth Amendment

Office who shall not have attained to the Age of thirty five Years, and been fourteen Years a Resident within the United States.

[In Case of the Removal of the President from Office, or of his Death, Resignation, or Inability to discharge the Powers and Duties of the said Office, the Same shall devolve on the Vice President, and the Congress may by Law provide for the Case of Removal, Death, Resignation or Inability, both of the President and Vice President, declaring what Officer shall then act as President, and such Officer shall act accordingly, until the Disability be removed, or a President shall be elected.][7]

The President shall, at stated Times, receive for his Services, a Compensation, which shall neither be encreased nor diminished during the Period for which he shall have been elected, and he shall not receive within that Period any other Emolument from the United States, or any of them.

Before he enter on the Execution of his Office, he shall take the following Oath or Affirmation:—"I do solemnly swear (or affirm) that I will faithfully execute the Office of President of the United States, and will to the best of my Ability, preserve, protect and defend the Constitution of the United States."

Section. 2. The President shall be Commander in Chief of the Army and Navy of the United States, and of the Militia of the several States, when called into the actual Service of the United States; he may require the Opinion, in writing, of the principal Officer in each of the executive Departments, upon any Subject relating to the Duties of their respective Offices, and he shall have Power to grant Reprieves and Pardons for Offences against the United States, except in Cases of Impeachment.

He shall have Power, by and with the Advice and Consent of the Senate, to make Treaties, provided two thirds of the Senators present concur; and he shall nominate, and by and with the Advice and Consent of the Senate, shall appoint Ambassadors, other public Ministers and Consuls, Judges of the supreme Court, and all other Officers of the United States, whose Appointments are not herein otherwise provided for, and which shall be established by Law: but the Congress may by

---

[7] Changed by the Twenty-Fifth Amendment

Law vest the Appointment of such inferior Officers, as they think proper, in the President alone, in the Courts of Law, or in the Heads of Departments.

The President shall have Power to fill up all Vacancies that may happen during the Recess of the Senate, by granting Commissions which shall expire at the End of their next Session.

Section. 3. He shall from time to time give to the Congress Information of the State of the Union, and recommend to their Consideration such Measures as he shall judge necessary and expedient; he may, on extraordinary Occasions, convene both Houses, or either of them, and in Case of Disagreement between them, with Respect to the Time of Adjournment, he may adjourn them to such Time as he shall think proper; he shall receive Ambassadors and other public Ministers; he shall take Care that the Laws be faithfully executed, and shall Commission all the Officers of the United States.

Section. 4. The President, Vice President and all civil Officers of the United States, shall be removed from Office on Impeachment for, and Conviction of, Treason, Bribery, or other high Crimes and Misdemeanors.

Article III

Section. 1. The judicial Power of the United States, shall be vested in one supreme Court, and in such inferior Courts as the Congress may from time to time ordain and establish. The Judges, both of the supreme and inferior Courts, shall hold their Offices during good Behaviour, and shall, at stated Times, receive for their Services, a Compensation, which shall not be diminished during their Continuance in Office.

Section. 2. The judicial Power shall extend to all Cases, in Law and Equity, arising under this Constitution, the Laws of the United States, and Treaties made, or which shall be made, under their Authority;—to all Cases affecting Ambassadors, other public Ministers and Consuls;—to all Cases of admiralty and maritime Jurisdiction;—to Controversies to which the United States shall be a Party;—to Controversies between two or more States;—[between a State and Citizens of another State;—][8] between Citizens of different States, —between Citizens of the same State claiming Lands under Grants of different States, [and between a State, or the Citizens thereof, and foreign States, Citizens or Subjects.][9]

In all Cases affecting Ambassadors, other public Ministers and Consuls, and those in which a State shall be Party, the supreme Court shall have original Jurisdiction. In all the other Cases before mentioned, the supreme Court shall have appellate Jurisdiction, both as to Law and Fact, with such Exceptions, and under such Regulations as the Congress shall make.

The Trial of all Crimes, except in Cases of Impeachment, shall be by Jury; and such Trial shall be held in the State where the said Crimes shall have been committed; but when not committed within any State, the Trial shall be at such Place or Places as the Congress may by Law have directed.

Section. 3. Treason against the United States, shall consist only in levying War against them, or in adhering to their Enemies, giving them Aid and Comfort. No Person shall be convicted of Treason unless on the Testimony of two Witnesses to the same overt Act, or on Confession in open Court.

The Congress shall have Power to declare the Punishment of Treason, but no Attainder of Treason shall work Corruption of Blood, or Forfeiture except during the Life of the Person attainted.

Article IV

Section. 1. Full Faith and Credit shall be given in each State to the public Acts, Records, and judicial Proceedings of every other State. And the Congress may by general Laws prescribe the Manner in which such Acts, Records and Proceedings shall be proved, and the Effect thereof.

---

[8] Changed by the Eleventh Amendment
[9] Changed by the Eleventh Amendment

Section. 2. The Citizens of each State shall be entitled to all Privileges and Immunities of Citizens in the several States.

A Person charged in any State with Treason, Felony, or other Crime, who shall flee from Justice, and be found in another State, shall on Demand of the executive Authority of the State from which he fled, be delivered up, to be removed to the State having Jurisdiction of the Crime.

[No Person held to Service or Labour in one State, under the Laws thereof, escaping into another, shall, in Consequence of any Law or Regulation therein, be discharged from such Service or Labour, but shall be delivered up on Claim of the Party to whom such Service or Labour may be due.][10]

Section. 3. New States may be admitted by the Congress into this Union; but no new State shall be formed or erected within the Jurisdiction of any other State; nor any State be formed by the Junction of two or more States, or Parts of States, without the Consent of the Legislatures of the States concerned as well as of the Congress.

The Congress shall have Power to dispose of and make all needful Rules and Regulations respecting the Territory or other Property belonging to the United States; and nothing in this Constitution shall be so construed as to Prejudice any Claims of the United States, or of any particular State.

Section. 4. The United States shall guarantee to every State in this Union a Republican Form of Government, and shall protect each of them against Invasion; and on Application of the Legislature, or of the Executive (when the Legislature cannot be convened) against domestic Violence.

Article V

The Congress, whenever two thirds of both Houses shall deem it necessary, shall propose Amendments to this Constitution, or, on the Application of the Legislatures of two thirds of the several States, shall

---

[10] Changed by the Thirteenth Amendment

call a Convention for proposing Amendments, which, in either Case, shall be valid to all Intents and Purposes, as Part of this Constitution, when ratified by the Legislatures of three fourths of the several States, or by Conventions in three fourths thereof, as the one or the other Mode of Ratification may be proposed by the Congress; Provided that no Amendment which may be made prior to the Year One thousand eight hundred and eight shall in any Manner affect the first and fourth Clauses in the Ninth Section of the first Article; and that no State, without its Consent, shall be deprived of its equal Suffrage in the Senate.

Article VI

All Debts contracted and Engagements entered into, before the Adoption of this Constitution, shall be as valid against the United States under this Constitution, as under the Confederation.

This Constitution, and the Laws of the United States which shall be made in Pursuance thereof; and all Treaties made, or which shall be made, under the Authority of the United States, shall be the supreme Law of the Land; and the Judges in every State shall be bound thereby, any Thing in the Constitution or Laws of any State to the Contrary notwithstanding.

The Senators and Representatives before mentioned, and the Members of the several State Legislatures, and all executive and judicial Officers, both of the United States and of the several States, shall be bound by Oath or Affirmation, to support this Constitution; but no religious Test shall ever be required as a Qualification to any Office or public Trust under the United States.

Article VII

The Ratification of the Conventions of nine States, shall be sufficient for the Establishment of this Constitution between the States so ratifying the Same.

Attest William Jackson Secretary

Done in Convention by the Unanimous Consent of the States present the Seventeenth Day of September in the Year of our Lord one thousand seven hundred and Eighty seven and of the Independence of the United States of America the Twelfth In witness whereof We have hereunto subscribed our Names,

G°: Washington –
Presid^t. and deputy from Virginia

Delaware	Geo: Read Gunning Bedford jun John Dickinson Richard Bassett Jaco: Broom	New Hampshire	John Langdon Nicholas Gilman
Maryland	James McHenry Dan of St Thos. Jenifer Danl Carroll	Massachusetts	Nathaniel Gorham Rufus King
Virginia	John Blair— James Madison Jr.	Connecticut	Wm. Saml. Johnson Roger Sherman
North Carolina	Wm Blount Richd. Dobbs Spaight. Hu Williamson	New York	Alexander Hamilton
South Carolina	J. Rutledge Charles Cotesworth Pinckney Charles Pinckney Pierce Butler	New Jersey	Wil. Livingston David Brearley Wm. Paterson Jona: Dayton
Georgia	William Few Abr Baldwin	Pennsylvania	B Franklin Thomas Mifflin Robt Morris Geo. Clymer Thos. FitzSimons Jared Ingersoll James Wilson. Gouv Morris

Amendments to the Constitution of the United States of America

Amendment I
Ratified December 15, 1791

Congress shall make no law respecting an establishment of religion, or prohibiting the free exercise thereof; or abridging the freedom of speech, or of the press; or the right of the people peaceably to assemble, and to petition the Government for a redress of grievances.

Amendment II
Ratified December 15, 1791

A well regulated Militia, being necessary to the security of a free State, the right of the people to keep and bear Arms, shall not be infringed.

Amendment III
Ratified December 15, 1791

No Soldier shall, in time of peace be quartered in any house, without the consent of the Owner, nor in time of war, but in a manner to be prescribed by law.

Amendment IV
Ratified December 15, 1791

The right of the people to be secure in their persons, houses, papers, and effects, against unreasonable searches and seizures, shall not be violated, and no Warrants shall issue, but upon probable cause, supported by Oath or affirmation, and particularly describing the place to be searched, and the persons or things to be seized.

Amendment V
Ratified December 15, 1791

No person shall be held to answer for a capital, or otherwise infamous crime, unless on a presentment or indictment of a Grand Jury, except in cases arising in the land or naval forces, or in the Militia, when in actual service in time of War or public danger; nor shall any person be subject for the same offence to be twice put in jeopardy of life or limb; nor shall be compelled in any criminal case to be a witness against himself, nor be deprived of life, liberty, or property, without due process of law; nor shall private property be taken for public use, without just compensation.

Amendment VI
Ratified December 15, 1791

In all criminal prosecutions, the accused shall enjoy the right to a speedy and public trial, by an impartial jury of the State and district wherein the crime shall have been committed, which district shall have been previously ascertained by law, and to be informed of the nature and cause of the accusation; to be confronted with the witnesses against him; to have compulsory process for obtaining witnesses in his favor, and to have the Assistance of Counsel for his defence.

Amendment VII
Ratified December 15, 1791

In Suits at common law, where the value in controversy shall exceed twenty dollars, the right of trial by jury shall be preserved, and no fact tried by a jury, shall be otherwise re-examined in any Court of the United States, than according to the rules of the common law.

Amendment VIII
Ratified December 15, 1791

Excessive bail shall not be required, nor excessive fines imposed, nor cruel and unusual punishments inflicted.

Amendment IX
Ratified December 15, 1791

The enumeration in the Constitution, of certain rights, shall not be construed to deny or disparage others retained by the people.

Amendment X
Ratified December 15, 1791

The powers not delegated to the United States by the Constitution, nor prohibited by it to the States, are reserved to the States respectively, or to the people.

Amendment XI
Ratified February 7, 1795

The Judicial power of the United States shall not be construed to extend to any suit in law or equity, commenced or prosecuted against one of the United States by Citizens of another State, or by Citizens or Subjects of any Foreign State.

Amendment XII
Ratified June 15, 1804

The Electors shall meet in their respective states, and vote by ballot for President and Vice-President, one of whom, at least, shall not be an inhabitant of the same state with themselves; they shall name in their ballots the person voted for as President, and in distinct ballots the person voted for as Vice-President, and they shall make distinct lists of all persons voted for as President, and of all persons voted for as Vice-President, and of the number of votes for each, which lists they shall sign and certify, and transmit sealed to the seat of the government of the United States, directed to the President of the Senate;—The President of the Senate shall, in the presence of the Senate and House of Representatives, open all the certificates and the votes shall then be counted;—The person having the greatest number of votes for President, shall be the President, if such number be a majority of the whole number of Electors appointed; and if no person have such majority, then from the persons having the highest numbers not exceeding three on the list of those voted for as President, the House of Representatives shall choose immediately, by ballot, the President. But in choosing the President, the votes shall be taken by states, the representation from each state having one vote; a quorum for this purpose shall consist of a member or members from two-thirds of the states, and a majority of all the states shall be necessary to a choice. [And if the House of Representatives shall not choose a President whenever the right of choice shall devolve upon them, before the fourth day of March next following, then the Vice-President shall act as President, as in the case of the death or other constitutional disability of the President.]11 —The person having the greatest number of votes as Vice-President, shall be the Vice-President, if such number be a majority of the whole number of Electors appointed, and if no person have a majority, then from the two highest numbers on the list, the Senate shall choose the Vice-President; a quorum for the purpose shall consist of two-thirds of the whole number of Senators, and a majority of the whole number shall be necessary to a choice. But no person constitutionally ineligible to the office of President shall be eligible to that of Vice-President of the United States.

Amendment XIII
Ratified December 6, 1865

Section. 1. Neither slavery nor involuntary servitude, except as a punishment for crime whereof the party shall have been duly convicted, shall exist within the United States, or any place subject to their jurisdiction.

Section. 2. Congress shall have power to enforce this article by appropriate legislation.

Amendment XIV
Ratified July 9, 1868

Section. 1. All persons born or naturalized in the United States, and subject to the jurisdiction thereof, are citizens of the United States and of the State wherein they reside. No State shall make or enforce any law which shall abridge the privileges or immunities of citizens of the United States; nor shall any State deprive any person of life, liberty, or property, without due process of law; nor deny to any person within its jurisdiction the equal protection of the laws.

---

[11] Superseded by Section 3 of the Twentieth Amendment

Section. 2. Representatives shall be apportioned among the several States according to their respective numbers, counting the whole number of persons in each State, excluding Indians not taxed. But when the right to vote at any election for the choice of electors for President and Vice President of the United States, Representatives in Congress, the Executive and Judicial officers of a State, or the members of the Legislature thereof, is denied to any of the male inhabitants of such State, being twenty-one years of age[12], and citizens of the United States, or in any way abridged, except for participation in rebellion, or other crime, the basis of representation therein shall be reduced in the proportion which the number of such male citizens shall bear to the whole number of male citizens twenty-one years of age in such State.

Section. 3. No person shall be a Senator or Representative in Congress, or elector of President and Vice President, or hold any office, civil or military, under the United States, or under any State, who, having previously taken an oath, as a member of Congress, or as an officer of the United States, or as a member of any State legislature, or as an executive or judicial officer of any State, to support the Constitution of the United States, shall have engaged in insurrection or rebellion against the same, or given aid or comfort to the enemies thereof. But Congress may by a vote of two-thirds of each House, remove such disability.

Section. 4. The validity of the public debt of the United States, authorized by law, including debts incurred for payment of pensions and bounties for services in suppressing insurrection or rebellion, shall not be questioned. But neither the United States nor any State shall assume or pay any debt or obligation incurred in aid of insurrection or rebellion against the United States, or any claim for the loss or emancipation of any slave; but all such debts, obligations and claims shall be held illegal and void.

Section. 5. The Congress shall have power to enforce, by appropriate legislation, the provisions of this article.

---

[12] Changed by Section 1 of the Twenty-Sixth Amendment

Amendment XV
Ratified February 3, 1870

Section. 1. The right of citizens of the United States to vote shall not be denied or abridged by the United States or by any State on account of race, color, or previous condition of servitude.

Section. 2. The Congress shall have power to enforce this article by appropriate legislation.

Amendment XVI
Ratified February 3, 1913

The Congress shall have power to lay and collect taxes on incomes, from whatever source derived, without apportionment among the several States, and without regard to any census or enumeration.

Amendment XVII
Ratified April 8, 1913

The Senate of the United States shall be composed of two Senators from each State, elected by the people thereof, for six years; and each Senator shall have one vote. The electors in each State shall have the qualifications requisite for electors of the most numerous branch of the State legislatures.

When vacancies happen in the representation of any State in the Senate, the executive authority of such State shall issue writs of election to fill such vacancies: Provided, That the legislature of any State may empower the executive thereof to make temporary appointments until the people fill the vacancies by election as the legislature may direct.

This amendment shall not be so construed as to affect the election or term of any Senator chosen before it becomes valid as part of the Constitution.

Amendment XVIII[13]
Ratified January 16, 1919

Section. 1. After one year from the ratification of this article the manufacture, sale, or transportation of intoxicating liquors within, the importation thereof into, or the exportation thereof from the United States and all territory subject to the jurisdiction thereof for beverage purposes is hereby prohibited.

Section. 2. The Congress and the several States shall have concurrent power to enforce this article by appropriate legislation.

Section. 3. This article shall be inoperative unless it shall have been ratified as an amendment to the Constitution by the legislatures of the several States, as provided in the Constitution, within seven years from the date of the submission hereof to the States by the Congress.

Amendment XIX
Ratified August 18, 1920

The right of citizens of the United States to vote shall not be denied or abridged by the United States or by any State on account of sex.

Congress shall have power to enforce this article by appropriate legislation.

Amendment XX
Ratified January 23, 1933

Section. 1. The terms of the President and Vice President shall end at noon on the 20th day of January, and the terms of Senators and Representatives at noon on the 3d day of January, of the years in which such terms would have ended if this article had not been ratified; and the terms of their successors shall then begin.

---

[13] Repealed by the Twenty-First Amendment

Section. 2. The Congress shall assemble at least once in every year, and such meeting shall begin at noon on the 3d day of January, unless they shall by law appoint a different day.

Section. 3. If, at the time fixed for the beginning of the term of the President, the President elect shall have died, the Vice President elect shall become President. If a President shall not have been chosen before the time fixed for the beginning of his term, or if the President elect shall have failed to qualify, then the Vice President elect shall act as President until a President shall have qualified; and the Congress may by law provide for the case wherein neither a President elect nor a Vice President elect shall have qualified, declaring who shall then act as President, or the manner in which one who is to act shall be selected, and such person shall act accordingly until a President or Vice President shall have qualified.

Section. 4. The Congress may by law provide for the case of the death of any of the persons from whom the House of Representatives may choose a President whenever the right of choice shall have devolved upon them, and for the case of the death of any of the persons from whom the Senate may choose a Vice President whenever the right of choice shall have devolved upon them.

Section. 5. Sections 1 and 2 shall take effect on the 15th day of October following the ratification of this article.

Section. 6. This article shall be inoperative unless it shall have been ratified as an amendment to the Constitution by the legislatures of three-fourths of the several States within seven years from the date of its submission.

Amendment XXI
Ratified December 5, 1933

Section. 1. The eighteenth article of amendment to the Constitution of the United States is hereby repealed.

Section. 2. The transportation or importation into any State, Territory, or possession of the United States for delivery or use therein of intoxicating liquors, in violation of the laws thereof, is hereby prohibited.

Section. 3. This article shall be inoperative unless it shall have been ratified as an amendment to the Constitution by conventions in the several States, as provided in the Constitution, within seven years from the date of the submission hereof to the States by the Congress.

Amendment XXII
Ratified February 27, 1951

Section. 1. No person shall be elected to the office of the President more than twice, and no person who has held the office of President, or acted as President, for more than two years of a term to which some other person was elected President shall be elected to the office of the President more than once. But this article shall not apply to any person holding the office of President when this article was proposed by the Congress, and shall not prevent any person who may be holding the office of President, or acting as President, during the term within which this article becomes operative from holding the office of President or acting as President during the remainder of such term.

Section. 2. This article shall be inoperative unless it shall have been ratified as an amendment to the Constitution by the legislatures of three-fourths of the several states within seven years from the date of its submission to the states by the Congress.

Amendment XXIII
Ratified March 29, 1961

Section. 1. The District constituting the seat of government of the United States shall appoint in such manner as the Congress may direct:

A number of electors of President and Vice President equal to the whole number of Senators and Representatives in Congress to which the District would be entitled if it were a state, but in no event more than the least populous state; they shall be in addition to those appointed by the states, but they shall be considered, for the purposes of the election of President and Vice President, to be electors appointed by a state; and they shall meet in the District and perform such duties as provided by the twelfth article of amendment.

Section. 2. The Congress shall have power to enforce this article by appropriate legislation.

Amendment XXIV
Ratified January 23, 1964

Section. 1. The right of citizens of the United States to vote in any primary or other election for President or Vice President, for electors for President or Vice President, or for Senator or Representative in Congress, shall not be denied or abridged by the United States or any state by reason of failure to pay any poll tax or other tax.

Section. 2. The Congress shall have power to enforce this article by appropriate legislation.

Amendment XXV
Ratified February 10, 1967

Section. 1. In case of the removal of the President from office or of his death or resignation, the Vice President shall become President.

Section. 2. Whenever there is a vacancy in the office of the Vice President, the President shall nominate a Vice President who shall take office upon confirmation by a majority vote of both Houses of Congress.

Section. 3. Whenever the President transmits to the President pro tempore of the Senate and the Speaker of the House of Representatives his written declaration that he is unable to discharge the powers and duties of his office, and until he transmits to them a written declaration to the contrary, such powers and duties shall be discharged by the Vice President as Acting President.

Section. 4. Whenever the Vice President and a majority of either the principal officers of the executive departments or of such other body as

Congress may by law provide, transmit to the President pro tempore of the Senate and the Speaker of the House of Representatives their written declaration that the President is unable to discharge the powers and duties of his office, the Vice President shall immediately assume the powers and duties of the office as Acting President.

Thereafter, when the President transmits to the President pro tempore of the Senate and the Speaker of the House of Representatives his written declaration that no inability exists, he shall resume the powers and duties of his office unless the Vice President and a majority of either the principal officers of the executive department or of such other body as Congress may by law provide, transmit within four days to the President pro tempore of the Senate and the Speaker of the House of Representatives their written declaration that the President is unable to discharge the powers and duties of his office. Thereupon Congress shall decide the issue, assembling within forty-eight hours for that purpose if not in session. If the Congress, within twenty-one days after receipt of the latter written declaration, or, if Congress is not in session, within twenty-one days after Congress is required to assemble, determines by two-thirds vote of both Houses that the President is unable to discharge the powers and duties of his office, the Vice President shall continue to discharge the same as Acting President; otherwise, the President shall resume the powers and duties of his office.

Amendment XXVI
Ratified July 1, 1971

Section. 1. The right of citizens of the United States, who are 18 years of age or older, to vote, shall not be denied or abridged by the United States or any state on account of age.

Section. 2. The Congress shall have the power to enforce this article by appropriate legislation.

Amendment XXVII
Ratified May 7, 1992

No law varying the compensation for the services of the Senators and Representatives shall take effect until an election of Representatives shall have intervened.

NOTES

Preface

[1] Tom Wolfe, "The Right Stuff," Farrar, Straus and Giroux, 1979.
[2] Thomas Carlyle, "On Heroes, Hero Worship, & the Heroic in History," Dent, 1908.
[3] Mark Levin, "Ameritopia," Threshold Editions, 2012.

Definitions

[1] Mark Levin, "Ameritopia," Threshold Editions, 2012.
[2] Mark Levin Radio Program.

Introduction

[1] Abraham Lincoln, "The Perpetuation of Our Political Institutions: Address Before the Young Men's Lyceum of Springfield, Illinois," http://abrahamlincoln.org, January 27, 1838.
[2] https://www.opm.gov.
[3] Data from http://wikipedia.org.
[4] Toni Morrison, "Clinton as the first black president," New Yorker, October 1998.
[5] James Cameron, "The Terminator," 1984
[6] David Horowitz, "Barack Obama's Rules for Revolution, The Alinsky Model," Freedom Center, 2009.

Dunham

[1] Samuel Adams (under pseudonym "Candidus"), Essay in The Boston Gazette, October 14, 1771.
[2] Barack Obama, "Dreams from My Father," Times Books, 1995

[3] Jonathan Martin, "Obama's mother known here as 'uncommon'," The Seattle Times, April 8, 2008.

[4] Pamela Geller, "HOW COULD STANLEY ANN DUNHAM HAVE DELIVERED BARACK HUSSEIN OBAMA JR. IN AUGUST OF 1961 IN HONOLULU, WHEN OFFICIAL UNIVERSITY OF WASHINGTON RECORDS SHOW HER 2680 MILES AWAY IN SEATTLE ATTENDING CLASSES THAT SAME MONTH?," http://pamelageller.com/2008/10/how-could-stanl.html, October 24, 2008.

[5] Barack Obama, "Dreams from My Father," Times Books, 1995

[6] Jones, Tim, "Obama's mom: Not just a girl from Kansas". Chicago Tribune, March 27, 2007.

[7] David Maraniss, "Barack Obama, The Story," Simon & Schuster, 2012.

[8] Bowers, Peter M., "Boeing Aircraft since 1916," Putnam, 1989.

[9] Herman, Arthur, "Freedom's Forge: How American Business Produced Victory in World War II," New York: Random House, 2012.

[10] Peacock, Lindsay, "Boeing B-29... First of the Superbombers, Part Two," Air International, September 1989.

[11] Knaack, Marcelle Size, "Post-World War II Bombers, 1945–1973," Washington, D.C.: Office of Air Force History, 1988.

[12] Morison, Samuel Eliot, "Victory in the Pacific, 1945, Vol. 14 of History of United States Naval Operations in World War II," University of Illinois Press, 1970.

[13] "Iwo To Japan", http://www.506thfightergroup.org, retrieved 2016.

[14] Inspired by presentation by Maj. Gen. David Harris, Society of Flight Test Engineers Symposium, Lancaster, CA, 2015.

[15] David Maraniss, "Barack Obama, The Story," Simon & Schuster, 2012.

[16] Pamela Geller, "HOW COULD STANLEY ANN DUNHAM HAVE DELIVERED BARACK HUSSEIN OBAMA JR. IN AUGUST OF 1961 IN HONOLULU, WHEN OFFICIAL UNIVERSITY OF WASHINGTON RECORDS SHOW HER 2680 MILES AWAY IN SEATTLE ATTENDING CLASSES THAT SAME MONTH?,"http://pamelageller.com/2008/10/how-could-stanl.html, October 24, 2008.

[17] "29 August 1949 - First Soviet nuclear test," http://www.ctbto.org/specials/testing-times/29-august-1949-first-soviet-nuclear-test, retrieved March 25, 2016.

[18] Knaack, Marcelle Size, "Post-World War II Bombers, 1945–1973," Washington, D.C.: Office of Air Force History, 1988.

[19] Boeing Co., "707/720 Commercial Transport, Historical Perspective," http://www.boeing.com/history/products/707.page, retrieved March 25, 2016.

Seeds

[1] Barack Obama, "Dreams from My Father," Times Books, 1995.

[2] Ibid.

[3] Ibid.

[4] Pamela Geller, "HOW COULD STANLEY ANN DUNHAM HAVE DELIVERED BARACK HUSSEIN OBAMA JR. IN AUGUST OF 1961 IN HONOLULU, WHEN OFFICIAL UNIVERSITY OF WASHINGTON RECORDS SHOW HER 2680 MILES AWAY IN SEATTLE ATTENDING CLASSES THAT SAME MONTH?," http://pamelageller.com/2008/10/how-could-stanl.html, October 24, 2008.

[5] Ibid.

[6] David Maraniss, "Barack Obama, The Story," Simon & Schuster, 2012.

[7] Ibid.

[8] Ibid.

[9] Ibid.

[10] Ibid.

[11] Ibid.

[12] Barack Obama, "The Audacity of Hope," Three Rivers Press, 2006.

[13] Franklin Roosevelt, "Executive Order 9066," U.S. National Archives & Records Administration. February 19, 1942.

[14] "Ralph Carr: Defender of Japanese Americans," Colorado Virtual Library.

[15] "Relocation and Incarceration of Japanese Americans During World War II," University of California - Japanese American Relocation Digital Archives.

[16] "442nd REGIMENTAL COMBAT TEAM," http://the442.org.

[17] Committee on Un-American Activities, United States House of Representatives, "REPORT ON THE HONOLULU RECORD," October 1, 1950.

[18] Ibid.

[19] Barack Obama, "Dreams from My Father," Times Books, 1995.

[20] Barack Obama, "Dreams from My Father," Times Books, 1995.

[21] David Remnick, "The Bridge, The Life and Rise of Barack Obama," Random House, 2010.

[22] Ibid.

Blackness

[1] Barack Obama, "Dreams from My Father," Times Books, 1995.

[2] "Mesopotamia: The Code of Hammurabi".

[3] Smith, Julia Floyd, "Slavery and Plantation Growth in Antebellum Florida, 1821–1860," University of Florida Press, 1973.

[4] "Mauritanian MPs pass slavery law," BBC News, August 9 2007.

[5] Bernard Lewis, "The Arabs in History," Oxford Press, 2002.

[6] Cynthia Yockey, "Obama's Kenyan ancestors sold slaves," http://aconservativelesbian.com/2009/07/13/obamas-kenyan-ancestors-sold-slaves, July 13, 2009.

[7] Ibid.

[8] David Remnick, "The Bridge, The Life and Rise of Barack Obama," Random House, 2010.

[9] Barack Obama, "Dreams from My Father," Times Books, 1995.

[10] David Mendell, "Obama, From Promise to Power," HarperCollins, 2007.

[11] Barack Obama, "Dreams from My Father," Times Books, 1995.

[12] David Maraniss, "Barack Obama, The Story", Simon & Schuster, 2012.

[13] Barack Obama, "Dreams from My Father," Times Books, 1995.

[14] Ibid.

[15] David Maraniss, "Barack Obama, The Story", Simon & Schuster, 2012.

[16] Ibid.

[17] Barack Obama, "Dreams from My Father," Times Books, 1995.

[18] Ibid.

[19] David Maraniss, "Barack Obama, The Story", Simon & Schuster, 2012.

[20] Ibid.

[21] Ibid.

[22] Ibid.

[23] Ibid.

[24] Ibid.

Direction

[1] Booker T. Washington, "My Larger Education," Start Publishing, 1951

[2] James M. McPherson, "Battle Cry of Freedom," Oxford University Press, 1988.

[3] "Case of Somerset (Somersett)," Freedom's Journal, 1827.

[4] Encyclopaedia Britannica, "slavery," http://academic.eb.com/blackhistory/article-24157, retrieved March 25, 2016.

[5] "Abolition of Slavery", Historica-Dominion Institute, Black History Canada.

[6] Hobhouse, Henry, "Seeds of Change: Six Plants That Transformed Mankind," Counterpoint, 2005.

[7] James M. McPherson, "Battle Cry of Freedom," Oxford University Press, 1988.

[8] Ibid.

[9] Ibid.

[10] Ibid.

[11] Ibid.

[12] Woodrow Wilson, "Constitutional Government of the United States," 1908.

[13] Heckscher, August, "Woodrow Wilson," Easton Press, 1991.

[14] Ibid.

[15] Ibid.

[16] Lewis, David Levering, "W. E. B. Du Bois: A Biography," Henry Holt and Co., 2009.

[17] Ronald Kessler, "Inside the White House," Simon and Schuster, 1996.

[18] Mark Levin, "Men in Black," Regenry, 2005.

Community Organizer

[1] Ronald Reagan, Speech to Fourth Annual Conservative Political Action Conference, February 6, 1977.

[2] Berger, Dan, "Outlaws of America: the Weather Underground and the Politics of Solidarity," AK press, 2006.

[3] Haitch, Richard, "Hurdle for Dohrn," The New York Times, February 10, 1985.

[4] Nicolaievsky, Boris and Maenchen-Helfen, Otto, "Karl Marx: Man and Fighter," Pelican, 1976.

[5] Wheen, Francis, "Karl Marx," Fourth Estate, 2001.

[6] Dennis Prager, "Still the Best Hope," Broadside Books, 2012.

[7] Allen West, "Guardian of the Republic," Crown Forum, 2014.

[8] David Horowitz, "Barack Obama's Rules for Revolution, The Alinksy Model," Freedom Press, 2009.

[9] David Maraniss, "Barack Obama, The Story", Simon & Schuster, 2012.

[10] Ibid.

[11] Ibid.

[12] Ibid.

[13] Barack Obama, "Dreams from My Father," Times Books, 1995.

[14] Ibid.

[15] David Remnick, "The Bridge, The Life and Rise of Barack Obama," Random House, 2010.

[16] Ibid.

[17] James H. Cone, "Black Theology & Black Power," Orbis, 1969.

[18] Anthony B. Bradley, "The Marxist Roots of Black Liberation Theology," Action Institute, http://www.acton.org/pub/commentary/2008/04/02/marxist-roots-black-liberation-theology, retrieved March 25, 2016.

[19] Barack Obama, "Dreams from My Father," Times Books, 1995.

[20] David Mendell, "Obama, From Promise to Power," HarperCollins, 2007.

[21] Grossman, Ron, "Family ties proved Ayers' point," Chicago Tribune, May 18, 2008.

[22] David Remnick, "The Bridge, The Life and Rise of Barack Obama," Random House, 2010.

[23] Ibid.

[24] Ibid.

Politics

[1] Eric Hoffer, "The True Believer," Harper & Row, 1951.

[2] David Remnick, "The Bridge, The Life and Rise of Barack Obama," Random House, 2010.

[3] Ibid.

[4] Ibid.

[5] Ibid.

[6] Ibid.

[7] Ibid.

[8] Ibid.

Stealing Senate

[1] David Mendell, "Obama, From Promise to Power," HarperCollins, 2007.

[2] David Remnick, "The Bridge, The Life and Rise of Barack Obama," Random House, 2010.

[3] David Mendell, "Obama, From Promise to Power," HarperCollins, 2007.

[4] Ibid.

[5] Ibid.

[6] Ibid.

[7] Ibid.

[8] Ibid.

[9] Ibid.

¹⁰ Ibid.

¹¹ Ibid.

¹² Ibid.

¹³ Ibid.

¹⁴ David Remnick, "The Bridge, The Life and Rise of Barack Obama," Random House, 2010.

¹⁵ Brian Montopoli, "National Journal: Obama Most Liberal Senator In 2007," CBS News, January 31, 2008.

¹⁶ David Mendell, "Obama, From Promise to Power," HarperCollins, 2007.

¹⁷ David Remnick, "The Bridge, The Life and Rise of Barack Obama," Random House, 2010.

Serendipity

¹ Super-Tuesday speech in Chicago, February 19, 2008.

² David Freddoso, "The Case against Barack Obama," Regnery, 2008.

³ Jess Henig, "ACORN Accusations," http://www.factcheck.org/2008/10/acorn-accusations/, October 21, 2008.

⁴ "Michelle Obama Rallies SEIU Staff Heading to Battleground States," https://www.gwu.edu/~action/2008/interestg08/seiu08releases.html, Sep 20, 2008

⁵ Ken Timmerman, "Obama Ignores Credit Card Donation Fraud," http://www.newsmax.com/KenTimmerman/obama-illegal-donations/2008/10/21/id/339941/, 21 Oct 2008

⁶ Michelle Malkin, " Black Panther intimidation at the polls?; NBPP: 'We will be at the polls in the cities and counties in many states to ensure that the enemy does not sabotage the black vote, which was won through the blood of the martyrs of our people'," http://michellemalkin.com/2008/11/04/black-panther-intimidation-at-the-polls, November 4, 2008

⁷ Saul Alinsky, "Rules for Radicals," Random House, 1971.

⁸ Unscripted Barack Obama campaign speech, May 21, 2008.

⁹ Simba, M., "The Obama Campaign 2008: A Historical Overview". Western Journal of Black Studies, 2009

¹⁰ Saul Alinsky, "Rules for Radicals," Random House, 1971.

[11] Jake Tapper, "A Biden Problem: Foot in Mouth," ABCNews.com, January 31, 2007.

[12] "Financial Summary Report Search Results," http://fec.gov, 2008.

[13] "National Exit Poll". CNN. January 28, 2013.

Myth-Building

[1] John F. Kennedy, "Commencement Address at Yale University", 1961.

[2] James Pierson, "How Jackie Kennedy Invented the Camelot Legend After JFK's Death," The Daily Beast, http://www.thedailybeast.com/articles/2013/11/12/how-jackie-kennedy-invented-the-camelot-legend-after-jfk-s-death.html, November 12, 2013.

[3] David Remnick, "The Bridge, The Life and Rise of Barack Obama," Random House, 2010.

[4] Ibid.

[5] Ibid.

[6] Ibid.

[7] Ibid.

[8] Ibid.

[9] Ibid.

[10] Ibid.

[11] Colin Powell Interview, NBC Meet the Press, 2008.

[12] Ibid.

[13] Franklin Delano Roosevelt, "State of the Union", January 11, 1944.

[14] Peter J. Wallison, "Dissent from the Majority Report of the Financial Crisis Inquiry Commission," American Enterprise Institute, January 2011

[15] Steven A. Holmes, "Fannie Mae Eases Credit To Aid Mortgage Lending," September 30, 1999.

[16] Gretchen Morgenson, "Fannie Mae Chief Is Dismissed From Investors' Suit" The New York Times. September 21, 2012.

[17] Unscripted Barack Obama campaign speech, July 3, 2008.

[18] William J. Bennett, "America, The Last Best Hope, Volume I: From the Age of Discovery to a World at War," Thomas Nelson, 2006.

[19] Scott Wright, "The Northwestern Chronicle and the Spanish–American War: American Catholic Attitudes Regarding the 'Splendid Little War,'" American Catholic Studies, 2005.

[20] Brands, Henry William," TR: The Last Romantic," Basic Books, 1997.

[21] Mike Allen, "Obama Sounds Economic Warning," Politico, January 8, 2009.

[22] Ibid.

[23] Jonathan V. Last, "Being Obama," Weekly Standard, September 5, 2011.

[24] Hugh Hewitt, "The Brief Against Obama," Center Street, 2012.

[25] Ibid.

[26] Douglas Brinkley, "The Wilderness Warrior: Theodore Roosevelt and the Crusade for America," Harper Collins, 2009.

[27] Nick Sorrentino, "Federal Land as a Percentage of Total State Land Area", http://www.againstcronycapitalism.org/2014/04/federal-land-and-a-percentage-of-total-state-land-area/, April 18, 2014

[28] Lewis L. Gould, "Four Hats in the Ring: The 1912 Election and the Birth of Modern American Politics," University Press of Kansas, 2008.

[29] Woodrow Wilson, Speech in Columbus, Ohio, September 4, 1919.

[30] Fredrik Logevall, "Embers of War: The Fall of an Empire and the Making of America's Vietnam," Random House, 2012

Residency

[1] Eric Hoffer, "The True Believer," Harper & Row, 1951.

[2] Judicial Watch, "Obama Breaks Transparency Promise," https://www.judicialwatch.org/blog/2008/12/obama-breaks-transparency-promise, December 29, 2008

[3] IBM Center for The Business of Government, "Obama Announces Reform Agenda," http://www.businessofgovernment.org/blog/obama-announces-reform-agenda, September, 2008.

[4] Michelle Malkin, "Culture of Corruption," Regenry, 2009.

[5] Judicial Watch, "Cover-up, Corruption and Czars," https://www.judicialwatch.org/press-room/weekly-updates/16-cover-corruption-and-czars/, April 22, 2011.

⁶ "List of U.S. executive branch czars," https://en.wikipedia.org/wiki/List_of_U.S._executive_branch_czars, retrieved March 25, 2016.

⁷ Michelle Malkin, "Culture of Corruption," Regenry, 2009.

⁸ Thomas Sowell, "Wealth, Poverty and Politics," Basic Books, 2015.

⁹ https://www.justice.gov/about, retrieved March 25, 2016.

¹⁰ Steve Charnovitz, "Reinventing the Commerce Dept.," Journal of Commerce, July 12, 1995.

¹¹ "President Establishes Office of Homeland Security," http://georgewbush-whitehouse.archives.gov/news/releases/2001/10/20011008.html, retrieved March 25, 2016.

¹² Meg Sullivan, "FDR's policies prolonged Depression by 7 years, UCLA economists calculate," http://newsroom.ucla.edu/releases/FDR-s-Policies-Prolonged-Depression-5409, August 10, 2004.

¹³ http://www.demog.berkeley.edu/~andrew/1918/figure2.html.

¹⁴ https://www.ssa.gov/.

Barack Obama Comes Out

[1] Eric Hoffer, "The True Believer," Harper & Row, 1951.

[2] Amy Clark, "Obama Record May Be Gold Mine For Critics," CBS News/AP, January 17, 2007.

[3] David Freddoso, "The Case against Barack Obama," Regenry, 2008.

[4] Hugh Hewitt, "The Brief Against Obama," Center Street, 2012.

[5] Obama Golf Counter, http://obamagolfcounter.com.

[6] Heritage.org, "Obama's $4 Million Hawaii Vacation", Hawaii Reporter, December 19, 2011.

[7] Alex Pappas, "Taxpayers spent $1.4 billion on Obama family last year, perks questioned in new book," Daily Caller, September 26, 2012.

[8] David Limbaugh, "The Great Destroyer," Regenry, 2012.

[9] Eric Owens, "Nobel Peace Prize Committee OUSTS Chairman Who Crowned Obama with $1.4 Mission Award," http://thefinaledition.com/article/nobel-committee-asks-obama-nicely-to-return-peace-prize.html, March 4, 2016.

[10] Matthew Diebel, "Former Nobel chief: Obama Peace Prize a failure," http://www.usatoday.com/story/news/2015/09/18/former-top-nobel-official-says-maybe-obamas-peace-prize-was-not-such-a-good-idea/72396794/, September 18, 2015.

[11] NORM DE PLEUME, "Nobel Committee Asks Obama "Nicely" To Return Peace Prize," http://thefinaledition.com/article/nobel-committee-asks-obama-nicely-to-return-peace-prize.html, March 6, 2016.

[12] Richard Brinkley, "Obama: Constitutional Scholar or Despot?," https://arizonadailyindependent.com/2015/03/23/obama-constitutional-scholar-or-despot/, March 23, 2015.

[13] AP, "Obama: If Congress won't act I will," Newsday, October 31, 2011.

[14] "Obama's State of the Union address: Criticism of the Supreme Court campaign finance ruling," LA Times, January 27, 2010.

Preparations

[1] Kyle Willyard, "The Battle of Great Bridge," http://www.continentalline.org, December 9, 1775

[2] Freedman, Russell, "Washington at Valley Forge," Holiday House, 2008.

[3] "Life and Legacy," http://www.johnmarshallfoundation.org/john-marshall/life-legacy, Retrieved 25 March 2016.

[4] "MARBURY v. MADISON," Decided February 1, 1803.

[5] Jefferson, Thomas, "The Writings of Thomas Jefferson, Letter to William Jarvis," September 28, 1820.

[6] Ibid.

[7] Bernard Schwartz, "A Book of Legal Lists: The Best and Worst in American Law," Oxford University Press, 1997.

[8] Junius P. Rodriguez, "Slavery in the United States: A Social, Political, and Historical Encyclopedia, Volume 1," ABC CLIO, 2007.

[9] Arthur E. Sutherland, "Segregation and the Supreme Court," The Atlantic, July 1954.

[10] "Brown v Board of Education Decision," http://www.crmvet.org, Retrieved March 25, 2016.

[11] Mark Levin, "Men in Black," Regenry, 2005.

[12] 317 U.S., "Wickard v. Filburn, Argued: May 4, 1942, Decided: November 9, 1942," Cornell University Law School, https://www.law.cornell.edu/supremecourt, Retrieved March 25, 2016.

The Real Campaign

[1] Saul Alinsky, "Rules for Radicals," Random House, 1971.

[2] "Dragnet, The Big Departure," Mark VII Limited, 1967.

[3] Ibid.

[4] Michael Savage, "The Savage Nation: Saving America from the Liberal Assault on Our Borders, Language, and Culture," Thomas Nelson, 2000.

[5] "American Suicide - A Warning By Former CO Gov Dick Lamm," http://rense.com/general87/amsu.htm, September 14, 2009.

[6] Michelle Malkin, "'I have a plan to destroy America'—by Richard D. Lamm," http://michellemalkin.com, February, 9, 2008.

[7] Thomas Sowell, "Wealth, Poverty and Politics," Basic Books, 2015.

[8] Frances Fox Piven, Richard A. Cloward, "The Weight of the Poor: A Strategy to End Poverty," The Nation, May 2, 1966.

[9] Julia Preston, "White House Plan on Immigration Includes Legal Status", New York Times, November 13, 2009.

[10] Jessica Vaughan, "Deportation Numbers Unwrapped," Center for Immigration Studies, http://www.cis.org/ICE-Illegal-Immigrant-Deportations, October 2013.

[11] W. James Antle III, "Obama denounced 'signing statements' under Bush, now uses them as president", The Daily Caller, http://dailycaller.com/2013/01/03/obama-denounced-signing-statements-under-bush-now-uses-them-as-president, January 3, 2013.

[12] Barack Obama, "Statement on Signing the Omnibus Appropriations Act, 2009," March 11, 2009.

[13] Ibid.

[14] Ibid.

[15] NPR, "Obama Promises 'New Dawn' Of World Leadership," November 6, 2008

[16] "Campaign speech," August 1, 2007

[17] "Interview with Al-Arabiya," January, 2009.

[18] Sean Hannity, "Conservative Victory," Harper, 2010.

[19] Major Garrett, "Obama Endures Ortega Diatribe," FoxNews.com, April 18, 2009.

[20] Michael Bastasch, "Flashback: Obama admitted energy prices would 'skyrocket' under his policies," The Daily Caller, http://dailycaller.com/2013/06/25/obama-admitted-energy-prices-would-skyrocket-under-his-policies, June 25, 2013.

[21] Dinesh D'Souza, "Stealing America," Broadside, 2015.

[22] https://www3.epa.gov/captrade.

[23] Tom Wolfe, "The Right Stuff," Farrar, Straus and Giroux, 1979.

[24] Hugh Hewitt, "The Brief Against Obama," Center Street, 2012.

[25] Ben Shapiro, "The People vs. Barack Obama," Threshold Editions, 2014.

[26] "Flashback: Doug Shulman in March 2012: 'There is Absolutely No Targeting,'," FreeBeacon.com, May 13, 2013, http://freebeacon.com/national-security/flashback-doug-shulman-in-march-2012-there-is-absolutely-no-targeting/.

[27] David Limbaugh, "The Great Destroyer," Regenry, 2012.

[28] Ben Shapiro, "The People vs. Barack Obama," Threshold Editions, 2014.

[29] Raven Clabough, "Obama Administration Adds 11,000 Pages of Regulations," The New American, September 11, 2012.

[30] James Hammerton, "The Hidden Cost of Regulation," Freedomworks, June 10, 2011.

[31] Ibid.

[32] Alex Newman, "Federal Regulations Cost U.S. $2 Trillion Per Year, Study Shows," The New American, September 15, 2014.

[33] William F. Jasper, "Regulators R Us: Feds Crank Up Regulations—on Everything," The New American, November 16, 2012.

[34] Dinesh D'Souza, "Stealing America," Broadside, 2015.

[35] Raven Clabough, "Obama Administration Adds 11,000 Pages of Regulations," The New American, September 11, 2012.

[36] Ibid.

[37] Bob Adelmann, "Federal Regulations Cut Standard of Living by 75 Percent Over 56 Years," The New American, June 27, 2013.

[38] Matt Cover, "Obama Regulation Czar Advocated Removing People's Organs Without Explicit Consent," CNSNews, http://cnsnews.com/news/article/obama-regulation-czar-advocated-removing-people-s-organs-without-explicit-consent, September 3, 2009.

[39] Ken Blackwell & Ken Klukowski, "The Blueprint," Lyons Press, 2010.

[40] Data from usgovernmentspending.com.

[41] Mark Steyn, "After America," Regenry, 2011.

[42] Sean Hannity, "Conservative Victory," Harper, 2010.

[43] David Limbaugh, "The Great Destroyer," Regenry, 2012.

Failure Again

[1] Mark R. Levin, "Liberty and Tyranny: A Conservative Manifesto," Threshold Editions, 2009.

[2] Jo Becker and Scott Shane, "The Libya Gamble," http://www.nytimes.com/2016/02/28/us/politics/hillary-clinton-libya.html, February 27, 2016.

[3] Katie Pavlich, "Fast and Furious," Regenry, 2012.

Purpose

[1] Eric Hoffer, "The True Believer," Harper & Row, 1951.

[2] Data from National Conference of State Legislatures, http://www.ncsl.org.

[3] Data from Tax Policy Center, http://www.taxpolicycenter.org.

[4] Data from Internal Revenue Service, Tax Foundation, http://taxfoundation.org.

No More Distractions

[1] Aamer Madhani, "Obama tells Medvedev he'll have 'flexibility' after election," http://content.usatoday.com/communities/theoval/post/2012/03/obama-tells-russian-hell-have-flexibility-after-election-/1#.VuLaJ7P2bL8, Mar 26, 2012.

[2] Ibid.

[3] Mitch Rofsky, "Size Matters: Is Obama's Second Term Agenda Big Enough? It's Not Just About Talk -- It's About Performance," http://www.huffingtonpost.com/mitch-rofsky/obama-second-term_b_2031721.html, 31 December 2012.

Legacy

[1] Charles Babington, "Obama Agenda Provides Long Work List To Tackle When He Returns," http://www.huffingtonpost.com/2012/12/24/obama-agenda_n_2359400.html, December 24, 2012.

[2] Hans Christian Anderson, "The Emperor's New Clothes," C.A. Reitzel, 1837.

[3] Eric Hoffer, "The True Believer," Harper & Row, 1951.

[4] Dr. Michael D. Evans, "Even if Nuclear Ambitions Weren't Enough to Sanction Iran, Their Murderous IED Campaign Against Americans Is," http://www.theblaze.com/contributions/even-if-nuclear-ambitions-werent-enough-to-sanction-iran-their-murderous-ied-campaign-against-americans-is/, November 23, 2013.

[5] "Iran marks Army Day with cries of 'Death to Israel, US'," The Times of Israel, April 18, 2015.

[6] "5 Flaws in the Iran Deal," Global Jewish Advocacy, August 7, 2015.

[7] George Phillips, "Iran Deal: $150 Billion to Fund Obama's War," http://www.gatestoneinstitute.org/6225/iran-150-billion-dollars, July 28, 2105.

[8] Memet Walker, "USDA awards $6 million in grants to 10 schools to study climate change," http://college.usatoday.com/2014/04/30/usda-awards-6-million-in-grants-to-10-schools-to-study-climate-change/, April 30, 2014.

[9] Milman, Oliver, "James Hansen, father of climate change awareness, calls Paris talks 'a fraud'," The Guardian , 12 December 2015.

[10] Ronald Reagan, "Ronald Reagan Speaks Out Against Socialized Medicine," (Spoken Word LP), 1961

[11] Maxim Lott, "Government awards more contracts to company that created glitchy ObamaCare website," FoxNews, November 05, 2013.

[12] David Martosko, "Obamacare program costs $50,000 in taxpayer money for every American who gets health insurance, says bombshell budget report," http://www.dailymail.co.uk/news/article-2927348/Obamacare-program-costs-50-000-American-gets-health-insurance-says-bombshell-budget-report.html, 26 January 2015.

[13] "Disney lays off 250 employees, replaces them with Indian H1-B workers: NYT Report," http://economictimes.indiatimes.com/articleshow/47540612.cms, June 4, 2015.

[14] Michelle Malkin and John Miano, "Sold Out," Threshold Editions/Mercury Ink, 2015.

[15] Data from usgovernmentspending.com

[16] Mark Levin, "Plunder and Deceit," Theshold Editions," 2015.

The Campaign Continues

[1] Saul Alinsky, "Rules for Radicals," Random House, 1971.

[2] MacMillan Learning, "Personal Control", http://macmillanlearning.com, Retrieved March 2016.

[3] Martin E. P. Seligman, Ph.D., "Learned Helplessness," Annual Review of Medicine, Vol. 23, February 1972.

[4] Chriss W. Street, "Republican FCC Member Warns Net Neutrality Is Not Neutral," Breitbart, http://www.breitbart.com/big-hollywood/2015/02/09/republican-fcc-member-warns-net-neutrality-is-not-neutral, February 9, 2015.

[5] Boliek, Brooks, "FCC finally kills off fairness doctrine," Politico, August 22, 2011.

[6] Hans von Spakovsky, "Prosecuting 'Climate Change Deniers'," http://dailysignal.com, March 10, 2016.

[7] Tom Cohen, "Obama: 'Trayvon Martin could have been me'," CNN, July 19, 2013.

[8] Eric Deggans, " Trayvon Martin update: Story is now more covered that presidential race," Tampa Bay Times, March 20, 2012.

[9] Larry Celona, et. al., "Gunman executes 2 NYPD cops in Garner 'revenge'," New York Post, December 20, 2014.

[10] Ben Shapiro, " A complete Timeline of Obama's Anti-Israel Hatred," Breitbart, March 20, 2015.

[11] Debra Heine, "Divider in Chief: 'I will never Engage in a Politics in Which I'm Trying to Divide People…'," PJ Media, June 1, 2015.

[12] Interview Sept 8, 2004.

¹³ MacKenzie Weinger, "Evolve: Obama gay marriage quotes," Politico, May 9, 2012.

¹⁴ Jay Sekulow, "Undemocratic," Howard Books, 2015.

¹⁵ Daniel Jonah Goldhagen, "Worse Than War: Genocide, Eliminationism, and the Ongoing Assault on Humanity," PublicAffairs, 2009.

Matriculation

¹ Peanuts™ by Shultz, http://www.peanuts.com/characters/charlie-brown/#.VvgcWGb2ZCo.

² John Nolte, "Cruz Is Correct: Trump Supported Hillary's Libya Debacle", Breitbart News, 26 February, 2016.

³ Saul Alinsky, "Rules for Radicals," Random House, 1971.

⁴ Aaron Klein, "Anti-Trump Groups Threaten 'Largest Disobedience Action of the Century," Breitbart News, March 16, 2016.

⁵ "AFL-CIO All In Behind Democracy Spring," Common Dreams, http://www.commondreams.org/newswire/2016/03/03/afl-cio-all-behind-democracy-spring, March 3, 2016.

⁶ Jay Sekulow, "Undemocratic," Howard Books, 2015.

⁷ Saul Alinsky, "Rules for Radicals," Random House, 1971.

Corrective Action

¹ "The Declaration of Independence," July 4, 1776.

² Ryan Young, "EPA costs US economy $353 billion per year," Daily Caller, December 27, 2012.

³ Mark Levin, "The Liberty Amendments," Threshold Editions, 2013.

⁴ Robert C. Hilborn, "Sea gulls, butterflies, and grasshoppers: A brief history of the butterfly effect in nonlinear dynamics," American Journal of Physics, April 2004.

⁵ Claudia Rosett, "The Twisted Conundrum of Funding the United Nations," The Tower, February 2014.

⁶ James Dobbins, Testimony on "A Comparative Evaluation of United Nations Peacekeeping," before US House Committee on Foreign Affairs, 2007.

[7] Jacob Hornberger, "But Foreign Aid *Is* Bribery! And Blackmail, Extortion, and Theft Too!," The Future of Freedom Foundation, September 26, 2003.

[8] "Convention of the States," http://www.conventionofstates.com.

Conclusion

[1] Eric Hoffer, "The True Believer," Harper & Row, 1951.

[2] Mark Levin, "Plunder and Deceit," Theshold Editions," 2015.

[3] Ronald Reagan, "Encroaching Control (The Peril of Ever Expanding Government)," A Time For Choosing: The Speeches of Ronald Reagan 1961-1982, Regnery, 1983.

Index

Abolitionists 33, 34, 45
Adams, John 111, 122, 130
Adams, Samuel 17, 271
Affirmative Action 55
Affordable Care Act 135, 169, 237
Alchemy xvi
Alinksy, Saul 79, 87, 213, 220
Alinsky, Saul 10, 60, 61, 66, 137, 140, 188, 194, 271, 278, 283, 287, 288
Alinskyite 65, 86
Altgeld Garden 61
Austin, Stephen F. 103
Axelrod, David 74, 75
Ayers, Bill 57, 64
Benghazi, Libya 161
Biden, Joe 89, 97, 279
Black Liberation Theology 62
Black Panthers 68, 85
Blaine, James G. 53
Boehner, John 9
Boerner, Phil 38, 39
Braun, Carol Moseley 65, 74
Brown vs Education 52
Browner, Carol 115
Buchanan, James 48, 131
Bush, George H.W. xi, 95, 118, 148
Bush, George W. 94, 95, 149, 217
Cap and Trade 146, 184
Carter, Jimmy xi, 118, 143, 170
Cleveland, Grover 53
Climate Change xvi, 115, 145, 182, 184, 233, 287
Clinton Global Initiative 161, 181, 188
Clinton, Hillary 12, 92, 145, 196
Clinton, Hillary Rodham 12, 60, 83, 84, 92, 93, 94, 145, 196
Cloward and Piven 140
Columbia University 37, 38, 39, 40, 56, 140
Communism 21, 29, 30, 58, 91
Communist League 58
Communist Manifesto 58
Cone, James 62
Confiscation Act 50
Cook, Genevieve 40
Cooper, Gordon x
Copernicus, Nicolaus xv
Copperheads 50
Davis, Frank Marshall 10, 30, 35, 36, 37
Davis, Jefferson 47
DeBonnett, Pat 61
Department of Defense 5, 101, 118, 121, 148
Dershowitz, Alan 63
Desert Shield ix
Desert Storm ix
Developing Communities Project 40, 60, 61
Dohrn, Bernardine 57, 64, 67
Douglas, Stephen A. 48
DuBois, W.E.B. 54, 59, 64
Dunham, Ann 17
Dunham, Stanley 17
Eisenhower, Dwight D. 118, 174, 198
Electoral College 49, 53, 218, 222, 225
Emancipation Proclamation 50
EPA 115, 146, 230, 288
Executive Order 9066 28
Fairness Doctrine 193
Fast and Furious 162

Fitzgerald, Peter 73
Foggy Bottom xii, xvii, 167, 231
Ford, Gerald 38, 92, 106, 141, 215
Franklin, Benjamin 14, 227
Gates, Bob 148
German Ideology 58
Gingrich, Newt xii
GITMO 181, 182
Global Warming 83, 156, 183
Great Depression 4, 99, 119, 133, 153, 167, 174, 238
Great Society 4, 118, 137, 155, 173
Grissom, Gus x, 147
Harrison, Benjamin 53, 145, 201
Harvard University 11, 26, 63, 65, 67, 69
Hawaii 10, 21, 23, 25, 26, 27, 29, 30, 31, 33, 35, 69, 125
Ho Chi Minh 111
Hoffer, Eric 67, 113, 123, 167, 277, 280, 281, 285, 286, 289
Hoover, Herbert 99, 193
Hull, Blair 74, 75, 76, 77
Humphrey, Hubert 214
Hurricane Katrina 80
Hyde Park 56, 57, 61, 67, 68, 76
Iran 180, 181, 197, 232, 286
Iraq 75, 96, 143, 180, 232
IRS 148, 149, 170
Israel 179, 180, 196, 197, 286, 287
Jackson, Jesse Jr 92
Jackson, Jesse Sr. 76, 81, 89, 92, 93
Jefferson, Thomas 47, 130, 131, 231
Jim Crow Laws 52, 56, 133

Johnson, Lyndon B. 55, 155, 194
Jones, Emil 68, 69, 76
Kansas-Nebraska Act 48
Kellman, Jerry 40, 60, 61, 65
Kennedy, John 91
Kennedy, John F. 155
Kennedy, Robert 214
Kenya 25, 26, 34, 63, 82
King, Martin Luther Jr. 34, 55, 57, 79, 93, 124
Kusunoki, Eric 31
League of Nations 54
League of the Just 58
Learned Helplessness 192
Lenin Peace Prize 54
Lilydale First Baptist Church 62
Lincoln, Abraham 1, 48, 73, 124, 129, 216, 271
Lost Decade ix
Love, Reverend Alvin 62
Madison, James 227, 237, 258
Main Stream Media (MSM) *See* Praetorian Guard
Malcolm X 35
Marshall, John 130
Marshall, Thurgood 55, 133
Marx, Karl 17, 57, 58, 59, 229
Marxist 11, 36, 59, 60, 88, 135, 175, 202, 215, 229, 232
McCain, John 84, 85, 89, 94, 95, 97
McCarthy, Eugene 214
McGovern, George 242
McKinley, William 105
McNear, Alex 39
Mexican-American War 103
Monroe, James 104, 141, 147
NAACP 59, 133
National Labor Relations Board (NLRB) 100

New Deal 4, 99, 100, 119, 133, 153, 173
Nixon, Richard xi
Nobel Peace Prize 55, 125, 126, 281
Obama, Barack Sr. 17, 25
Obamacare 176, *See* Affordable Care Act
Occidental College 35, 39
Ockham's Razor xv, 202
Oxy *See* Occidental College
Perot, Ross 218
Pierce, Franklin 48, 159, 258
Polk, James K. 47, 103, 104
Powell, General Colin 95, 96, 279
Praetorian Guard 13, 87, 102, 127, 156, 160, 184, 189, 199, 208, 225, 237
Project Vote 65, 220
Reagan, Ronald xi, 57, 141, 148, 161, 175, 179, 184, 203, 215, 237, 240, 276, 289
Reconstruction Amendments 45, 51
Romney, Mitt 150, 169, 172
Roosevelt, Franklin 18, 28, 97, 99, 115, 117, 120, 133, 134, 153, 163, 173, 215
Roosevelt, Theodore 54, 94, 105, 110, 213
Roseland 40, 60
Rush, Bobby 61, 68, 70, 193
Ryan, Paul 9

Schakowsky, Jan 76
Scott, Dred 46, 52, 131
Second Bill of Rights 97
SEIU 76, 85, 278
Shomon, Dan 68, 69, 75, 81
Sidley Austin 56, 57, 64
Slavery 33, 34, 45, 46, 47, 48, 49, 50, 51, 104, 131, 132, 262
Taft, William Howard 54, 106, 110, 213
Taylor, Zachary 47
Terry, Brian 162
Terry, Don 36
The Right Stuff x
Tribe, Lawrence 63
Trinity United Church of Christ 62
Troubled Asset Relief Act (TARP) 101
Truman, Harry 117
United Nations 93, 142, 161, 180, 181, 184, 196, 231, 232, 288
USAID 232
Washington, Booker T. 45, 54, 59, 64, 275
Washington, George ix, 14, 130, 223, 228
Wickard v. Filburn 134
Wilson, Woodrow 53, 99, 106, 110, 111, 112, 117, 133, 173, 213, 218, 258
Wright, Jeremiah A. 62, 92, 93, 94

www.ingramcontent.com/pod-product-compliance
Lightning Source LLC
Chambersburg PA
CBHW020744160426
43192CB00006B/241